factual discourse from the school board to the halls of Congress. Not only does she inspire us to reach for the stars—but she nudges us forward, step by step, with action plans that can train us how to converse more effectively and learn together.

Is Backstrom being realistic? Frankly, I can't pretend to know. But I do believe, like Backstrom, if American democracy is to survive, with or without a civil war, learning to talk to each other is sure as hell necessary.

**—Denise H. Gibbon**
Publishing Consultant &Licensed Attorney at Law
(New York & California), Above the Dotted Line

I0092672

## PRAISE FOR *IGNITING A BOLD NEW DEMOCRACY*

### *Empowering Citizens Through Game-Changing Reforms*

Author Ruth Backstrom, in her powerful and heartfelt book *Igniting a Bold New Democracy*, invites us to embrace compassion and empathy towards our fellow citizens and political leaders while remaining true and respectful of our differences. Her book shares ways to communicate honestly and compassionately and work together to create a stronger, and more productive United States of America. Backstrom invites each of us to get off our couch, light our torch and join her dynamic journey to ignite a bold new democracy.

**—Nancy Kirkendall**
Real Estate Team Leader/ Associate REMAX Alliance
The Kirkendall Team

I so appreciated this book. I want to say the author means what the title says, the *whole* title; she shows up as a work in progress, an action figure for justice since girlhood and on that dynamic journey to this day. The book is full of surprises, speaking to and inviting depth. She winds a path as a deeply thoughtful guide, sending her reader off into many intriguing and verdant tributaries that are proof of an ever-emergent democracy, alive in the minds and hearts of past and present-day Americans.

**—Corrina McFarlane**
Peabody Winner World Without Oil
Program Coordinator, Wise Democracy
Santa Cruz County, CA

If you want a book that thoughtfully details what has worked in the past to change America and why it was successful, this book is for you. If you're looking for step-by-step processes that can augment past approaches and even design new ways forward, buy this book. This is a call-to-action guide for thought leaders to create the new democracy. Use this book as a springboard to get ready, get set, GO!!

—**Linda Bark**
Founder and CEO for Wisdom of the
Whole Coaching Academy
PhD, RN, MCC, NC-BC, NBC-HWC

In *Igniting A Bold New Democracy*, author Ruth Backstrom's goal is clear. For the sake of our democracy, we need to transform from cultural warriors into passionate reformers calling for a united America. How? By transforming our ruminations about a national civil war into a passion for a national civil conversation.

Before sharing how to achieve this American renaissance, Backstrom thoughtfully replays and re-evaluates the pivotal cultural and political events of the past and current century that have brought us to this divide. The author's analysis of events and public figures is not only thorough but accessible to any interested reader, including thought-leaders, municipal figures, media talking heads, NGOs, historians, academics, and most importantly, the civic-minded.

As she shakes up our pedestrian assumptions about how we arrived at the current impasse, Backstrom makes it clear this is no time for complacency. All of us, no matter what our political persuasion, must pick up the pace if we intend to outrun the dictators.

For the author, "understanding" is not a noun but an active verb—one that demands we get to work understanding the fellow citizens we rant about and oppose. We also must advocate for truthful and

# IGNITING A BOLD NEW DEMOCRACY

## Empowering Citizens Through Game-Changing Reforms

Ruth Backstrom

Copyright © 2023 Ruth Backstrom

RuthBackstrom.com

All rights reserved. **No part of this publication may be used or reproduced in whole or in part, stored** in a retrieval system or transmitted in any form or by any means including, but not limited to, electronic, mechanical, photocopying, recording, or otherwise, **without prior written permission from the author except in the case of brief quotations in critical articles or reviews. For information about permissions, contact** Ruth@RuthBackstrom.com.

ISBN: 979-8-9873127-0-4 (Paperback)
ISBN: 979-8-9873127-1-1 (eBook)
ISBN: 979-8-9873127-2-8 (Hardcover)
Library of Congress Control Number: 2022921690
Printed in Durham, NC, USA by Ruth Backstrom

**NOTICE AND DISCLAIMER**
**This book is designed to provide general advice and strategies about the subjects discussed and may not be suitable for every situation.** Although the author has made every effort to ensure that the information in this book was correct at press time, **no warranties or guarantees are expressed or implied by the author's choice of content for this volume** and the author assumes no responsibility for errors, omissions, or contrary interpretations of the subject matter. References to other sources are provided for informational purposes only and do not constitute an endorsement of those sources.

This work is sold with the understanding that the author is not responsible for the results accrued from the information in this book. Use of this book does not establish any advisory, counseling, or professional relationship with the author. **The author shall not be liable for damages of any kind, including but not limited to physical, psychological, emotional, financial, legal, or commercial, resulting from the use of this book.**

For more information, visit RuthBackstrom.com.

For bulk book orders, contact Ruth@RuthBackstrom.com.

# A Special Bonus from Ruth

Now that you have your copy of *Igniting a Bold New Democracy*, you are on your way to knowing how to help reform our country. You will get loads of information about the transformations that are necessary and how to create them. I also included many inspiring stories of how change has happened in the past.

You can also receive a special bonus which is a comprehensive list of the various organizations that are working on these issues, so you can find ways to help change our country.

There are books out there that complain about our broken politics, but there are few that explain how to catalyze the transformations that are needed. With this additional information, you'll be armed with the skills required to become one of the sparks that helps ignite a new bolder approach to citizens improving our country.

Go to https://Ruthbackstrom.com/bonus to register for your gift. You'll also receive additional information about progress that organizations are making on creating deep reforms. You may, of course, unsubscribe at any time.

The sooner you start to become a powerful change agent, the better! Never underestimate the power of one person to help create profound transformations.

Let's come together and shift our country back towards being the democracy that reflects our best values and inspires us.

Let's create the game changing reforms that are needed together!

*Ruth Backstrom*

This book is dedicated to my tribe:

for my mother who was always my north star,

my father, and my husband Steve who has a heart of gold,

my siblings and their spouses Chris, Ellen, Alexandrea,
Jeffery, and Kim,

my beloved children and their spouses Lars & Jenny,
Elsa & Simon,

and my grandchildren Gavin, Hans, Niels, Rens, and Siana,

may we build a just and wise democracy for them to grow up in.

# TABLE OF CONTENTS

# ACKNOWLEDGMENTS

I realize it takes a village to write a book. First, I am grateful for the support my husband gave me with all the IT issues and for letting me steal into the quiet of my study to write this book which stole many hours out of our life together. Other people were especially helpful because they forced me to rethink my assumptions and convinced me to bring more of my voice into the process. For that, I am especially grateful to my editor Nanette Levin for providing me so much direction, beyond what others had offered. Thanks to George White for his editorial help as well.

I am also grateful for my great beta readers who diligently sent me back valuable feedback: Chris and Ellen Jones, Michael Cuddehe, Betsy Crites, Sandy Smith-Nonini, Denise Gibbon, Corrina McFarlane, Linda Bark, Louise Maidment. Thanks to Cheri Torres, and Jackie Stavros for their help in the chapter on Appreciative Inquiry. Special thanks also go to Rosa Zubizarreta for help on my chapter on Dynamic Facilitation and to Manfred Helrigl for input on his experiences in Vorarlberg. Jim Rough and Susan Michael also helped through their support over the years. Nancy Fields brought my ideas to life with her great visuals and wordsmithing on my website and with helpful marketing tips. Thanks also to Nancy Cox and Nancy Kirkendall for long talks and shared books.

# INTRODUCTION

It was an overcast day, the rain was just around the corner, and I decided to try and drive to the grocery store before the storm hit. I went to my local Food Lion which is the closest cheap store near my house. Cheap always satisfies my Scottish nature, and it has the least expensive organic produce to help me avert putting too many poisons in my body. I got this frugal nature from my mother, who told me when I was getting married, that she didn't want me to spend too much money on my wedding dress because I would only wear it one day. (Although, I thought that was maybe overdoing it.)

I parked my car in the Food Lion lot and this stranger came up to me and pointed to my Obama bumper sticker. He asked if I had voted for him. (At the time, Obama was a couple of years into his first term.) I knew from the man's negative tone of voice, that I was supposed to catalog my regrets. Instead, I thought, yes, I voted for him two years ago and will probably vote for him in another two years, but I responded with a simple yes.

"I think he's the worst president we've ever had," he complained.

"That honor goes to George Bush," I retorted defensively.

"Yeah, well, he was pretty bad too," he agreed, shaking his head affirmatively.

"Do you think, I should pay for people who don't work?" he asked.

"It's really bad now at our workplace," he lamented in a more plaintive tone.

"That is what they do in Europe and all the other industrialized countries," I said replying to his question about paying for people who don't work.

"Yeah, well, you should move to one of those countries," he blasted back.

"You should educate yourself about how the rest of the world lives," I blurted back.

Then there was a tremendous clap of thunder as the threatening rain began. I darted into the store to escape the bad feelings and the streams of rain coming down, while he went to his car. Yet I was troubled by the conversation, mostly because I knew there was an opening for a deeper conversation when he expressed his concern for the people at his workplace. I had blown it with my canned talking points that spilled out before I realized what I was doing. It was one of those moments where the words raced out impulsively, triggered by my emotions before my mind kicked into gear.

That interaction has rumbled around in the back of my mind for years, and I imagine we have all been having conversations like this across our country for a long time now – those of us who are still talking to people who don't think like us. We just throw our slogans back and forth at each other, pushing us further and further apart. The fights have intensified so that even people who should be allies are now seen as enemies. Yet, at the same time, we yearn for different conversations.

Years later, after my conversation in the Food Lion parking lot, I learned a facilitation method developed by Jim Rough called Dynamic Facilitation, and it was a transformative experience for me. We discussed problems in groups and yet instead of arguing the whole time, we came together around solutions. Each group started as a collection of individuals with diverse perspectives and ended with a collective sensibility, after integrating the learnings that they experienced through their conversations. It was astounding to watch, and even more exhilarating to experience. These encounters stretched what I thought was possible and gave me more hope about the ability of well-guided groups to solve problems and shift to more effective ways of interacting.

From these pivotal experiences, I felt more optimistic about the chance of integrating diverse perspectives into a solution that could shift our conversations towards a more positive orientation. I also realized that we could use facilitation techniques throughout our society to bring us to a more emotionally intelligent orientation in our national discourse. This doesn't mean that everyone would shift to a better approach, but we could reach a tipping point where our conversations became more effective, possibly even seeding new narratives that could tilt us in a more positive direction.

The value of diversity became evident when we worked in these groups and began to talk about solving some of our most intransigent problems. In the past, I generally resisted discussions with others who disagreed with me. However, in a safe space, I realized different points of view are enormously useful in crafting more comprehensive solutions, as more diversity generates an opportunity to refine a solution to address multiple aspects of a challenge.

When I took my niece to Europe for a tour after graduating from high school, we stopped in Salzburg, Austria. While there, I talked to someone about how the state of Vorarlberg, Austria had developed a whole system for using Dynamic Facilitation embedded in Citizen Councils that were designed to bring the voice of the people to the attention of the government. They systematized its use, so Citizen

Councils consistently expressed the common-sense voice of the people, as Jim Rough says. It was so successful that they institutionalized the process into their state constitution.

As I was writing this book, my friend Cheri Torres, author of the popular book *Conversations Worth Having*, introduced me to Appreciative Inquiry. I saw that this approach also offers powerful tools for structuring conversations that could shift our attention towards creating a vision of the future we want, pulling us gently towards it. The positive approach of Appreciative Inquiry stresses examining what is working and finding ways to expand on the parts of the culture of an organization that is already doing well. It also encourages groups to examine their underlying assumptions and remember the basic vision that they started with. Then the goal is to focus on how they could re-enliven their mission and move closer to it. There was no blaming or shaming – as we do in so much of our culture. This approach is like a breath of fresh air to counterbalance the negative conversations that continue to undermine our connections and destroy our integrity as a nation.

I wrote this book for people who are part of what the organization More in Common calls the "exhausted majority;" those who want the fights to end, and long for common sense to return to our national discourse. It is for moderate conservatives, independents, and liberals, who want our democracy to survive and know that we need a dramatic shift to strengthen it. It is also written for change agents and thought leaders who will instigate those changes. We don't have to agree on everything, we just have to find a better way to navigate through our differences. My goal is to focus on bringing us together to rise up to meet our current and future challenges. While each political side tends to blame the other side, in many ways, we are all caught in a system that has become dysfunctional.

At the same time, we are also potentially powerful actors who could change our collective quality of life. Groups in our past have pushed the pendulum back towards a more reform-minded sensibility when it grew out of line. The first step to shifting in that direction is to switch our attention and work to inspire people to take a new direction where more honest and positive conversations can be seeded and take root.

The intellectual and experiential path that led me to these concerns started with my interest in education. I got a Ph.D. in education, after receiving a B.A. in history, but after a while, I began to see that the problems confronted within our society were much broader and that changing the school system was not enough. Although I wrote my dissertation about the positive effects of small schools (and am still impressed by what the Small Schools movement accomplished), deeper social changes are needed, ones that could support all children growing up in a healthy environment.

While this book is written from a liberal-progressive orientation, I try to focus on broad issues that affect us all and recognize the value of diverse perspectives coming together to find the best, well-honed solutions. However, because we are in the midst of a time when huge shifts are necessary, conservative voices may be the most valuable in keeping us rooted in our best traditional values as we make the essential adaptations.

Historically, most large-scale change has been generated by small grassroots groups pushing for change, creating a movement with a powerful coalition that reaches into the halls of government. While I have highlighted many of the important issues and suggested some new narratives, ultimately the narratives must be forged and promoted through civic conversations that inspire organized action. People will be more likely to take ownership of an agenda they created and be more compelled to generate the momentum needed to implement it.

Systemic change, though, is not enough because we also need internal shifts in our mindsets and better ways of being and thinking together. If we are to find our way back to each other, it may help to use new tools and approaches that touch our hearts and inspire more compassionate listening. These experiences can cultivate the collective wisdom necessary to navigate these tumultuous times. Remembering some of our finest moments can also motivate us to come back together and advocate for the changes we want.

I realize that it is hard to write a book about politics these days without offending someone. Then being bold enough to suggest that neither party has got it quite right and that we need a new democracy - well that's heresy these days in a world where politics has become like a religion. There is little room for agnostics in the current scheme of things. Furthermore, who would want to craft a new system at a time when people are barely talking to each other?

So, I want to apologize in advance for any time that I offend you. I think we all have our blind spots and biases. Of course, that is the advantage of coming together – we begin to perceive them more clearly. While I recognize that there are diverse political persuasions and many independents who are unhappy with both parties, the two primary parties still largely determine what happens in our government. So, when I use the terms Republican and conservative interchangeably, or Democrat and liberal, I am referencing the voting blocks that give power to each party.

Furthermore, I contend this is just the time to begin to have new kinds of conversations among citizens as a way to leapfrog over the barriers that have kept us from talking effectively. It would be useful to escape the toxic political slogans and come together as citizens to steward our country toward a 21st-century democracy that serves us all.

Yet, we don't have to re-create it from scratch, we just have to revitalize our best impulses from past eras, when we transformed our country. The first chapter takes you on a journey back in time to a moment when we were brave, and a few visionary civic leaders led us toward one of the most remarkable experiments in our history. We can stretch our imagination about what is possible by drawing on our past and use those memories to instruct us on how to design a more functional future. The rest of the book is designed to help answer the question "How can we make such a transition and what changes should we take on?"

# PART I.

## HOW LEADERS STIR
## OUR IMAGINATIONS

As citizens of the United States, we have more power than we think. In fact, most of the major change in our history has happened as a result of grassroots efforts. In order for our democracy to survive, citizens must reform it. Moderate conservatives, independents, and liberals need to band together to model healthier norms of interaction and create a new vision for the democracy we want. This can happen by creating a modern 21$^{st}$-century democracy with institutions that are designed to rise to the challenges of this era.

Large-scale reform is only possible, however, through virtuous leadership, strong movements, new narratives, powerful forces of resistance to the trend toward autocracy, and a new vision of what we want. In the process of generating the changes we need, people will have to experience different ways of coming together, ones that tap into our shared sensibilities and create a stronger sense of "we." Movements should demonstrate it, and leaders should model it.

Our society has become fractured by fights about many things and between many groups. There are generational battles and fights within the political parties. Furthermore, there are these battling approaches that have been going back and forth for more than half a century over issues of race, religion, and economics. The journey back to connecting to each other in a healthy way has to be forged by courageous leaders who stand above the crowd, helping us reconnect to our best values.

This section focuses on leaders who have stirred the imaginations of people through their words and actions. We've had a lot of dynamic leaders over the years, often coming from surprising places. Civic leaders have dramatically shifted our circumstances in the past.

Strong leaders can make all the difference, even when the trend is against investing in wise solutions. The truly talented are able to reframe problems in a way that helps even those strongly opposed to certain ideas see the merit in considering a different perspective.

When integrity is in short supply, that's the most important time for courageous leaders to step up. It helps to examine and understand what has worked and what hasn't in the past before forging ahead to craft a richer future. The first section of this book illustrates some of the challenges former and current leaders have when trying to bring meaningful change along with the dynamic approaches they've taken to move a nation.

Civic leaders, presidents, and legislators can all stir our imaginations in new ways. They can help us claim rights that have never been claimed before, and challenge authority when necessary. They can also remind us of important values that are being challenged and persuade us to have the courage to resist when it is an unpopular choice. For example, the truth also matters because we cannot build a democracy on dishonesty, as Liz Cheney has been suggesting in her January 6th hearings.

Our task of firming up our democracy is critical to the success of other endeavors. Part of taking the animosity out of our culture must also include building a stronger democracy that strengthens our institutions, so they work for everyone and reflect our alleged values. Leaders should also stir our imaginations in ways that allow us to escape the limits of this period and begin to envision the more generous and virtuous country we want to become.

# 1

## VISIONARY CIVIC LEADERS
## WHO CHANGED OUR DESTINY

### *How to produce a thriving, growing middle class*

Right after the 9/11 attacks on the twin towers, my sister-in-law, Ellen, and I were driving across the country from North Carolina to Iowa. The roads were eerily quiet and deserted. Feeling a little raw from the events that had transpired, we talked and listened to music, avoiding the news. Three hours into the first part of our thousand-mile journey, I pulled the car into a small convenience store nestled deep in the mountains of rural West Virginia. After filling up our gas tank, we went inside to buy snacks.

Several people were gathered around a small TV set in the back of the store. Moving closer to see what was captivating everyone, we saw that same iconic scene of the first plane flying into the twin tower. It was strange to see it again, as though it was an eternal image that had somehow become frozen in time and was replaying in a continual loop. I stood there mesmerized by the scene, staring in anguish at it, and tears started streaming down my face.

Tears come easily to me, and it usually is embarrassing. However, this time it was so instantaneous that it caught me off guard, and I stood frozen like a deer in headlights. A stranger standing next to me turned and hugged me gently for a moment. After we left, both Ellen and I commented on what a kind gesture that was. There was something uplifting and soothing about feeling linked together through our shared grief as Americans around what had just transpired.

Feeling connected in times of emergencies is a natural response, but it isn't always what happens. It can either be supported or discouraged, depending on our leaders and the national conversations that are shaping the culture at the time. Our national discourse is like the lifeblood of our society; it keeps us involved in ongoing conversations that bond us together and help us understand and interpret the world. It is made up of stories or popular concepts that shape the way we think about issues. These narratives come from many sources as they work their way into mainstream awareness.

They also feed our collective imagination, expanding and/or limiting what we think is possible and shaping our course of action. A rich imagination can be a foundation for more complex problem-solving around our most difficult problems. On the other hand, polarizing words that demonize others have had a toxic effect. They generate distrust and resentment while limiting our imaginations. Such divisive approaches damage the natural bonds between citizens in times of emergency.

Nineteen years after 9/11, Tony Green, a consultant, and coach for prisoners, described in a newspaper article in the *Dallas Voice* how he became convinced that the pandemic was a "scamdemic" because he read and followed conspiracy theories that peddled that line. He bought into the idea that the mainstream media and the Democrats wanted to create a panic by spreading false rumors that would then lead to a crashed economy and demolish Trump's chances of getting re-elected. Tony described himself as participating in the extreme behavior embraced by Trump's most ardent followers.[1]

On Saturday, June 13, 2020, he and his gay partner decided to throw a family party. This was at a time when the COVID pandemic was raging. By Monday, his partner and his parents were sick. On June 24th, Tony and his father-in-law went to the hospital. The medical staff said the virus was attacking Tony's central nervous system, requiring quick intervention to avoid an imminent stroke. The medical staff put him on a ventilator that vibrated through his entire body and sounded like an old-fashioned electric heater. Tony's partner's grandmother died on July 1st.

Tony was so wrought with guilt that he felt compelled to write an article to discourage people from making the pandemic a political issue. He regretted causing such pain and suffering for the people he loved through political grandstanding. Whether your views lean right or left, it's clear this level of polarization causes deep pain and is also destroying the social fabric that connects us together to make democracy work.

These stories illustrate the different approaches to coming together to comfort and protect each other in times of emergencies, or not. Something is deeply broken in our country's psyche. How did we get so divided, and what can we do to turn it around?

Over the past 50+ years, our partisanship practices have grown to cover more and more territory. Lilliana Mason, author of *Uncivil Agreements,* says our political identities have grown really big as these things stack together and become more forceful as they encompass more aspects of our lives. So, when one small issue gets triggered, it activates more anger and leads to a state of perpetual irritation on both sides. Mason notes that policy preferences are less important in such an environment than identity markers. This means, for example, people will vote for politicians whose policies they do not support if those politicians exhibit the right identity markers.[2] This exerts a dysfunctional effect on our democracy and undermines the bonds that allow policymaking to reflect the majority's views.

## How Can We Create a Better Future?

Focusing specifically on modeling new ways of being together as we discuss issues with nuance and compromise, is a reasonable place to start in creating more productive interchanges. Our national discourse wasn't always this dysfunctional, but humans tend to model what they see, and now they need new models to counter the effects of years of divisive discord.

Stephen Prothero, a professor of religion at Boston University and historian who wrote about culture wars in his book *Why Liberals Win (Even When they Lose Elections)*, makes the point that culture wars are where nuance is destroyed.[3] We need unifying leaders, and shared narratives refined through constructive conversations, to unravel the extremism that is so prevalent.

Prothero defines a culture war as a time when there are ongoing outraged public disputes that are focused on moral and religious issues that question the direction our country should take, and the very definition of what it is to be an American. They are characterized by several factors. First, they touch on moral, religious, and cultural issues, rather than simply economic concerns. Secondly, people are less open to compromise. Finally, they are often fueled by rhetoric that suggests that the people who oppose their views are also enemies of the state or not real Americans.[4]

He dates the rise of our current culture wars to 1966 when Reagan launched his bid for governor of California. The wars began over how to handle the protestors at the University of California, Berkeley, and they didn't go national until the late 1970s.[5]

When politicians and the media dial up the rampant divisive strategy, that encourages people to blame each other, rather than look towards real solutions. Voters are manipulated by politicians' needs to draw people into a particular camp and solidify their base as warriors against the other side. For-profit news media are driven by a desire for sensationalism to attract more viewers, sell more advertising, and keep audiences coming back for more. I am not suggesting that there is a conspiracy to divide and conquer us, it is rather that the incentives for these groups don't serve the public's interests.

This divisive strategy was frequently used by English colonizers. It kept the native inhabitants in their colonies too contentious to effectively resist their conquerors. This formula was the central strategy that allowed England to develop such an impressive empire. They stoked ethnic and religious differences to keep attention away from counterattacks against their colonial ambitions. They used this strategy with success first in Ireland, then extended it to India, Africa, and the Middle East.[6]

We are currently suffering a similar fate. New memes should stress how the majority of us are losing out under this routine. While the media and politicians gain committed followers from this divide-and-conquer mentality, the public has become addicted to the fight. We, like fools, turn on our TVs every day and get another hit – focused on hearing that a conservative or liberal did something deplorable today or watching as talking heads yell at each other.

If politicians and inflammatory news outlets can keep the public focused on petty differences, predatory practices that are allowing our collective wealth to race unevenly into the upper echelons of our society can stay obscured. In order for that redistribution to stop, we have to stop fighting and see that our concerns overlap. Our polarization makes it impossible to create significant changes that require large coalitions—the kind of citizen movements that brought significant progress to our country in the past.

During this delicate time of transition when a lot of changes are necessary, it is especially important for leaders to deepen the discourse and inspire people to, instead of resisting change, be part of designing it. President Roosevelt's famous fireside chats, for example, were geared towards helping explain the New Deal as a way to get us out of the depression through the creation of government jobs.

Roosevelt's approach also prevailed because he was able to put together a broad coalition of groups to support his tactics and enough people to cluster around certain central ideas to create a foundation for his policies to endure. Historian William Leuchtenburg, professor emeritus at the University of North Carolina, at Chapel Hill talked about FDR's legacy as bringing together a coalition that was so diverse and broad that it kept the Democrats in power for the next thirty years.[7]

What people find acceptable depends on the influence of both the narratives promoted by our leaders and the coalitions we put together. For example, we have to make a persuasive case for rethinking our policies around income distribution. Sacrifices the wealthy might make in the form of higher tax rates and lower CEO pay rates, for example, will be worth it because they will be living in a healthier society.

To illustrate how people could feel about the choice between higher pay rates or better social safety nets, here is an example from Finland. Anssi Rantanen, a 23-year-old Finnish student, plans to get a degree in London and work a few years abroad before going home. He explained that once you become accustomed to a higher quality of life with excellent government health insurance, good quality state-funded education, and a comprehensive social safety net, it's hard to give it up. Therefore, he makes the point that he has no interest in immigrating to the United States after his studies either because he doesn't want to live permanently in a country without such a social safety net. Surveys showed that few Nordic executives want to give up their quality of life and move to the United States for higher salaries.[8] Americans should be persuaded by those arguments to support creating a more equitable society that leads to a higher quality of life for all.

Most of the other industrialized countries do a better job than we do of stressing the value of caring for all. New narratives should emphasize how we are all better off with a stronger social safety net. Our communities and families could be healthier, people would also have more time to care for each other and help attend to the collective needs of their community.

We also may be limited in our thinking about who can make changes in our national discourse. Some people assume that it was always framed by political leaders or brilliant visionaries in elite classes. However, major change has often been initiated by ordinary people enlisting broad-based support for new ideas. We are much more powerful than we think, both individually and collectively. To illustrate what is possible when leaders break out of the boundaries of the past, we just have to look back at our own history and remember some of our best moments.

⤮

This story begins at a time when WWII was winding down and soldiers were listening to tender love songs. They accentuated their sense of nostalgia and longing to return home to their normal lives— back to their sweethearts and unfinished hopes and dreams. They had left all that behind and lived in unfamiliar, cramped quarters for four long years, facing possible death or disaster.

Yet there was a problem brewing on the horizon. Congress was trying to come to grips with the issue of how to handle sixteen million returning vets. They were afraid that the veterans would swamp the labor market and send the United States back into a depression, or at least a recession.[9]

The federal government hadn't taken care of vets very well after WWI. The returning vets had been given $60 and a ticket home, but not much else. Later, there was a law passed that promised the WWI veterans bonus pay, in the form of certificates that they could cash in at a later date. However, the redemption date was delayed so long that a group of 45,000 vets and family members marched into Washington.[10] While the vets camped out, waiting for their funds from President Hoover, they were pushed out of the capitol without being paid. Those who didn't leave voluntarily were chased out by U.S. army troops that took over their campsite and burned all their belongings in the summer of 1932.[11] It was a very tumultuous time and not handled very effectively, an embarrassing time for the country.

After WWII, some leaders from the American Legion wanted to get returning vets more smoothly assimilated back into society. The American Legion was a nonprofit chartered by Congress to attend to the needs of veterans in 1919.[12] Many of their members had experienced the pain of being a poor WWI vet. Having lived through the indignities of limited resources, they were personally committed to a different response this time.

Warren Atherton, a California lawyer and head of the American Legion, complained to Congress in April 1944 that WWII vets were coming home with disabilities at the rate of 5,000 a week, and they needed immediate help because the VA Hospitals were full. He didn't want a G.I. Bill that would give resources to the vets held up any longer.[13]

Harry Colmery, head of the Republican National Committee and former director of the American Legion, wrote the initial ideas for the G.I. Bill on the back of an envelope. He incorporated all the lessons learned from WWI into the framing of the bill, making a case for a different approach.[14] However, Arizona Senator Ernest William

MacFarland, a Republican, was the true visionary behind the final bill that he and Atherton pushed through Congress because he added educational benefits and home loans.[15]

Newspaper tycoon William Randolph Hearst became a huge proponent of the bill and used his nationwide newspapers to get widespread support for it.[16] The final version of the bill included low-interest loans to buy a house, or a farm, or set up a business, free educational tuition to any college they could get into, or vocational training. It also had an unemployment section that ensured a $20 stipend to unemployed vets. The unemployment clause was the part that almost killed the bill.[17]

Yet it was a radical bill for its time with opposition from various interest groups. For example, University of Chicago Chancellor Robert Hutchins claimed it would make "Hobo Jungles" out of the universities.[18] Moreover, there were competing veteran bills that were much more modest. Franklin Delano Roosevelt had also imagined something much less ambitious.[19]

Despite all their efforts, the bill languished in committee and would have died if it hadn't been for some last-minute moves from the American Legion men. Through their connections, they were able to find someone to drive a recuperating committee member through the night to a plane that got him to Washington in time to cast the deciding vote. Then President Roosevelt signed the legislation in 1944, guaranteeing benefits extending until 1956.[20]

∽ঔৎ∽

The consequences of the bill were so widespread and uplifting that it created what author Tom Brokaw called "the greatest generation" due to their success resulting from a free college education boost.[21] Yet, it's probably not that they were inherently any more talented than any generation; they were great because the government invested so much in them, and our country benefitted as well. Congress estimated that the payoff was seven dollars for every dollar spent due to the increased taxes paid to the government by college graduates. That generation also created 14 Nobel Prize winners and two dozen Pulitzer Prize Winners.[22]

It was considered the greatest sociological experiment of all time, expanding the middle class to new heights. In the end, it has been deemed one of the most important pieces of legislation ever passed by the federal government.[23] It transformed America. Before that bill, college and home ownership were out of reach for most people. Not only did the American Legion switch the country's orientation away from a sense of scarcity towards veterans, but it also created a whole new society—one much more financially comfortable.

There were 7.8 million who benefitted from free college out of the returning 16 million.[24] They were also able to capitalize on $2.4 million worth of home loans.[25] Educators who were skeptical of the bill before it was passed, praised its successes by 1951.[26]

African American citizens were included in the bill, but they had trouble accessing the benefits because it was arranged so that it went through local authorities who discouraged African Americans from applying to college. They told Black vets that they would have a hard time getting hired for jobs that required a college degree and suggested technical training instead. Furthermore, they were unable to access mortgages because the bank and various subdivisions refused to loan money or sell houses to Black families.[27]

This is our legacy – we were the first ones to invest like that in the middle class, and we should expand it to others today who are struggling to maintain their place in the middle class. We need the same sort of imaginative thinking to reshape our future and to improve our quality of life today – so we can have the same standards as other industrialized nations.

Reparations could start by giving African Americans the same boost that we gave white veterans after WWII. While the G.I. Bill illustrated the power of civic leaders to persuade Congress to invest in people in new ways, it also permanently established the idea that veterans have rights. Presidents have also been responsible for modeling new perspectives to inspire action.

# 2

## ESCAPING THE RACIAL STALEMATE

### *Creating a win-win scenario*

As I stood watching Obama deliver his last speech before his first election, I couldn't help thinking that many of us had dreamed of this day. Obama spoke about how a "righteous wind" was moving across America. I wished my mother had been alive to see it.

> If there is anyone out there who still doubts that America is a place where all things are possible; who still wonders if the dream of our founders is alive in our time; who still questions the power of our democracy: Tonight is your answer.
>
> It's been a long time coming, but tonight, because of what we did on this day, in this election, at this defining moment, change has come to America...[28]

It was an impressive triumph. Despite our past, Americans had elected an African American president in the hopes he would take us further toward the multicultural society that many of us envisioned. Obama's acceptance speech captured the magic of that moment. Oprah cried as she listened and leaned against a stranger in the crowd. The tough and sturdy warrior Jesse Jackson had tears trickling down his face, too. Even Fox News dug down deep and found someone to applaud the moment, saying only in America could a candidate from an oppressed minority win the presidency.

The honeymoon was short-lived, even though President Obama offered an olive branch to Republicans as he asked Christian evangelical Rick Warren to pray at his inauguration.[29] Fox news complained when he wore a tan suit or used Dijon mustard on his burger. They found one thing after another to complain about. Nothing was too trivial to mention.[30]

Tribalism intensified when Obama was working on the Affordable Care Act. He carefully worked with the "Gang of Six," comprised of three Republicans and three Democrats, to create a bipartisan healthcare bill. Yet before they got very far, talks began to break down because minority leader Mitch McConnell indicated he would not support bipartisan recommendations for fear it could reduce the number of Republican winners in midterm elections.[31] There are hidden agendas behind the rhetoric that drives political discourse, making honest conversations and good-faith negotiating nearly impossible.

Nevertheless, Congress addressed the healthcare needs of 20 million uninsured Americans by passing the Affordable Care Act (ACA).[32] Of course, there were problems with the ACA. All the premiums were expensive, and while subsidies reduced the costs based on income levels, the premiums were higher than the fees many had previously paid for individual coverage.[33] Affordable healthcare has still not been achieved, despite the fact that most other industrialized nations accept it as a basic right. These shortcomings illustrate how deeply broken some of our systems are.

Another telling sign that the country is being run by corporations was the 2008 mortgage meltdown where bank executives sailed through without any of them going to jail. Senator Dick Durbin explained why succinctly when he said that the bank lobby is the most powerful lobby, "they frankly own the place" (Congress).[34]

Obama also inherited a flawed criminal justice system with a long history of abusing African Americans in many ways. Over the last 40 years, the U.S. jail and prison population increased by approximately 500%, according to the Sentencing Project, an organization working on better criminal justice practices.[35] This led to disastrous consequences for Black communities, our society, and individual lives as people spent more time in jail.[36]

A study by the Justice Policy Institute found that under President Clinton, federal prisoners numbers doubled, increasing to a level higher than in the previous twelve years under Republican administrations.[37] His mandatory sentencing policies forced judges to give unreasonably long periods of incarceration, taking away judges' usual discretionary powers.

For example, when he was 24 years old, Weldon Angelos was convicted of selling marijuana. The judge was forced to give him a 55-year sentence because he also had a gun, even though, he never displayed it during the transaction. Judge Paul Cassel talked about how unfair this was because aircraft hijackers get 24-year sentences, and terrorists 20-year sentences.[38]

Another brutal tactic in the war on drugs is using SWAT (Special Weapons and Tactics) teams to invade peoples' houses with military-grade weapons, often in the middle of the night. While they were developed in response to 1960s conflicts, the increased militarization of police forces in the 1990s has made this tactic more frequent and lethal today.[39]

One of the more well-known stories of SWAT team excesses involved Breonna Taylor, a 26-year-old emergency room technician working at several hospitals and making plans to become a registered nurse. Three policemen started banging on her door at midnight on March 13, 2020. When her boyfriend, Kenneth Walker, came to see who was there, he says they knocked down the door with a battering ram without announcing who they were.

At that point, Walker shot in self-defense. The police returned fire and shot five rounds of ammunition, hitting Taylor several times. This story was even more disturbing because they had already apprehended the suspect, an accused drug dealer, and were entering her apartment to search for drugs.[40] There was no need to do this search with a SWAT team in the middle of the night. They found no drugs and left Breonna Taylor dead.

The ACLU (American Civil Liberty Union) estimates that about 45,000 SWAT raids occur yearly, or about 124 daily. Approximately 80% of these raids involve searches for small amounts of drugs in communities of color. [41] States should restrict their use, reminding criminal justice officials that citizens are not enemy combatants, and neighborhoods should not be treated like war zones. How and why did our policing become such an abusive system?

## POLICING AS A REVENUE GENERATING SYSTEM

A 2016 class action lawsuit by 12 policemen in New York City explained how crime fighting has become abusive. The plaintiffs described the quota system that rewards the targeting of specific neighborhoods. Each officer got points for the number of felonies they turn in; police need points to get a vacation or to be considered for overtime hours.

Sergeant Miranda, a 20-year veteran, described how arrests throughout New York City focused on the same three low-income neighborhoods to maximize their number of arrests. Policemen face pressure to constantly turn in tickets and warrants to retain their job.[42]

These practices are pervasive across the country. Cities use trivial infractions to fund their budget deficits through petty fines. Small-town courts sometimes implement a rotating system to quickly shuffle people through. For example, Ferguson, Missouri, one of the most egregious examples, collected 20% of its revenue from fines taken mainly from African Americans.

Beginning in the 1990s, Peter Edelman, a law professor at George-town University, observed that the government was running a loan shark operation to the tune of $50 billion. This involved 10 million poor, currently and formerly incarcerated people who were being charged interest on fines they couldn't pay to make up for city revenue shortfalls. Meanwhile, white-collar criminals owe $450 billion in back taxes. In effect, we have come to a place where being poor in America is a crime for far too many people.[43]

This kind of policing is not a criminal justice system but a revenue-generating system that preys on the most vulnerable people in our society. Their crime is being poor and unable to leverage the legal or financial resources to fight back against police harassment. Furthermore, it is a soul-crushing system that dehumanizes both the police and the victims as well.

## COSTS OF EXCESSIVE POLICING

The National Research Council did a study in 2014 called *The Growth of Incarceration in the United States: Exploring Causes and Consequences.* There are three essential points in the study. First, they highlighted the fact that the crime rate rises in the 70s and 80s was mainly due to the migration north of African American families; research shows that significant population shifts historically result in crime waves. When the Irish migrated and landed in slums, their crime levels were high. The difference was that we didn't throw them in jail. Instead, we invested in more schooling and social services.

Secondly, the report says we need to switch out of our punitive prison orientation to a rehabilitation model. Finally, and most importantly, it notes that there has been a bidding war in the political arena where leaders compete to see who can seem toughest on crime. Little political discourse during the 1970s and 1980s discussed true justice or actual rehabilitation. [44]

This whole approach is expensive and brutal. It has an easy fix—we end these expensive and destructive practices. Breonna Taylor's case resulted in a $12 million settlement;[45] George Floyd's family received $27 million.[46] But these lives are irreplaceable. With a better system, that $39 million in reparations could have been invested in programs designed to save lives by uplifting communities, like we did with the Irish.

*This system can be deadly for innocent people.* No amount of money, prestige, or propriety can save you if you find yourself in front of the wrong policeman having a bad day. This also means Black parents must prepare their children for living in a world that is constantly a potential threat to them. It also underscores how being Black in America means you are always living in perpetual fear, as the author Ta-Neishi Coates highlights so masterfully in his book written to his son titled *Between the World and Me*.[47]

Now that I have a biracial grandchild, I worry about these things in a much more personal way. I realize that we should think about these losses of lives and lost potential as though we were their parents and imagine the unbearable anguish of such unwarranted excesses. Beyond the criminal justice system, there is also the problem of the marginalization of African Americans in segregated, under-resourced communities, with many families bogged down by multi-generational poverty.

## SEGREGATION AND POVERTY

The myth that we live in a post-racial society because we elected Barak Obama as president has to be rejected. For example, while the mechanisms for housing segregation have changed so that financial barriers have replaced racial prejudice, it still persists, and the consequences are bleak.

Richard Rothstein, a distinguished fellow at the nonpartisan Economic Policy Institute, describes how government policy perpetuated segregation in his book *The Color of Law*. He explains how zoning laws were written after WWII to allow the growth of federally subsidized suburban communities to enable people to own an affordable single home. Yet the Federal Housing Administration manual required a provision in these developments, built outside metro areas across the country, that the developers would never sell to African Americans. There was also a clause in every house deed that prohibited resale or rental to African Americans.

After this explicit policy, the government didn't have to create new policies; these homes just appreciated, white families enjoyed the benefits of subsidized housing, and others were excluded. Zoning regulations prohibited the addition of apartment buildings or duplexes in these neighborhoods, so they could remain prohibitively expensive. The consequences of segregation are that African Americans often live in areas where people have less access to jobs and transportation, and without access to healthy food.[48]

When schools and communities resist integration, social mobility becomes more difficult. A report looking at school integration, "Brown at 50: King's Dream or Plessy's Nightmare," by Gary Orfield and Chungmei Lee, examine the data around integration and conclude that there has been little progress in the fifty years since the 1954 (Brown vs. Board of Education) ruling.[49] The consequence is that this level of isolation leads to higher and more sustained levels of poverty.

Multigenerational poverty, is the most debilitating impediment to upward mobility and has devastating outcomes. A 2020 Brookings Institute study revealed children who grow up in the second generation of poverty are more likely to end up in jail or face an earlier death than those who do not. Their *Panel Study of Income Dynamics* extended the analysis to third-generation families living in poverty. One in five Black adults came from three generations of poverty. At the same time, only one out of a hundred white families lived in impoverished circumstances for three generations.[50]

## HEALING PAST AND PRESENT INJUSTICES

A study by Pew Research surveyed 3,912 Black Americans in October 2021. Six out of ten Black responders said that police brutality and racism were the most significant problems in their lives. Economic inequality came next, with 54% saying it was a major problem. Affordable healthcare, efforts to limit voting, and low-quality schools were also cited as problems by more than 40% of the responders. The solutions they stressed included more support for Black businesses, reparations through educational assistance, and home ownership assistance.[51] This is essentially like extending the G.I. Bill to people of color, making up for the adverse effects of being excluded from the bill and unable to accrue generational wealth.

Models of how to create thriving neighborhoods can also draw on the work of the Harlem Children's Zone project. Their mission is to end intergenerational poverty in Central Harlem. The project began in the 1990s with one block in Harlem, where they provided wraparound services to address drug abuse, crime, dilapidated housing, healthcare, and school issues. They were so successful that they created additional charter schools and a series of 13 programs that support children from birth to college graduation and beyond. Over the years, they have enlarged their target to cover 97 blocks in Harlem, serving 22,500 youth and adults annually.[52] What's so compelling about this approach is that it provides additional resources and a support system that allows for internal shifts to occur while encouraging economic mobility.

Yet more extensive changes depend on Americans shifting to a more caring, generous space, as Obama pointed out, and escaping the racial stalemate we are caught in. He modeled a path forward to do that by holding the tensions that existed in America, both good and bad, about race. He explained that he could hold a space of love for his white grandparents, who said things about Black people that made him cringe inside, and for his minister, Reverend Wright, who some considered harsh in his railings against the shortcomings of America.[53] He demonstrated his ability to do that in his famous "A More Perfect Union" address given during his campaign on March 18, 2008:

> The fact that so many people are surprised to hear that anger in some of Reverend Wright's sermons simply reminds us of the old truism that the most segregated hour of American life occurs on Sunday morning. That anger is not always productive, indeed, all too often it distracts attention from solving real problems. It keeps us from squarely facing our own complicity within the African-American community in our condition. It prevents the African-American community from forging the alliances it needs to bring about real change. But the anger is real, it is powerful. And to simply wish it away, to condemn it without understanding

its roots, only serves to widen the chasm of misunderstanding that exists between the races...

In fact, a similar anger exists within segments of the white community. Most working and middle-class white Americans don't feel that they have been particularly privileged by their race... They've worked hard all their lives, many times only to see their jobs shipped overseas or their pensions dumped after a lifetime of labor. They are anxious about their futures, and they feel their dreams slipping away. And in an era of stagnant wages and global competition, opportunity comes to be seen as a zero-sum game, in which your dreams come at my expense...

And yet, to wish away the resentments of white Americans, to label them as misguided or even racist, without recognizing they are grounded in legitimate concerns, this too widens the racial divide and blocks the path to understanding. This is where we are right now. It's a racial stalemate we've been stuck in for years.[54]

Naming the problem so clearly was a powerful public stance. It opens up the possibility of examining perspectives and motives around zero-sum game thinking and intentional manipulation designed to sow division between us. The stalemate will only stop when we come to believe that both groups deserve more and that resources well invested will bring huge rewards, both financial and social, now, as they have before.

In many ways, Obama was a bridge between two worlds, modeling a way forward for our multicultural society by helping soothe the pain behind some of our most troubling moments and capturing our experiences through eloquent speeches that resonated deeply with the emotional tenor of the moment. One of the most powerful speeches Obama gave reflected the sense of empathy that has to be cultivated in our culture to open up a space for the shifts we need. At the Emanuel African Methodist Episcopal Church in Charleston, South Carolina, on June 26, 2015, he consoled the grief of a nation, a church, and its members, while simultaneously honoring the lives of the murdered. A white supremacist killed nine African Americans in that church, yet Obama immortalized them that night. Obama said, at the Charleston funeral, we must come to see that:

> My liberty depends on you being free, too. ...He (God) knew that the path of grace involves an open mind -- but, more importantly, an open heart...

> That, more than any particular policy or analysis, is what's called upon right now, I think -- what a friend of mine, the writer Marilyn Robinson, calls that reservoir of goodness, beyond, and of another kind, that we are able to do to each other in the ordinary cause of things. That reservoir of goodness. If we can find that grace, anything is possible. If we can tap that grace, everything can change.[55]

His speech illustrated how words can heal and chart a path forward. First, he humanized the victims of the violence who had been dehumanized by their assailant. He told us about Reverend Clementa Pinckney, preaching at the tender age of 13 and ordained when he turned 18. The Reverend then went on to become a South Carolina state senator. Obama then contextualized the situation by saying that the Black church was where dignity was restored to African Americans, and they felt whole, implying that killing them in their sanctuary was especially cruel.

Obama said these things simply to recognize and hold their pain. In the end, he had recognized their pain, acknowledged how it was reminiscent of past wrongs, and still held out hope for a different future. It's a powerful vision we should hold on to as we navigate these tumultuous times … a north star in a chaotic time.

Yet he not only addressed our pain through his speeches, but he also inspired people to take action when it was needed. After the speech in Charleston, South Carolina, Obama said that Confederate flags belonged in museums only. Asking for the flags to come down was not an act of political correctness, he pointed out, making an important distinction between the overreach that sometimes happens with the left and legitimate complaints. There was a picture of Dylann Roof, who murdered the nine people at the Charleston church, displaying a confederate flag on social media. So, a push to bring down the flag intensified across the country.[56]

The next day, inspired by Obama's words, thirty-year-old activist and filmmaker Bree Newsome Bass drove from Charlotte, North Carolina, to Charleston, South Carolina. She proceeded to the Capital to scale the flagpole and bring the Confederate flag down. A Greenpeace member showed her how to climb the pole with her climbing gear. She worked with ten other activists to plan the event.

She waited until the coast was clear and began scaling the 30-foot flagpole, realizing she might be shot. While ascending the pole, the police arrived and told her to come down. She explained that her act was a nonviolent protest that involved taking the flag down and being arrested. Bass told the police they were coming towards her with hate, but she was coming against them in the name of God. And the flag was coming down. She described afterward how the adrenaline was pumping through her body at the time. Still, she felt peace as well, as her attention settled to a more profound realm.

After she got to the bottom of the pole, they arrested her and her accomplice. They booked them on charges of defaming a monument with penalties of $5,000 and/or a prison term of up to three years.

The charges were dropped against Bass and her accomplice. The image of her scaling the flagpole became an iconic symbol of the movement to remove confederate flags. She gave talks about how she tore hatred out of the sky. Artists depicted her as a superhero overnight, and people donated to her defense. On July 10, 2015, the flag was taken down for good and sent to a museum.[57]

Over time, the battle reached a tipping point. Confederate flags came down across the country as the tide turned after the brutal death of George Floyd in 2020. South Carolina, Alabama, Mississippi, and Virginia took their flags down. Pressure from sports teams and businesses helped to convince states that it was time to accept the adverse effects of the symbolism behind it.[58]

If we are to escape our racial stalemate, it will be through coming to terms with our past and mapping out a different future that holds promise for all of us. It must go beyond taking down flags to eliminating multigenerational poverty. Yet the most critical part of mapping that different future entails not only taking down confederate flags to get the hatred out of the air but taking it out of our hearts, as well.

# 3

## WOMEN RISING UP

## *Saving Democracy for our Children*

In many ways, Liz Cheney, the former representative from Wyoming, was an unlikely candidate for becoming a champion in the drama surrounding Trump's January 6th activities. She had few disagreements with Trump ideologically and was a consummate politician. Through her grit and connections, Cheney had achieved the third most revered position in the Republican Party as head of the House Republican Conference.

Yet perhaps her role is even more heroic because she stood up to Trump when she had everything to lose and no history of taking on such challenges. We tend to discredit our leaders by pointing out all their flaws. The only real heroes we allow ourselves to admire are the superheroes on the silver screen. Yet her courageous handling of the January 6 investigations broke the rules and brought praise from both sides. She received the prestigious John F. Kennedy Profiles in Courage Award on May 22, 2022, after voting to impeach Trump and losing her position in the House Republican Conference.[59]

She also received an invitation to speak at the Reagan Institute on June 29, 2022, where Cheney explained why she decided to confront Trump. She said:

> ... I come to this choice as a mother, committed to ensuring that my children and their children can continue to live in an America where the peaceful transfer of power is guaranteed. We must ensure that we live in a nation that is governed by law and not by men... we have to choose... Because Republicans cannot both be loyal to Donald Trump and loyal to the constitution.[60]

She was courageous in many of her choices. Other Republican renegades just gave up on their party and threw their lot in with the Democrats. Of course, she may still do that, but Cheney was trying something bold. She decided to stay and change the minds of people in her own party by bringing reasonable conservatives to the forefront in her hearings. She brought new faces, names, and narratives to light as she started her work with the January 6th Commission.

Cheney wanted people to understand the full implications of the January 6 events. Trump tweeted that people should not watch the hearings, and she responded, "no citizen of this Republic is a bystander. All of us have an obligation to understand what actually happened." Then she proceeded to take people through the story of what happened blow by blow. Her goal was to get her audience to see the world through the eyes of the witnesses and participants in the drama that unfolded. These witnesses were chosen to discount claims that the objections to Trump's behavior were merely partisan attacks on him. They showcased the experiences of loyal Republicans who were part of Trump's staff and found themselves caught in a precarious place where they could either do his bidding or follow the laws.

Objectively stating the facts, Cheney methodically countered the popular narratives and dramatically let the true story unfold. They heard how many people within Trump's inner circle, including his daughter and attorney general William Barr, tried to tell him that there was no evidence that the election was stolen. Then, while the riot at the Capitol was going on, Trump's family members and Fox News staff sent messages to him, asking him to call off the violence. Instead, when the rioters talked about hanging Mike Pence, the former president said they might have the right idea. Trump ultimately asked the protestors to leave but did so while stating he loved them and told them they were very special.[61]

 Cheney also discredited the idea that it was a peaceful protest that got out of hand or fomented by left-wing radicals like Antifa followers. One of the most riveting moments was when 31-year-old capitol police officer Caroline Edwards described the violent battles around her. It was clear from this testimony that this encounter was premeditated, and the protestors purposely brought weapons to use them.

She was knocked unconscious and, when she came to, continued trying to catch her fellow officers as they fell. While doing that, she described how she slipped in blood everywhere she turned. It was chaos and mayhem. Edwards was a four-year police veteran who pointed out that nothing in her training had prepared her for this. She explained it was like a war scene with hours spent in hand-to-hand combat.

After her injury, she was called a traitor and other names, sometimes a hero or a villain, but she said she was neither. She was shocked to be standing face-to-face in combat with other Americans and asked herself, how did we get here? Edwards said her grandfather was a marine veteran from the Korean War, and she was proud to be a protector of the country's Capitol. Her patriotism had never been questioned before, but she explained that she would give up everything so that the America her grandfather had defended was around in the future.[62]

Footage of the event shared some of the most harrowing moments. Viscerally putting people in someone else's shoes helped break down some of the "us vs. them" mentality that has been ramped up in the rhetoric. It was hard not to feel sympathetic and admire her patriotism as she lived through these harrowing experiences. The story became personal, moving it beyond the confines of the slogans. People lost their lives. The consequences of Trump's actions were highlighted through the innocent testimony of a young woman caught in a war scene that left her and other officers injured.

Another part of the investigation highlighted the fact that people went to jail due to Trump's lies about the stolen election and then regretted it. Cheney pointed out how tragic this was.

> Here is the worst part: Donald Trump knows that millions of Americans who supported him would stand up and defend our nation where it threatened. They would put their lives and freedom at stake to protect her. And he is preying on their patriotism. He is preying on their sense of justice. And on January 6, Donald Trump turned their love of country into a weapon against our Capitol and our Constitution... [63]

This illustrates another aspect of this tragedy. Cheney highlighted how callous Trump's behavior was as it damaged the social fabric of our country. While many of these rioters were violent and brutal in their actions, not innocent victims, he goaded them on. He says he loves his supporters but uses them to achieve his own personal aims. Cheney tried to get her viewers to see the incident in a new light as she stressed the consequences of his deception that rippled out to affect first his followers, then the innocent police, and ultimately our entire country.

In the end, though, the critical question is: are the hearings shifting peoples' perspectives? A July 22 online Reuters/Ipsos poll of 1,005 adults found some comforting shifts from a poll done six weeks earlier, before the hearings. There was a 12% decrease in Republicans who thought the election was stolen (from 67% to 55%) using the same poll. Furthermore, 30% of Republicans now believe Trump should not run for president again, up from 25% in June.[64] The percentage of Republicans who think Trump is partly to blame for the riot went up from 33% to 40%.[65] A solid 67% of Independents polled in late September 2022 said he should not run for president again. Perhaps, though, one of the most important effects of the hearings is they started to undermine Trump's control over media messaging.

If a tipping point is coming, it makes sense that a woman should bring Trump down. After all, women were the ones that rose up the day after his inauguration in protest, as an estimated half a million women gathered in Washington D.C. to protest Trump's rise to power. Another three million held protest marches around the world.[66] Suburban women gave the election to Biden in 2020.[67] Women instinctively knew that Trump's toxic masculinity and divisiveness would not benefit them or the country.

Building on Liz Cheney's work, civic groups could help to create the tipping point needed to reject this rise of autocracy. Sometimes, the only way to restore balance is by building up to a place where people suddenly shift their awareness and see that the person who captivated everyone is not a positive force. Here's an example of how that has worked in the past.

With the rise of Wisconsin Senator Joseph McCarthy in the 1950s, there was a second red scare around the idea that the country was being overrun by communists. He attacked all levels of the government, and his popularity soared as he fed off the anxiety about the possible spread of communism. In February 1950, he claimed, without any evidence, that 205 communists were employed by the State Department.[68]

Famous actors were also put on blacklists and had trouble getting work. Some of the more prominent names on the list were Charlie Chaplin, Langston Hughes, Orson Welles, and Lena Horne. Orson Welles wrote a film that mirrored the times called *Touch of Evil,* where a crooked law enforcement official creates witch hunts instead of protecting people.[69]

Three years into his work, Senator McCarthy asked a well-respected and heavily decorated World War II Brigadier General to testify before his committee. He asked the general to give him the names of people responsible for interfacing with an army dentist who had pleaded the fifth rather than cooperate with the senator. The army then gave the dentist an honorable discharge, and the senator wanted the names of everyone who interfaced with him. The general refused, and an irate McCarthy berated the general's intelligence and reputation, ending by saying he wasn't fit to wear his uniform.

The broadcast journalist Edward R. Murrow then did a TV special where he used the senator's words to highlight his abusive behavior. He ended by pointing out that McCarthy was exploiting people's fear.[70] This tarnished McCarthy's reputation, but the final blow came when the army took on McCarthy.

The army exposed a report of the senator using persistent pressure tactics to get favors from the armed service for an associate's friend. The last tactic McCarthy used, the 44th one revealed in the army report, was a threat to use his influence to destroy the army. When McCarthy tried to turn the table by attacking the legal firm assisting the military, claiming they had some vague ties to the communist party, the army counsel suggested that McCarthy had done enough damage.

The army counsel's last refrain is what people from that era remember the most. He asked McCarthy if he had no sense of decency left. With those words, the general restored balance to the political discourse, and McCarthyism ended, along with the frenzy that had supported it.[71] Our task is to restore a sense of balance and stability to our system so decency can return to our country, as it did after McCarthy lost his influence. Those changes could then create a foundation for the conversations necessary to move our country towards the important reforms that can strengthen and protect our democracy in the future.

It may take some time to take down the web that Trump has spun to encourage factions and violence. Still, Liz Cheney's January 6 investigations have made him vulnerable. Others will follow her lead. In her hearing's closing remarks, she quoted Margaret Thatcher, who said, "Let it never be said that the dedication of those who love freedom is less than the determination of those who would destroy it."[72] It will require the dedication of all of us to address the perils before us. Citizens and political leaders must come together in large numbers to succeed.

⚭

Never doubt your ability to make a difference, even under challenging circumstances. So often, people think they need the proper skill set or a particular type of personality or charisma to effect change. Greta Thunberg, a 15-year-old Swedish climate activist with Asperger's syndrome, is an unlikely candidate for being a mover and shaker in the world.

Yet, with her soft power, she has created a global student movement and claims that her Asperger's syndrome is actually her superpower. On September 20, 2019, she inspired 4 million people to participate in 2,500 events worldwide. Forbes listed her as one of the hundred most influential women that year. Individuals like her will catalyze the movements that will shift our world so that it becomes worthy of our highest aspirations.[73] The secret is to lean into your special powers and find an arena where you can ignite change. This is a difficult time that calls for all of us to lean into our superpowers in order to save our democracy.

# PART II.

## MOVEMENTS GIVE US A TASTE OF A BETTER FUTURE

Political organizing can be both exhilarating and frustrating at the same time. Movements speak to our unfulfilled hopes and dreams of a better future. They activate our deepest desires to affect the world, yet the pace of change is often slow, and the wins are few. When it does work, an exciting sense of solidarity restores our lost sense of community and gives us hope that change is possible.

To keep groups going, there have to be solid ties, and there has to be a sense of purpose that can sustain them when the difficult times come along … and they will. The organization More in Common showcases an analysis of how to create effective movements. Giuliane da Empoli, a Swiss and Italian writer and journalist, writes in his report *The End-less Sea* that you have to build in a taste of the future you are working towards. For example, if you want more green spaces in your town, start by planting beautiful plants around, so people will see what they have been missing. He explains that if you hire seamen to go out and fish, you don't start by giving them tasks. Instead, you tell them stories about the sea, so they develop a love of it and yearn to be a sailor.[74]

Organizers and protestors in movements also need to hear stories and tales of success so they will want to be part of the call toward justice and become inspired activists. These messages should not just be positive but also address citizens' underlying fears: their sense of lost trust, and a feeling of not having a voice in their country.

Organizations that have energized activism in these challenging times, where incremental change is not enough, also have narratives that unify and advocate for significant transformations. Nevertheless, there also has to be a sense of fun that lets people escape cynicism and hopelessness while providing joy and empowerment.

Another essential facet of movement building is having people involved help create a clear vision. Creating drama is a helpful way to accentuate the issues and draw attention to the promises, so people will hold on to their dreams and complain when they are not fulfilled. Giuliane da Empoli gives the wonderful example of the comedic group the Yes Men, who did a prank the week after Obama's election where they created a copy of the New York Times printed out with all the visions of what they would like to have happen in the first six months. This prank was a way to create accountability around Obama's promises.

While building a movement, people also must get personal satisfaction and recognition for what they do. They need to understand the population they are trying to influence, preferably because they have a similar background. Sensitive leadership also is essential, where empathy and other qualities of emotional intelligence are expressed.

For example, female governors in the U.S. kept their death rates lower during Covid than their male counterparts. That was because they were good at getting information out quickly and recognizing the various needs of their constituents while speaking to them empathetically. They were also both optimistic and realistic about what they could do, serving as a powerful antidote to the polarized political games that led to more deaths in some states. Finally, the style of our reform efforts must be vibrant and appealing and shake us out of the sense of hopelessness and despair that prevails in a country where so much power has been concentrated in the hands of such a small segment of the population.[75]

# 4

## THE QUEST FOR DEEPER TRUTHS

*Uncovering more accurate accounts of events creates a healthier society*

When I was little, the block I lived on encompassed my whole world. I rushed out after breakfast to play with my neighborhood friends on the weekends and long summer days, staying out until my parents called us home for dinner. It wasn't until I was around seven that I went for a drive with my family into an adjoining, poor African American neighborhood on the south side of Chicago. Until that drive, I had been unaware of the economic differences in nearby areas. The gray, weather-beaten, wooden apartments stacked on top of each other looked cheap and unsubstantial against the cold, snowy winds of the Chicago winters, especially compared to the solid brick houses on my block. Laundry was drying on clotheslines on the back landings, suggesting the absence of dryers.

Turning to my mother, I asked, "Why don't we give them more money?"

"We work hard for our money," she replied, not so much as a denial of my observation but more likely a response designed to avoid explaining the whole racist state of affairs to a seven-year-old. My mother was very committed to integration. We lived in the integrated neighborhood of Hyde Park because of it. That response, however, didn't really acknowledge the unfairness I was trying to draw attention to, so I retreated into a silent melancholy space and returned to surveying the neighborhood.

That sense of dissatisfaction with inequities continued, though. Six years later, as I was listening to the radio, I heard a man's deep, resonant voice talking with the cadences of a preacher. It wasn't so much his words that impressed me. His voice's calm, steadiness and confidence spoke directly to my concerns. I thought this is a man who lives in a place that most people never even visit, a place of profound moral clarity and strength. I learned that he was the head of the civil rights movement, and his name was Dr. Martin Luther King Jr.

At the time, I was going to an integrated school on the south side of Chicago. In truth, the population was almost all Black, as most whites had fled to the suburbs or private schools. The high school was built for a much smaller student population. We traveled like schools of human fish bundled together as we swam through the hallways, navigating the one-way up and another way down staircases needed to handle the overflow. Outside were makeshift classrooms in mobile trailers. We called them Willis Wagons after the superintendent who maintained the segregated schools.

By now, the consequences of racism were pretty clear to me but still as repugnant and disconcerting as they were when I was seven. There were food fights in the high school occasionally when the stress of the whole scene spilled over into the lunchroom. I never witnessed one, but my friends warned me to hide under the tables when the trays started flying.

Then one day, when I was a freshman in high school, my best friend Barbara told me about plans for a school boycott and a march to demand that the Chicago public schools be integrated. We took the

Illinois Central train downtown from Hyde Park to join the marchers at Balboa Drive. The organizers had planned to march to superintendent Benjamin Willis's office to talk to him when we arrived. We found out, though, that he had no intention of talking with us, so instead, the organizers directed us to sit down in protest.

After we sat down, the police attacked and beat some leaders, including Dick Gregory, a famous comedian, civil rights leader, and author. I had never seen a scalp wound before and was terrified at the sight of blood pouring like thick dark red rivers down the victims' faces. It was the first time I'd seen police use their billy clubs on protestors. But it wasn't the last time.

When the police came towards me and my friend Barbara, I told her to hold on tight as fear surged through my heart and mind. A burly-looking cop turned towards his partner and said, "I'll get that one," interpreting my remark as a challenge. With visions of blood pouring down my face, I stood up and offered to walk into one of the paddy wagons instead. It was a liberating moment as I saw this as a chance to foil his plans.

They took us in paddy wagons to the police station and began processing our arrests. Since the people I was with we were all minors, our parents had to pick us up. Arrangements were made for them to retrieve us in clusters, so fewer people had to take off from work. Later that evening, my friend Barbara and her parents watched footage on the news of the police yanking her arm behind her back as they tossed her roughly into the paddy wagon.

The disappointing reality is that, despite the efforts of the 250,000 who participated in the first Chicago school boycott, the Chicago Public Schools are as segregated today as they were in 1963. Chicago community organizer Bob Lucas describes the limited long term effects of these struggles in Gordon Quinn's documentary on the event (Quinn was also the director of the movies *Hoop Dreams* and the *Interrupters*).[76] This was not the future I hoped for on that fateful day.

∽⊛∾

One of the questions I continued to wonder is, why didn't schools make more progress on integration? What happened in Charlotte, North Carolina, is an example of how our country reneged on our initial commitment to school integration. In 1970, the school system worked to break the pattern of segregation, successfully eliminating most high-poverty segregated schools for many decades.[77] Anthony Foxx attended one of these integrated schools, then went on to attend Davidson College, one of the best liberal arts schools in the South, before being chosen to head Obama's U.S. Department of Transportation.

Foxx described his experience in an integrated Charlotte school and said it was the first time he saw his white counterparts as equals. In 1999, a conservative judge ordered the school system to undo its busing efforts as the political winds shifted. White parents sued for reverse discrimination and won. The schools are now as segregated as they were in the 1960s. Those five white families who went to court overturned 29 years of progress for 28,000 students.[78] Foxx's achievements illustrate how maintaining our commitment to the civil rights movement's aspirations could have further improved the quality of life for a large segment of our society. Stalling or reversing promises to fully integrate African Americans into the schools ultimately hurt everyone in our nation.

One result of Charlotte's return to segregated schools was that high schoolers in high-poverty areas graduated at a 77.6% rate versus 95.2% for their affluent counterparts.[79] Another consequence was the police killings of innocent Black people as they congregated around their schools. On September 20, 2016, an unarmed Keith Lamont Scott was shot by a policeman as he waited in his truck for his son at a school bus stop in Charlotte.[80] Black Lives Matter came to Charlotte to protest Scott's murder.[81]

This chapter focuses on three significant movement outcomes. First, the civil rights movement strongly repudiated the myth of separate but equal facilities by displaying the ugly underbelly of violence that held segregation in place. Second, it gave birth to an alternative narrative emphasizing how out of sync racism is with Christian morals and democratic claims of equality. Finally, the movement pushed for integrating public facilities, voting access, and additional job opportunities. It called for an end to segregated schools and housing, white supremacy terrorism, and police violence.[82]

One of the early protests around segregated dining took place in 1960 when four black college students dreamed up and organized a protest at a local Woolworths in Greensboro, North Carolina. Franklin McCain, one of the four original organizers, was 19. He said it was transformative to reclaim some of his personal dignity because the racism in our culture had made him feel suicidal in high school. It was a taste of what the future might bring and what it would feel like to be less restricted by the Jim Crow laws of the South. Hundreds of students joined him three days later. Copycat sit-ins emerged across the country as students in 55 cities replicated this strategy in 13 states. After six months of repeated protests, Woolworth switched to integrated dining.[83]

Voting rights was another long-desired goal for Black southerners. Although federal laws gave everyone the right to vote, southern states had created poll taxes, literacy tests, and threats of violence that made it impossible for African Americans to register to vote from 1900- 1965.[84] A pivotal moment for the civil rights

movement occurred after a march for voting rights in Selma, Alabama, in 1965.

The first protest march was led without a permit, resulting in the
famous Bloody Sunday event where 600 marchers were beaten,
attacked, and tear-gassed by policemen on horseback and men
on foot wielding billy clubs. Hundreds were injured and had to be
treated at a local hospital. Meanwhile, the white onlookers cheered.
This was all caught on video by news teams who got the footage to
their offices in time to play it on the evening news.

That night, ABC interrupted an award-winning documentary on
the Nazi trials at Nuremberg to show clips of people brutally beaten
in Selma. About 48 million people watching German WWII atrocities suddenly saw scenes from the attacks in Selma—the similarities
between Nuremberg and Selma were not lost on the viewers.[85]

This was the moment when the brutality of the caste system was on
full display. It was not separate but equal, as the Supreme Court had
suggested in the past; it was an oppressive, debilitating system that
disenfranchised Black people in every possible way, held in place by
the continual threat of violence. A dozen legislators spoke the next
day about the parallels between the Nazi stormtroopers and Governor George Wallace's troopers who attacked the marchers. Public
opinion in the halls of Congress swelled up to support the efforts of
Dr. Martin Luther King Jr. Racism was becoming an embarrassment
with these scenes rippling out in newscasts worldwide.[86]

King invited those who were morally opposed to what happened
in Selma to come the next day and join in the fight for justice.
His speeches stirred up a sense among some of the clergy that if
they stood with King, they could take a moral stand for the better
world he spoke about. The numbers grew as 2,000, primarily white

clergymen, joined King.[87] On March 25, after being granted a permit, 25,000 made the four-day, 50-mile walk from Selma, Alabama, to Montgomery to listen to King's celebratory words. This was a significant turning point in the movement's history because Selma, Alabama, was considered one of the most intransigent and brutal places in the South. The outcome of those efforts was the Voting Rights Act of 1965, which provided federal oversight to prevent the use of bogus literacy tests or other obstructions to prevent African Americans from voting.[88] While we made progressed in some areas, the victories were not easily won.

## THE TURBULENCE OF THE TIMES

In her book *America on Fire*, Yale historian and law professor Elizabeth Hinton details the many battles between 1968 and 1972 that occurred.[89] She describes the cycle that led to 1,949 uprisings across the country.[90] The violence was at a level not seen since the civil war, and it led to the destruction of millions of dollars of property. Hinton documents the events, showing how they created the foundation for our current climate of excessive policing, mass incarceration, and ongoing violence.[91]

Many rebellions came out of a cycle of police harassment that led to community retaliation. For example, Black residents picketed a local store in downtown Decatur, Illinois, in 1969, demanding more Black jobs. That evening, in response, police ticketed Black teens for drag racing. Meanwhile, white teens in another part of town were committing the same offenses without any objections from the police. This kind of prejudicial treatment brought on retaliation. The next night when a policeman arrived, two hundred Black teens trapped him in his car until reinforcements fired tear gas to disperse the crowd. Many incidents of harassment persisted across the country.[92]

Some of the fights were further exacerbated when white supremacists joined the fray. In Cairo, Illinois, 600 vigilantes were deputized,
calling themselves the White Hats, and they terrorized Black neighborhoods with shotguns. In the summer of 1969, they shot guns into
the Pyramid Courts housing project in response to an article in a
local newspaper condemning them as a repressive white supremacist
group.[93]

The newly integrated schools had conflicts, as well. Often racial disputes started over issues like including Black girls on the cheerleading
squad. Violence erupted in 1969 in Burlington, North Carolina, after
white students booed at the girls when they tried out and refused
to consider including them. While both Black and white parents
complained, confrontations escalated to a point where the National
Guard was called in, and one Black student was killed.[94] During this
time, some young Black men were killed in these types of fights, others were incarcerated.

Elizabeth Hinton further describes how the Omnibus Crime
Control and Safe Street Act of 1968 increased the use of military
hardware in policing these incidents. The result of these rebellions
was that the incarceration rate of young Black males increased so
much that 75% of the Black people incarcerated were under 30 in
the 1970s.[95]

California deputy attorney general Charles O'Brien (in office from
1962-1971) summed up the issue well when he pointed out that passing new criminal laws does not solve our problems. Inequality, poverty, and lost potential are not directly caused by the police, but they
are left to deal with the consequences and young peoples' yearnings
for opportunities. Consequently, he suggested, other social agencies
need to do more, find creative solutions, and take more responsibility
so that policemen are not scapegoated and forced to bear the burdens of all the failures within our systems.[96]

Yet that was a rare framing of the problem. Mostly it was presented in a way that supported an escalated level of policing and pushing back rather than addressing the underlying issue of harassment and repression. President Johnson called the retaliations to excessive policing "riots brought on by hoodlums."[97] This framing deflected attention from the repressive nature of policing and the damaging consequences of neglected neighborhoods at the root of these protests.

There was also an emerging sensibility that our culture needed to amplify our moral sensibilities by creating a stronger connection between our religious tenets and the way we lived our lives. Historians Maurice Isserman and Michael Kazin, co-authors of *America Divided: The Civil War of the 1960s*, claim that some of the most significant changes in our culture came on the religious front during that decade. More than a third of all Americans left their usual places of worship and sought a more direct connection with God.[98] Yet even these religious shifts went in different directions depending on political leanings.

The right-wing evangelical preacher Billy Graham had a magazine, *Decision*, with a subscription level that climbed into the millions as it promised an unchanging gospel in times of change. Evangelicals also offered help to people strung out on drugs. Vonette Zachary Bright and Dr. William Bright founded the Campus Crusade for Christ in 1951.[99] It grew over time so that by the '70s, they had a staff of 6,500 and a budget of $42 million to help convert young people to the evangelical ranks where they could "get high on Jesus, instead of drugs."[100]

Author Peter Russell suggests that our culture began to experience a spiritual crisis in the 1960s when, for the first time, a considerable segment of society wanted a different orientation - one not so centered on a materialistic worldview.[101] Sages from the East came to the

United States, stressing a need for everyone to develop more inner awareness as a prerequisite for happiness and a more generous and compassionate society.

Philip Goldberg describes in his book, *American Veda*, how Eastern knowledge about these inner dimensions of life came to the West as the Beatles met Maharishi Mahesh Yogi and changed our expectations for what was possible in human development. By 1968, our understanding of spirituality shifted. Meditation practices changed from being counterculture to being mainstream. By 1976, more than a million people had learned the Transcendental Meditation® technique.[102] While spiritual paths differed, there was a mutual recognition that our culture had overlooked some of the critical spiritual components necessary to build a strong foundation for a more connected and compassionate society.

## LESSONS FROM THIS PERIOD

The civil rights movement illustrated the strength of large numbers coming together to confront the Jim Crow laws. It showed that there was more safety in numbers and that as protestors gained a sense of their increased power, it also restored some of their personal dignity. The movement grew in numbers and effect over time. King's famous speeches articulated a new vision that began to emerge.

Yet structural forces of repression continued as police continued to harass Black residents in low-income neighborhoods. These forces have persisted into our current policing system. Some cities, though, managed to escape these trends through interventions. The few successes illustrate how we could reform policing practices across the country. Cincinnati was one of them. In 2001, after the death of 19-year-old Timothy Thomas, Cincinnati erupted into the largest disturbance the country had seen since the Los Angeles riots ten years earlier. Three other Black men had been killed in

Cincinnati five months before Timothy Thomas, so tensions were already high.[103]

After the uprising, the mayor brought in federal help. The police department entered into an agreement with federal overseers that required officers to focus less on arrests and more on getting to know the needs of residents. Federal monitors who oversaw departmental practices were treated with contempt and resentment at first. Over time, new policies were implemented, but it took 12 years to reach the goals stipulated in the agreement. Cincinnati Police Chief Streicher stressed that it was necessary to create accountability to avoid people slipping back into their old patterns. In the end, use-of-force incidents were reduced by more than half, and misdemeanors diminished by approximately a third of what they were before the intervention.[104]

Perhaps there is a question about whether we can afford such interventions. Yet we should examine what the current system is costing our society. A first-of-its-kind study by scholars at Washington University in St. Louis looked at all the costs associated with our incarceration policies. They concluded the price is $1.2 trillion a year in 2020 dollars (or 6% of our GDP). Poor communities and families bear the brunt of those expenses. Every dollar the criminal justice system spends is accompanied by a ten-dollar loss by communities and families. This ten-dollar loss results from lost wages, lower lifetime earnings, higher mortality rates, and increased criminal behavior after incarceration.[105]

Finally, the way issues are framed determines how they are handled. If Blacks are being harassed, that situation requires a different solution than if they are random hoodlums rioting in the streets. Whatever narrative prevails determines the course of action taken; therefore, creating a more nuanced and accurate picture of events is critical.

Understanding how progress became stalled helps to understand how contested this period was. While many of the movements that characterized this period had their roots in earlier times, Andrew Hartman, a history professor at Illinois State University, claims in *A War for the Soul of America* that the current culture wars are just a continuation of the deep divide that was first created in the 1960s and never resolved.[106] As the consensus around the need for change eroded over time, maintaining a commitment to it became more difficult. The next chapter examines two other movements of the 1960s that copied many of the techniques of the civil rights movement, as they also sought to create a more humane society in other arenas.

# 5

## CHANGING HEARTS AND MINDS

### *Committed civic groups can unlock a society's social conscience*

One early afternoon on July 22, 1964, Mario Savio and Robert Osman were walking towards the Freedom Project's downtown Jackson headquarters in Mississippi after registering Black voters. Suddenly, two Klansmen pulled up and jumped out of an older model white Chevy. They chased them with baseball bats. Savio was tall and able to outrun them. Osman, on the other hand, ended up with injuries that sent him to a nearby hospital.[107] While Osman escaped with his life, others were not so lucky. A week after the Freedom Project began, three civil rights workers were reported missing in Philadelphia, Mississippi, and later found dead.[108]

The Freedom Project was organized by Robert Moses, director of SNCC (the Student's Nonviolent Coordinating Committee). The goal was to involve college students—Black and white—in a campaign to register disenfranchised Black voters over the summer.[109] The potential voters experienced humiliation and intimidation during registration attempts—not success. At the end of the summer, 1,000 volunteers helped 17,000 people try to register; 1,600 succeeded.[110]

Despite the brutal attacks and their limited success, Savio said he thought the work was sacred; the divine working in the world.[111] As a 21-year-old, these experiences had a huge impact on his future.[112] Since he was the eldest in an Italian Catholic family, his spiritual sensibilities inspired dreams of becoming a priest, but his experiences in Mississippi drew him in another direction.[113]

Savio returned to the University of California at Berkeley, inspired to do more for the movement. Shortly after Savio arrived on campus for the fall semester, though, Chancellor Strong abruptly decided to prohibit organizations from coordinating off-campus political activities on the campus grounds after September 21, 1964.

Jack Weinberg, another civil rights advocate, challenged the prohibition by setting up an organizing table for CORE (the Congress of Racial Equality) on October 1st. Weinberg went limp and refused to move when they told him to leave. A police car drove onto the campus and put him inside to take him to the station. Immediately, students swarmed the car, engulfing it in bodies extended ten yards long on all sides.[114] The arrest took place at lunchtime, with a crowd estimated at 7,000 as people spilled out from class and joined the protest.[115]

After the car became immobilized, it became a podium for speakers. Graduate students  spoke about the culture of conformity and the fear of Communism—both leftovers from the '50s. This cast a long shadow inhibiting activism among left leaning liberals at Berkeley. The Sproul administration, pressured by the university's board of regents, had required faculty to take loyalty oaths that denounced any affiliation with Communism in 1949. These oaths chased away 131 faculty members who refused to sign.[116] In 1960, protesting faculty and students went to a meeting of the House Un-Americans Activity Committee (HUAC) in San Francisco and were washed down the stairs of City Hall by high powered water hoses.[117]

Michael Rossman, a graduate student at the time, explained that telling these stories cemented a collective appreciation of the long-term struggle for a less repressive society. He stressed that it was the first public dialogue that he'd ever witnessed where the sense of a public "we" emerged. Large numbers protested, even though peoples' careers were on the line. There was high potential for violence as 600 plus cops hid behind Sproul Hall, waiting, if needed.[118] Savio stressed how the hyper-individualism built into American life was replaced by the rediscovery of solidarity in these times. He described it as a process where new possibilities open up, and you realize what you've been missing in your life.[119] The standoff dragged on throughout an entire day and night of negotiations. The protestors finally accepted the administration's terms, leaving 36 hours after the protest began.[120]

Members represented a wide range of political orientations—from Young Students for Goldwater at one end, to Communists at the other. There were fifty groups that sent representatives to the executive committee meetings.[121] The local press falsely portrayed the FSM (the Free Speech Movement) as mostly radical communists.[122]

In the end, the administration did not press charges against Weinberg, but they still decided to charge the organizers of the October 1 activities. On December 2, the FSM organized a protest demonstration against that decision; 4,000 students converged on Sproul Hall. Savio, who was a powerful orator, gave his most famous speech at this event. He stressed that President Clark Kerr had described the university as being in the "knowledge industry" to defend the decision to forbid voter registration advocacy on campus and avoid becoming embroiled in the politics of the civil rights movement.

Eloquently expressing his frustration with Kerr's bureaucratic indifference, the speech became known as the "Operation of the Machine" speech. Savio complained that the impersonal bureaucracy had become like a machine, dehumanizing students. He complained that students weren't "raw materials" or people to be purchased by future employers. There comes a point when the ways of the machine are so troubling that you have to make it stop, he claimed.[123]

The speech was also a broader condemnation of the problems in our society as a whole. It was the complacency from years of institutions ignoring racism that created the need for a civil rights movement in the first place, highlighting the fact that indifference to immoral acts also has a destructive impact on the society. This speech became famous over time because it so powerfully captured the sense of dehumanization in our culture, inspiring songs and literary works, and has been quoted extensively. As recently as 2008, it was referenced by Occupy Wall Street protesters.[124]

Vaclav Havel, a former political dissident who later became president of Czechoslovakia, makes the point that the root problems in modern societies go deeper than economic issues of socialism or capitalism. The problem, he observes, is that humans are often feeling an overwhelming sense of powerlessness in big systems that are impersonal and operating counter to their moral sensibilities.

Havel also states that political parties are not the solution; they deprive humans of their own connections with their ethical sensitivities, good judgement, and genuine speech (free of slogans). What is needed instead is a group of engaged people (a parallel polis) that can help direct the political actors by illustrating effective moral ways to interact.[125]

In some ways, the FSM acted as a parallel polis, trying to spark the conscience of the university community by members simply speaking from their hearts. Several people wrote about the incredible level of authenticity in Savio's speeches and his whole way of being. Doug Rossinow, who is now a professor in the History, Religion and Women's Studies department at Metropolitan State University in Minneapolis, spoke about Savio's stunning ability to tap into deeper realms that awakened so many students' moral sensibilities.[126]

Savio's speech inspired students to take over Sproul Hall at 7:30 PM and stay until 3AM, when the police arrested the remaining 773 people who refused to disperse.[127] It was the largest mass arrest of students in American history.[128] This brought the university to a screeching halt. Classes were cancelled, rallies increased, and a hundred volunteer lawyers came to the aid of the students. Until this point, the battles had been largely between the administration and the students. However, the faculty now got involved; many exchanges took place as the various sectors of the campus community tried to process the whole event.[129]

The next day the faculty convened an academic senate meeting to debate the joint proposal of a liberal committee. Faculty broadcast their three-hour debate for students to hear. They voted 824 to 115 to support the students. Some members of the faculty were in tears as they came out of the proceedings to the applause of the students.[130] Bettina Aptheker, an FSM organizer, observed that both the faculty and students came to believe that the repression of the 1950s was finally over.[131]

President Clark Kerr, on the other hand, tells the inside story of the administration's perspective in his essay in *The Free Speech Movement, Reflections on Berkeley in the 1960s*. He explains his desire to keep the university free of too much politicization, the kind of political activism he'd seen in Germany in 1936 and 1939. He was involved in bringing Jewish refugees to the United States and became familiar with how the Nazis came to oppress student and faculty dissent.

Kerr, though, weakened his own ability to negotiate with the students when he fed into the red-baiting in the media as a political ploy to distance himself from the negative publicity. This undermined the students' trust in him and their belief that he was a fair arbitrator. The students also exaggerated Kerr's shortcomings, misrepresenting him, and ignoring his own liberal defense of freedom of speech over the years.[132] The inability of these two groups to mediate their differences left room for other forces to intervene.

Ronald Reagan ran for governor in 1966 and won on the platform that he would "clean up the mess at Berkeley," and "send welfare bums back to work." He made exaggerated claims about Berkeley and used it repeatedly in his campaign speeches. Both Kerr, and Earl Cheit, the executive Vice Chancellor at the time, observed that the FSM aided Reagan's run for the governor's office. Voters believed that the movement was a group of radical communists who needed a tough leader like Reagan to end their activities.[133] Of course, much of the media portrayed the FSM as a communist-inspired movement, a notion that the FBI endorsed. As a result, a statewide poll showed 74% of the people polled disapproved of the protesters.[134]

FBI Director Herbert Hoover wanted Kerr to label the protestors as communists and get rid of them. After he failed to gain Kerr's support, Hoover turned his attention to Reagan. Three weeks after Reagan was elected, he got Kerr fired.[135] The university community was appalled that a politician could exercise such power over the running of a university.[136]

There were also positive changes, however, that came to the university. Sean Burns from the Center for Developing Economies at UC Irvine points out that community engaged scholarship with their diverse roots had many influences, but the 1960s demands for relevance was perhaps one of the biggest milestones.[137] The movement built what Burns called a culture of "social transformation" where issues like white supremacy were debated in public venues and students requested that their courses examine these issues. Consequently, faculty became involved in community-engaged scholarships and continue to ask those same questions today.[138] In the end, Savio's legacy has been commemorated in multiple ways, including a plaque where he spoke at Berkeley, a downtown square named after him, a lecture series, and an activist award given posthumously, due to his early death in 1996.[139]

The Free Speech Movement set Berkeley up to become a strong center for change and engaged advocacy, and, along with other universities, it helped spread the anti-war movement.[140] President Eisenhower at the end of his presidency, in 1961, lamented the fact that the military industrial complex had become so powerful. He stressed, therefore, that it is especially important that it not be left to determine our foreign policy.[141] The Vietnam War, however, was a poster child for how difficult it was to stop an ongoing war, even when the majority of the public came to oppose it.

## THE ANTIWAR MOVEMENT (1965–73)

Bill Zimmerman, an organizer in the anti-war movement, wrote an opinion piece in the New York Times describing the four phases of the initiative. The first part of stage one (1964-67) involved educating the public through campus teach-ins staged across 120 campuses over a three-month period, ending with an April rally that brought 20,000 people to oppose the war.[142] The teach-ins provided opportunities for discussing important questions like why are we fighting in Vietnam? How are we waging the war? Can we win it?

Louis Menard, author of *The Free World: Art and Thought in the Cold War,* makes the point that we spent 30 years involved in Vietnam, including financial, diplomatic, and finally military involvement. We dropped three times as many tons of bombs on Vietnam as the Allies did in WWII, and Vietnam is a country the size of New Mexico. Yet in the end we had nothing to show for it; at no point was there any sign that the anti-communist forces were on track to prevail. The military advisors both misunderstood the enemies' true motives for independence and the military situation on the ground.[143]

Professor Hans J. Morgenthau, a conservative political science professor at the University of Chicago, wrote a New York Times article at the time, arguing that we should get out of Vietnam because it's a civil war that the Vietnamese should handle on their own. Furthermore, he suggested the way to create strong democracies was not through military acts, but through economic development and support.[144]

The other disturbing issue was the cruel tactics of the war and its effects on civilians. Napalm, a sticky tar like substance, caused excruciating pain because it burned at very high temperatures. When people tried to wipe it off, it spread instead, creating panic and huge, often deadly burns. The use of Agent Orange to improve visibility also destroyed 20% of Vietnam's foliage and caused terrible burns and after effects.[145] Protestors complained that civilians were too often the primary targets, and in addition to that problem, we were supporting a corrupt dictatorship under President Diem.[146]

Diem also jailed 100,000 people without trial, torturing, and executing some.[147] However, the worst exposé of our brutality occurred with the My Lai Massacre. A photojournalist captured an image of a small girl running through the street in terror as American soldiers wiped out an entire village consisting of 347-504 unarmed civilians. Along the way they raped 20 women and girls, some as young as ten. According to reports in The New York Times, U.S. soldiers in that unit admitted committing these atrocities and explained rape had become so endemic that it occurred routinely in their killing operations.[148]

The Communists, on the other hand, were also guilty of inhumane practices and repressive measures. When they finally took over, they followed the usual protocol that Communist countries did at that time; they took over the schools and ended the free press. Hundreds of thousands fled the country with estimates of 200,000 deaths among those who tried to leave. Some on the left had romanticized the Vietcong, thinking that Ho Chi Minh was just a nationalist fighting for independence or that Communism would look different than it did when he took over.[149]

After the successful education phase was implemented, the second phase involved uniting the resistance through marches and protests. A new level was achieved in November 1969, when 500,000 people protested in New York, the largest gathering of this sort in history. Draft resistance increased as celebrity figures like Muhammed Ali inspired others to go to jail or flee to Canada.[150]

The third stage was more militant and chaotic with a less clear strategy (1969-71). While the mainstream anti-war movement itself never condoned violence, some extremist elements emerged on the fringes. The Weathermen was an anti-war group that had 300 members who went underground because of their radical politics. At the trial of the Chicago Seven in 1968, they vandalized shops along Chicago's Gold Coast while the trial was going on in what came to be known as the "Days of Rage."[151]

What drove these secure middle class young people to take such extreme measures? Emile de Antonio created a documentary about them. Mark Rudd, one of the people in the film, explains that the frustration was so strong as nothing seemed to be working to discourage the war, so they became filled with hate and a demented logic took over. He said he took on an air of moral superiority that also prevailed in his thinking.[152]

The war continued and took a draconian turn in 1969. The U.S. had 500,000 troops in South Vietnam[153] and yet the intervention was still failing. So a frustrated President Nixon, on April 28, 1970, announced his decision to expand bombings into neighboring Cambodia.[154] Protests broke out on campuses across the country.

The most infamous protest was at Kent State, Ohio, where 28 national guardsmen fired into a crowd of unarmed college students, killing four and wounding nine. The killings sent shock waves across the country.[155]

On May 1, several days before the Kent State massacre, Nixon had gone to visit the Pentagon. There he referred to the protestors as "bums," while calling the soldiers involved in the war "the greatest."[156] Later, a father who was looking at the corpse of his dead daughter in the pictures of the Kent State killings, responded angrily that his daughter was not a bum.[157]

These comments demonstrate the deep disconnect between the left and right's perceptions of protestors during this time. James Rhodes, the Republican governor of Ohio, compared the protestors to Hitler's brown shirts and said they need to be eliminated. Vice President Agnew used similar language. Ronald Reagan, governor of California by this time, said, "If it takes a bloodbath, then let's get it over with."[158]

Nixon's expansion of the war not only lead to large student protests, but the bombings destabilized Cambodia, as well. A leading scholar, Ben Kiernan, estimates that between 50,000 and 150,000 Cambodians were killed by the U.S. bombings.[159] The Khmer Rouge used the chaos to wage war against vulnerable ethnic minorities, professionals, and Buddhists, killing approximately 1.7 million in their genocidal acts (21% of the population), according to most estimates.[160]

The fourth stage of resistance, that comprised the anti-war movement, heightened after the My Lai massacre in 1971. In the documentary film *Sir! No Sir!* by Displaced Films, they made the point that as the war wound down, there were more and more desertions and killings of officers because of the brutality of the tactics of the war.[161] Finally, after ten years and five presidents, the long crusade against the Vietnam War brought to a close one of the most unpopular wars ever fought.

## LESSONS FROM THE 1960s MOVEMENTS

One important take away from the Free Speech Movement (FSM) is that it is better to find compromises within a shared ideology than to exacerbate the differences and allow a more extreme approach to prevail. This is, of course, easier to say than to accomplish. The differences between generations are always hard to bridge – especially in times of large-scale change.

Another key point is that the FSM was so successful because of the heartfelt way that Savio spoke to people, touching their emotions and stirring others' moral sensibilities. He freed their movement from the deadness of political slogans and the limits of ideology by embracing students all across the political spectrum who appreciated free speech. The collective feelings of the groups that had emerged from their joint discussions were expressed in his famous speeches. It was a great model for how to create solidarity in movements – lessons for this time where a huge democracy movement is necessary. As the push to resist autocracy increases, we will want to create a large, diverse coalition for a tipping point towards the deep reform that is needed.

 One of the most powerful lessons from the anti-war movement was that people can change their minds through meaningful educational experiences that allow them to explore an issue without pressure to agree with one side or the other. The teach-ins had an extensive impact, especially when coupled with celebrities speaking out against the war. Large educational events organized around climate change concerns could have a similar impact to the teach-ins that happened in the 1960s. A tipping point can be reached more quickly when groups coalesce through open dialogues.

The issues of that time are still with us today. The Vietnam War is just one of the many wars that have been an embarrassment to the U.S. If we want to strengthen our democracy, it has to start with improving it both at home and abroad - in times of war and peace. What we could benefit from, instead of more wars, is more innovative approaches like the investments made through the Marshall Plan after WWII-efforts that rebuilt Europe. We could use more actions like Reagan's negotiations with Russia that led to the reduction of nuclear weapons. Also, more talks like Kennedy's conversations with Khrushchev – those talks ended the Cuban missile crisis, a standoff that could have led to a nuclear war with Russia. This is especially important today as nuclear powers like China and Russia continue to act more aggressively.

However, the power of the military industrial complex has grown extensively over time, making it a source of campaign funding, and potential jobs for retiring Congressmen. The use of more diplomacy will probably only happen if the public demands more civilian control over the military. Yet even more central to creating significant change is the necessity to take money out of politics; that is the prerequisite for real systemic shifts in the military industrial complex.

# 6

## A Bold Democracy Movement

### *We need game-changing reforms to shore up our democracy*

What we need now is a democracy movement that is as powerful as some of the movements of the 1960s. One that can create a reform agenda that can be bold because it is backed by a broad majority of people. It should also be conceived and created through interactive civic discussions with people from different perspectives across the country. These conversations could begin to restore nuance to our political narratives. They also should focus on restoring integrity to all our institutions, so they reflect our highest ideals. Instead of seeking genuine solutions, our politics has become a grandstanding exercise, won not by the candidates who have the best ideas, but by the ones who have the most money and the best marketing gurus.

It is a critical time when people need to experience a new alternative rather than just maintaining the status quo or choosing an autocrat. What is called for is a new living democracy that can honestly address the needs of the people rather than pandering to the worst tendencies in our country.

Our country has also been naive about the power of public relations firms to shape our elections by manipulating our emotions.

Al Gore, in his book *Assault on Reason,* describes how his analysts were able to accurately predict what kind of emotional appeal would produce an 8.5% jump in his poll rating.[162] When he used their prescribed tactics, he got precisely what they projected. Mass media and public relations firms have learned how to manipulate outcomes so that the winners of elections are often those with the strongest emotional appeal rather than those with the most effective solutions.

An agenda that confronts five critical issues could begin to take our society into a healthier place. Our goals should be to:

1. increase the power of citizen input into our governance,
2. end the winner takes all system within our politics,
3. regulate social media,
4. finance high-quality news, and
5. create stronger accountability.

## INCREASING THE POWER OF CITIZENS IN GOVERNMENT

Our national discourse used to be a powerful tool for addressing the concerns of the people. We were a country capable of genuine debate based on shared facts, a real concern for solving problems, and caring for each other. Now, most of the analysis and discourse is around cherry-picking and twisting information so that the parties appeal to their political donors and their group's voting bloc. It is important to find our way back to that earlier situation where real issues were addressed and significant legislation was passed. We could decrease the influence of special interests and big donors if we capped the amount of money that is spent on campaigns and/or provided government funds.

Other democracies do not spend the kind of money we do on elections. According to the Center for Responsive Politics, the total amount spent on the 2020 United States election was $14 billion, more than double what was allocated in 2016.[163] In 2017, Germany spent $109.6 million for all their candidates at election time. Their election cycle is much shorter than the U.S. and is funded chiefly by the state.[164]

The U.S. outspends every country in the world per capita on elections. Since 1971, the Supreme Court overturned restrictive laws against campaign contributions, opening doors to what amounts to legalized bribery.[165] Money in political campaigns also tends to favor affluent donors so that they have an undue influence on who gets to run for office and who gets elected.

Our broken politics is at the heart of most of our problems. It is the one thread that, if it was unraveled, would open up a world of new possibilities. There is a growing recognition that getting money out of politics is central to producing an effective government, but the problem is that any reform initiatives go through a system that is unwilling to change itself.

Therefore, citizens should assert their power in innovative, bold ways. For example, they could convene citizens' constitutional conventions in states across the country and then weave those ideas together and create a national agenda. Also, we should discuss changes to the constitution that would help us deal more effectively with the limitations we are up against as we navigate a 21st-century world with an 18th-century document.

Citizens could focus on what needs to change and the fastest way to implement reforms, working with experts as necessary. At these gatherings, powerful facilitation methods, described in the next section, could help generate inclusive, and collaborative thinking. New kinds of conversations outside of politics could allow us to escape this stuck place that we've been in for so long.

Another important outcome of these conventions should be the popularization of new narratives that could guide us away from our toxic discourse towards more positive citizen-driven messaging. These groups could also partner with state-level politicians to encourage reforms from the grassroots up.

Change is more likely to come from the bottom up because no political party can jeopardize its funding streams without the security of a full-scale popular movement behind them. Maine shows what is possible locally when the influence of money is reduced. In 1996, a bipartisan team of local politicians passed the Clean Election Act, which allowed candidates to get state funds if they secured a large number of small donations ($5) that indicated broad-based support. They had to agree to forgo raising significant contributions to be eligible.

This system allowed many more blue-collar candidates to run and win. For example, Deb Simpson was a waitress and a single mom before she served in the Maine House of Representatives from 2000 to 2008. In 2008, 85% of their legislators were elected from state funds. Firefighters, teachers, and other workers were able to run for office. Women gained the most from the state funds.

The consequences were that the little state of Maine created the most robust public policies in the country, primarily geared towards meeting the needs of the working class. This demonstrates the enormous impact public funding could have on who represents the citizens and what legislation gets passed. The problem is that in 2010, the Supreme Court ruled against state matching funds in the Arizona Free Enterprise Club vs. Bennett. In Arizona and Maine's matching funds program, the state could help add additional funds to finance a state-funded candidate if his opponent started outspending him. After this provision was struck down, the Maine system was reduced to only 51% of the candidates using state funding in the 2014 election.[166]

This story of Maine's experiments illustrates how state funding enables people with less money to get adequate representation. Kagan, an associate justice of the Supreme Court said that only in a backward world would competition from publicly funded candidates be seen as an attack on free speech.[167] Securing state funding for elections should be included in a democracy movement in order to bring the voice of the people back into government.

Another major problem is that our political system has turned our politics into a winner takes all approach where whichever party wins the majority determines who controls everything. Yet this actually works against the best way to create policies, which is to have vibrant debates and carefully crafted compromises that help legislators design the best laws.

## MOVING TOWARDS TEAMS INSTEAD OF WINNER TAKES ALL POLITICS

So often in our current system, we get leaders who are selected because they all profess the same policies in order to satisfy their donors. Since the best policies come from cooperative teams, why don't we encourage our congressmen to work together in diverse groups? This would discourage the extremism on either side and allow more people to run on a platform that had more universal appeal.

Lincoln used a diverse team approach described in Doris Kearns Goodwin's book, *Team of Rivals: The Political Genius of Abraham Lincoln*. The book highlights Lincoln's team's diversity; political representatives from every strand, conservative to radical, worked with him. In a talk on NPR, Goodwin describes how emotionally intelligent Lincoln was as he negotiated peace between all these different factions.

He felt that if he could keep them all talking together under the same tent, he could keep the country together.[168] This would be a powerful new approach to start by using it locally and refining it through experience. Teams could be organized around topics like local sustainability or business growth and less around political parties. Another critical step is for our country to regulate social media and change our media model, as well.

## SOCIAL MEDIA EFFECTS

Jonathan Haidt, a social psychologist at New York University, discusses his concerns about social media and the problems with our political parties in an article in the Atlantic Magazine titled *Why the Past 10 years of American Life Have Been Uniquely Stupid*. It highlights the destructive force social media has played in our lives, making us stupider by amplifying the worst tendencies on both sides.[169]

Haidt makes the point that on the right, social media has helped further spread the belief in conspiracy theories, and on the left, it has stifled dissent, reducing tolerance for diverse points of view. This has been problematic on the left, where younger progressives often attack older liberals, and the universities cater to the demands of the students, sometimes firing professors for questionable reasons.

For example, David Shor, a Civic Analytics employee, was fired after responding to protests after George Floyd's death with a tweet that linked to a 1960s study showing that violent demonstrations led to electoral losses for Democrats. He was clearly trying to be helpful, but he was accused of antiBlackness. This term is used to highlight that someone is uniquely prejudicial towards African Americans, as opposed to all people of color.[170]

Haidt says that Civic Analytics denied they fired him for that reason. It's in line with a trend, however, since 2020, where questioning policies, or actions, may cost you your job. The result of this period,

Haidt claims, is that dissent has been stifled in most of the cultural institutions that the left controls – Hollywood, Silicon Valley, and educational institutions. The traditional liberals went silent, and the radical ones prevailed. Many reporters resigned from the New York Times during this time.[171]

We have lost a sense of balance in both our political parties. The extremes on either side tend to be too powerful in our society, making constructive dialogue difficult and inhibiting consensus or compromise even within similar orientations. It is often hard to translate experiences from generation to generation. There was a considerable generation gap during the 1960s because the pace of change was so fast, and there is one today for similar reasons.

It would be helpful to use powerful facilitation tools to create a safe space for more discussions about the two generations' different perspectives. These conversations could benefit from more nuance, with people talking face to face, coming to understand each other's motivations better, sharing power, and seeking compromise.

Regulating social media companies could also discourage them from pandering to our worst tendencies. Haidt claims that anonymity encourages more extreme behavior, so insisting people identify themselves might help. It would be in the same vein as requiring banks to identify their customers, so they do not launder money for criminals. This could go a long way toward reducing death threats and the most destructive behaviors executed by a small number of people using the Internet. The advancement of artificial intelligence will also make things worse, Haidt suggests. People will be able to churn out misinformation in droves – we could get even stupider, much faster.[172]

Tristan Harris is an American technology ethicist, executive director, and co-founder of the Center for Humane Technology. Harris calls for a digital constitutional convention to discuss how to regulate social media, so it supports our democracy.[173]

Furthermore, restoring respect for the truth is a prerequisite to enhancing our national discourse. It is an essential guardrail for generating a shared reality to guide our conversations. Historically, the truth has been discerned through a well-developed process that distinguishes fact from fiction, curating it carefully through institutions and journals.

In his book *The Constitution of Knowledge*, Jonathan Rauch details the history of the development of respect for the truth, as brought out through the scientific method. It is a collective enterprise whose fruits we all enjoy, but it is maintained through a rigorous set of underlying rules, guidelines, and agreements. This accomplishment has taken time to develop and should not be dismissed lightly.[174] In addition to valuing truth, we must honor the value of diverse perspectives. Bringing groups together to be exposed to different points of view can bring attention to our own personal biases and broaden our thinking.

Culturing a commitment to restoring more effective patterns of political interaction is an important part of the process of rebalancing our democracy. The dysfunction in our system expresses itself in multiple ways. Over time the standards in our political discourse have become increasingly dishonest and lacking in substance. Candidates use trivial and contrafactual information to peddle outrage with great emotional gusto, making one passionate issue override attention to all others. Extensive publicly funded news and regulation could bring a more profound and less partisan approach to the coverage of issues.

## REGULATE NEWS MEDIA

Al Gore points out that our news is supposed to be like the immune system of our democracy; it filters out the things that are false and unhealthy for our society. What went wrong? The public discourse is no longer as discriminating as it once was. Too many media and political forces ramp up the use of fear and other emotional filters to undercut our ability to ferret out the truth.[175]

Robert McChesney, a professor at the Institute of Communications Research, points out in his book *Rich Media, Poor Democracy* that the more democratic a country is, the better its public broadcasting system. Governments committed to democracy realize that news should have high standards so that people can meaningfully participate in the political process.

He suggests that the drive to improve media should be part of a broader social movement to convince legislators to make changes. The Netherlands, Germany, and Japan have a much different model of news broadcasting that includes public funding to get higher-quality news. Once commercial television has taken over, it is hard to turn a country back to subsidized information that serves the public.[176] A bold democracy movement should create enough momentum to rethink how we disseminate news.

The concentration of power in the hands of fewer media companies means that a handful of people, with a revenue that is equivalent to the size of what some small countries have, can now determine our news. From the 1960s to the 1980s, news media went down to 6 major companies. Cable news followed a similar consolidation pattern, so by 1999, 6 firms controlled 80% of the nation's programming.[177] This has led to a strong current of protecting the status quo and made the media an anti-democratic force in the United States. The consequence of this is a state of hyper-commercialism and the degradation of journalism.[178]

Junk news has also grown in our country through programs labeled news, but they are instead either propaganda or outright entertainment. Due to the shrinking of the companies that report news, information has been dumbed down. The trouble is that it distorts our worldview, and our news has become inundated by attention to sensational but insignificant events.

These practices undermine our national discourse and our ability to sustain a truly informed citizenry. Jefferson claimed that educated citizens are necessary for the survival of democracy, and today much of the erosion of our democratic sensibilities is due to the toxic effect of false news. [179]

Neither the level of critical skills taught in public education nor mass media have kept up with the pace of change and prepared citizens for the public relations tactics of the 21st Century. The public needs better reasoning skills, more sophisticated tools of analysis, citizenship knowledge, and broader global awareness.

It is not only a problem of money in media, but in both Congress and the presidency, money plays too central a role in who gets to run for office and who gets elected. Special interests have too much power in determining our elections. All these troubles have undermined the quality of our democracy and our ability to hold all our representatives accountable.

## ACCOUNTABILITY

There are four categories for determining the robustness of a democracy: full democracy, flawed, hybrid, and authoritarian. Since 2016, the U.S. has been downgraded to a "flawed democracy" and was rated number 25th from the top out of 167 countries, as analyzed by the Economist Intelligence Unit, which ranks countries yearly. The rating is based on five aspects of governance that are individually scored and then averaged: electoral process, civil liberties, functioning government, political participation, and political culture. Our score has continued to fall; in 2019, it was 7.96, and in 2020 it fell to 7.92. In 2021, the U.S. fell further to number 26 with a score of 7.85.[180]

Norway ranked number one with a rating of 9.81 in 2020. The reasons for our low rating were described in the report. It was due to a low level of trust in our institutions and our political parties, and deep dysfunction in the government. They also highlighted our polarization that makes consensus extremely difficult to achieve.[181]

One way to change our counterproductive practices and broken institutions would be to create an independent agency funded by Congress yet designed to reform our democracy by creating enforceable ethical standards. Too many institutions have become corrupted by narrow special interests that undermine what the majority wants.

We should reach a point where every institution is analyzed in terms of how they uphold our democratic ideals. That could be the north star that guides everything. The Supreme Court, for example, has ended the federal constitutional right for women to have an abortion, for the EPA to regulate carbon emissions, and undermined safety by expanding the right to carry concealed guns. Representative Jamie Raskin, formerly a constitutional scholar, pointed out that the Court has been on a reactionary binge. It is also clear that they have more disturbing decisions on the way. In the past, stacking the Supreme Court seemed like too extreme a measure, but now in light of the justices' behavior, it is seen as a way of saving the Court and giving it more legitimacy by bringing it in more accord with the majority's views.[182]

It also raises the question should six judges on the Supreme Court have the power to dictate what millions of women choose to do with their bodies? Their authority should not include dictating their religious preferences over the beliefs and desires of millions of women; otherwise, we cease to have a democracy and are well on our way to a theocracy instead.

Mechanisms must be established to prevent a country of more than 330 million people from being held hostage by a handful of extremist judges. Too many of our systems are outdated and operate with little accountability. We need more oversight over our institutions, so they are able to reflect the values necessary to create a functional modern democracy. This is where an outside agency or a civic constitutional convention could propose useful strategies to counterbalance our institutions when they go rogue.

Isn't it more important that our policies reflect the people's will than follow a system that is no longer working and was designed more than 200 years ago? The authority to determine whether we rise to meet climate change aspirations concerns the fates of all of us, and we should have ways of weighing in on a decision that could end life as we know it. Without adequate accountability, rogue actors can manipulate our system without any consequences. This is how we got to a point where the Supreme Court is undermining democracy instead of upholding it.

There are two courageous approaches that the president could take to address the Supreme Court issue. First, the president could defy the Court. Alternatively, he could stack the courts with four more justices. Andrew Jackson proceeded with his relocation of Native Americans even though the Supreme Court ruled that it was unconstitutional because the president has the right to enforce or refuse to follow the Court. [183] But these are both troublesome choices because they set a terrible precedent.

Ultimately, it would help to have a less political process for appointing candidates to the Supreme Court. They should not think of their obligation to a party, over their role as a true arbitrator for justice. They need to uphold values that best serve our ideals. Disturbing decisions like Citizens United that allowed more money to flow into our elections show how far they have retreated from that position.[184]

An agency outside the government could force Congress to adopt higher standards. The agency could also oversee state-level civic panels that serve as an interface between the people and their representatives. The civic leaders of these committees could help the public make better judgments about the news and reduce the toxic effects of false information. Citizen panels, with a new federal agency with teeth, could create more mechanisms for strengthening the role of citizens in stewarding our government.

The citizen panels might set up regular interactive sessions with a group of experts to help educate their communities about important issues. These panels could also bring concerns from the people to the attention of their local and state representatives. They could further inform the public about what their representatives are doing, serving as a secondary source of verification. Another task they could take on would be to modernize our systems, so there are better incentives for our representatives to work together to accomplish big things. Ultimately, it is also critical to avert our slide toward autocracy.

## RESTORING HEALTHY STANDARDS

One of the goals of these civic groups connected to the panel could be to work to re-establish lost standards and enhance our democratic standing. For our democracy to survive, our legislators should put attention and money into strengthening and modernizing our institutions and creating higher accountability standards.

Our biggest problem, though, is recovering from the damage that comes from the aftermath of this period of divisiveness. Bullies and power-hungry leaders may not be stopped by others espousing values they do not hold. Our society needs better guardrails against future strongmen. Restoring ethical behavior and accountability is critical to shifting towards a more robust government.

This is a time when bold shifts must pull us in the right direction. Game-changing reforms are necessary now to avert the danger of the collapse of our democracy. Civic leaders in the past have engaged in activities that have profoundly impacted our country. Sometimes large, convincing, populist movements can break through concentrated networks of power.

That is what the Bank of North Dakota did when it drove power down to their state, taking it away from the wealthy out-of-town bankers. This makes sense because one of the problems we face is that we are such a big democracy it is difficult to feel effective at creating change across the entire country. We should take a page from our history about how to act boldly to reclaim our power.

Civic leadership can leapfrog over existing hierarchies by simply persuading people to take their power back. A.C. Townley and Frank Wood turned the placid State of North Dakota into a hotbed of radical change where socialist ideas took root in the early twentieth Century. Townley was an inspiring orator who made novel socialist ideas seem like obvious solutions. His friend, Frank Wood, was a charismatic organizer. Together they persuaded 100,000 farmers to join a nonpartisan league that would create a new political party. Farmers banded together and developed alternatives to the banks' high commercial lending rates. At that time, 78% of the people in North Dakota were involved in agriculture, so most of the state was impacted by these issues.

Its mission was to help fund agriculture, business, and commerce; it could give low-interest loans to individuals and the state as needed. In 1917, the nonpartisan party took over, and two years later, it created a state bank (the Bank of North Dakota – BND) to help farmers get more reasonable terms on loans. In the 1940s, they sold foreclosed farmland back to farmers after the depression had subsided.[185]

The benefits from that bank were not only immediate, but they continued and grew for over a century.

While the rest of the country was falling into a recession after the 2008 financial meltdown, North Dakota was humming along. At the time, the reckless behavior of the financial industry cost us $22 trillion in economic wealth, according to the Government Accountability Office. Our annual gross domestic product is $13 trillion, so if we had all taken off from work for almost two years, we would have lost the equivalent of what the bankers lost through their reckless behavior.

Twelve months after the meltdown, the foreclosure rate in North Dakota was minimal, plus they had a state surplus of $1.2 billion. Neighboring Minnesota was looking at a deficit of $5.2 billion. North Dakota's unemployment rate was 3.4%, while nearby states were double-digit. They were doing so well because the state bank shielded them from the economic vagaries of the market since its inception.[186]

The BND operates like a public utility with complete transparency; it can handle loans for state emergencies, fund these things with low-interest loans, and repay itself without draining its operating cash. No other state has this kind of financial power for public emergencies.[187] One prominent businessman at the bank also explained that they did only legitimate loans, avoiding the risky unsecured ventures that led to the 2008 debacle. While many cities and states were on the brink of bankruptcy, BND paid out an annual dividend and put 50% of their profit back into the state's general fund.[188]

These tactics shifted the welfare of an entire state and are the kind of approaches needed now to cut through the status quo and rearrange our power dynamics. As the BND illustrates, large groups can re-imagine what is possible and make it happen. Ultimately, what is needed is a new party that really represents the people.

❧

The strength of movements is that they can shift norms and take us towards a different future, away from the limitations of the past. They are powered by solid narratives and dramatic actions that question the status quo. They are a vital part of the tapestry of progress. Once momentum is attained, individual initiatives sponta-neously arise, and people find many creative ways to keep the focus on the necessary changes.

# PART III.

## TOOLS FOR GAME-CHANGING CONVERSATIONS

Have you ever had a conversation where your perception shifted from something that someone said, and it had a profound impact on your thinking? Exchanges can have significant and long-lasting effects, catalyzing new behaviors you never imagined undertaking.

In the past, we have shifted our perception as a nation because of bold new approaches launched due to a compelling new vision or idea. When President Kennedy suggested going to the moon, it was a radical idea, but ideas become a reality when we move toward them. Before the G.I. Bill, veterans had never been offered long-term support when they returned.

Right now, we need better tools to focus our country's future

toward more connection and hope and away from fear and violence. Many of us want those things; we just have to let go of some of our past assumptions and beliefs and reconnect with each other so we can come together to master the challenges of the 21st Century.

Deep change is necessary, and it will take all our collective intelligence and wisdom to figure out how to introduce it in a timely way. What is needed now, more than ever, is catalyzing conversations that inspire actions and can have a transformative effect on our society by giving us a sense of inner renewal and inspiration as we take on the necessary reforms. This section provides examples of tools that can help us create those conversations.

# 7

## CULTURING OUR COLLECTIVE INTELLIGENCE

### *Tools for helping groups work in the zone*

Have you ever watched a flock of birds cross the sky in V formation, marveled at their orderliness and harmony, and wondered why
humans can't function in those ways? Deborah Tannen observes that
we have a warlike culture that approaches everything, including public dialogue, in a combative way.[189] We tend to become attached to
our points of view and cling to them. Opposition and conflict are the
themes that prevail in the news; stories of unity and bridge-building
are rarely told. The idea that everything must be presented in the
frame of an argument has gone to such extremes that completely
false ideas are presented as just one side of a dispute.

Tannen describes how a holocaust denier got TV coverage because
he represented an alternative point of view. The danger of this is that
it casts doubts about well-accepted understandings and undermines
the credibility of all facts.[190] Furthermore, this approach destroys
the genuine nuances that exist and the possibility of discovering the
subtle facets of a subject.

Of course, all conversations don't have to be like that; most of us
have had conversations where we sit with old friends and hang on to

each other's words. They remind us of what is possible in chats with friends or lovers, where the connections run so deep that they can finish each other's sentences. Why can't more of our conversations be like those? With careful facilitation, group conversations can be more stimulating and enjoyable; they can even be a way to diffuse tensions and increase connections.

Have you ever seen people having a fight, and then they somehow make their way through to a reconciliation that makes them feel closer than before the battle? The Gottmans, famous marriage therapists, say this is the best possible outcome of a fight between couples. People who develop their conversational skills expand their capacity to experience connections even under challenging circumstances.[191] We could experience multiple benefits if we tooled up our communication capacities and cultured new ways of interacting.

In this chapter, I'll review examples of an approach that creates spaces that can help develop our collective intelligence so groups can function at their peak. In these spaces, groups can tap into their most productive ways of interacting, ways to resolve conflict and handle past grievances. These techniques cultivate new kinds of conversations. Then, in the next chapter, I will focus on the most critical question: How could we have more conversations that bring this collective intelligence into our national discourse?

## UNCOVERING COLLECTIVE INTELLIGENCE

Tom Atlee, the author of *The Tao of Democracy*, describes how he was on an eight-month, 1,200-person, cross-country Great Peace March for Global Disarmament that commenced in 1986. Three months into the journey, the group became embroiled in an extended fight for days and threatened to break up the group. It is ironic that people on a peace march would end up in such a fight, but it shows how susceptible we all are to squabbles. Even the most refined peace-loving people can become caught up in disputes.

Finally, one rainy day, they sat in a fertilizer factory and were asked to discuss their deepest feelings about the issue. They talked for two hours about the problem that was tearing them apart. After everyone had spoken and felt heard, a calm settled over the group, and the answer emerged spontaneously. No decision was made, but the idea emerged as a natural consequence of the lengthy discussion. The trouble was that one faction wanted to walk in close proximity to emphasize their numbers, and the others wanted to spread out so they could have one-on-one conversations. They saw how they could satisfy both desires by staying close together in the cities and walking separately in the countryside where no one was watching them.

Atlee explains how he felt like he had witnessed a miracle and wondered about it until he came across a passage describing a meeting with the Turtle Clan of the Onandaga Iroquois. Oren Lyons explained how the tribal council had met and talked until they had covered everything, and the truth emerged. Atlee called this experience the uncovering of the collective intelligence of groups, a process where the various gifts of all are integrated to produce an advantageous outcome for the whole.[192]

He had uncovered a moment when a group harmoniously inspired a more collaborative sensibility and operated like the birds that fly in a formation. This is a proven approach to resolution, one that some Native Americans have been practicing for a long time. We can learn how to replicate it in our work in groups.

A conversation is a powerful tool for bringing minds together. Research studies suggest a physiological change occurs when groups reach a consensus. A study by Dr. Sievers, a social neuroscientist at Dartmouth College, highlights how people synchronize their thinking on a neural level when they achieve agreement. After reaching a consensus, he mapped people's brains in groups and found that their brain waves continued to be synchronized even when thinking about other topics not discussed. He found that people with the same inherent dispositions had similar brain alignments as groups that had just reached an agreement.

Demonstrating people changing their minds, helped others do so as well. However, if a strident person drowned everyone else out, it was harder to reach an agreement. Mediators, though, could be a powerful force for generating unity by modeling their ability to switch positions.[193]

## GROUPS IN THE ZONE

In these moments when divisive conversations become more harmonious, it is as though groups turn on their collective intelligence and work at their maximum capacity. Like an athlete who excels and talks about working "in the zone," there is an experience like that for groups. Atlee describes this state as characterized by six qualities: 1) emotional intelligence and many other types of intelligence are used, 2) collaborative interchanges prevail (there is an enhanced capacity to share power and enter a group problem-solving state), 3) divergences are used wisely and incorporated into refining the solution, 4) holistic, systemic thinking arises, 5) deeper and wiser problem solving emerges, and 6) the self-organizing intelligence and underlying harmony in natural systems can prevail.[194] It is a hidden, deep capacity that should be cultivated, especially now.

The unique quality of this experience is that the dynamics shifted so that instead of each person thinking only like an individual, people began to also consider other perspectives and work as a unified group. Atlee calls this sharing power with each other instead of trying to establish dominance over others.[195] These experiences are incredible to watch but even more magical to experience because individuals come to work together as a well-functioning team in a heartening way where they feel part of something bigger than themselves. This experience satisfies some deep yearning to be connected to our shared humanity in a revitalizing way.

It also represents the best kind of democratic functioning—one in which we think holistically about the welfare of ourselves and others and we can bring all our emotions, intuitions, and profound wisdom into the conversation. As the group bonds through these shared feelings, they also become more invested in the needs of the collective. They expand their sense of self to include a larger field and become less attached to advocating for their ideas.

These groups draw out a broader, more holistic level of awareness. Groups could evoke this state by creating the right conditions for it to emerge. When groups enter this state, they have access to a collective consciousness that Atlee describes as being grounded in their shared humanity. The wisdom of the group emerges from this level.[196]

What is unique about this style of functioning is that because they listen empathetically to one another, these groups can consider all sides of a situation in all its complexities. They not only accept divergent points of view; they welcome them and consider them a valuable component of the problem-solving mechanisms needed to conjure up a profound solution. The big picture perspective can emerge, and people can take on a long-term view, examining various solutions objectively.

The answers they come up with are often common-sense responses, or sometimes, they offer out-of-the-box solutions. These groups can focus on local, state, national, or international problems. Wicked problems that are difficult and complex to solve are within their grasp. They can listen to experts without being pulled into the trap of advocating for the expert's personal solutions.[197]

They can also respond to problems more effectively than the masses because they can really study an issue collectively from many different angles without the force of one particular approach silencing other perspectives. Atlee describes an event in Canada that captures some of the features of these types of interchanges. This one was convened to bridge differences between the Quebec secessionist aspirations and those who didn't want a separation.

## BRIDGING DIFFERENCES

In June 1991, Maclean, Canada's leading magazine, sponsored and hosted a three-day meeting of a dozen diverse individuals to discuss the Quebec separatist movement. This group of individuals had been carefully selected because they were articulate representatives of all the various perspectives on the issue. After arriving, they soon started arguing, and the group looked like it might dissolve in anger. However, they began to have some breakthroughs when they split into small groups. At the end of three days, they had all signed a detailed agreement that charted a new course forward. They developed deep bonds through the process and left hugging each other goodbye.

How was this transformation possible? Roger Fisher, world-renowned negotiator and co-author of *Getting to Yes,* and two colleagues facilitated the event. The process began with everyone cataloging their grievances. While they disagreed on how to solve them, this process produced a growing understanding and agreement about the severity of the problems. The process was both educational and relational. People became educated about the high poverty and infant mortality rates that the Quebec separatists experienced and more sympathetic to their expressed pain and anger.

Through many intense interchanges, the group began to move towards solutions after the depth of pain had been heard, and everyone felt deeply heard and understood by their opponents. The twelve-person group came up with a four-page manifesto that suggested policy changes within schools, government, businesses, and within segments of society. The Canadian Broadcasting film crew that filmed the event called it a transformative event for everyone. This case study illustrates the power of bringing diverse facilitated groups together to have deep and constructive conversations.

Other attempts to have focus group conversations—a $27 million forum on Canada's future among them—had not yielded such powerful results. This conversation led to town hall meetings that discussed the manifesto and Maclean magazine wrote extensively about it, and a TV station recorded the one-and-a-half-day event. It illustrates that the depth of conversation is critical to creating the healing shifts needed.[198]

It was a powerful example of how civic interchanges can diffuse conflict. Unfortunately, some politicians felt threatened by the outcome and squelched any continuing conversations so that their work was not a foundation for something more. The key to having a practical result is that these conversations must ultimately penetrate into the power structure. These powerful voices that genuinely represent the public's needs must be given the authority to carry the weight they deserve.

The next example focuses on the transformative effects of Judith Glaser's work, which illustrates what becomes possible when the voice of collective intelligence is taken seriously and used to help guide businesses.

## OTHER WAYS TO EVOKE OUR COLLECTIVE INTELLIGENCE

In her book *Conversational Intelligence,* Judith Glaser describes another approach to evoking collective intelligence. As a coach for business executives, her consulting work allowed companies to transition from the bottom of their industries to the top by generating more authentic problem-solving conversations. Through her coaching, they could more effectively analyze the things they needed to do to move to the top of their industry. Her work helps shed light on how conversations can evolve to deeper levels.

Glaser outlines three levels of conversations: transactional (Level 1), positional (Level 2), and transformational (Level 3). A transactional conversation involves a simple exchange of information; people try to inform each other about something. A positional conversation entails inquiry and advocacy—often people are trying to persuade each other to adopt their point of view. A transformational discussion is characterized by sharing and discovering information so thoroughly that stunning new possibilities emerge from the conversation.

These different kinds of conversations have other characteristics. Glaser points out that all these types of conversations are necessary, but the transformative ones are where people explore issues and become more open to new questions that they don't have the answers for. To experience the gains from these types of conversations, Glaser taught groups how to create and maintain Level 3 conversations, and they became skilled at switching to these types of conversations when needed. The three levels are described in more detail below.

Level 1 – (Transactional) This is relatively straightforward. We use it a lot in our interchanges. Our intention at this level is to gather information or dispense it. We are listening to protect our ideas or ourselves from criticism and are hoping to promote our success. Our trust is shallow at this level, and we are not open to much influence by the other person.

Level 2 – (Positional) The goal in these conversations is to persuade others to either agree or disagree with a proposal, and people tend to want to win listeners to their side. Trust is conditional on how the conversation is going, and success is mainly viewed in terms of the speaker's ability to persuade others to his/her opinion. Power is slightly expanded in this level from focusing on one person to shifting to include the group.

Level 3 – (Transformational) These conversations engage the whole group and are a way to co-create new understandings from the group mapping their individual interpretations together to create a shared vision. The group participants influence each other through their interchanges. They listen to connect with each other rather than trying to simply inform or persuade a group. The members' aspirations for mutual success and trust are high during these interactions. They begin to focus on questions they don't have answers to and have limited knowledge about.[199]

Glaser found that she could shift a company's entire culture by changing their conversations. When they could have more authentic (Level 3) conversations and address their challenges more honestly, they could take on problems that had previously eluded them. Cultivating these powerful conversations within their organizations allowed them to move into a stronger position in their industry.

As a result, leaders created the conditions for breakthrough conversations that could uncover critical missing pieces of information that prompted new actions that led to much higher performance levels.[200] Glaser uses the term conversational intelligence to describe the skills needed to achieve a high level of collaboration. These are aspects of the art of conversation that people can learn and replicate and embed into their organizational discourse.

She found that certain qualities must be present in a group for it to function on Level 3 continually. People had to feel safe in the group. In addition, they had to think that diverse points of view were welcome so they could openly talk about their experiences and be heard. Also, there have to be high levels of trust because when someone experiences an emotionally uncomfortable confrontation, they tend to go into fight-or-flight mode and shut down.

If those conditions were met and they knew how to tap into these subtler levels of conversation, they could activate qualities like empathy, trust, and integrity. Then the ultimate goal was to map their different visions together and create a fuller picture of the whole situation.[201]

This serves as a good summary of the pre-existing conditions necessary for groups to work in their zone, as well, and express the collective intelligence that Atlee wrote about. Other groups could also begin to encourage the acquisition of such skills. They could start to map their views of a situation together and come up with clear and profound insights to help them solve wicked problems.

A case study shows how the process worked in one company. Glaser worked with Clairol, the hair dye company when their sales were down. The marketing department thought their promotions were too weak, and the sales department thought the salespeople needed better incentives. The advertising executives felt they should have younger people in their ads. No one was on the same page.

Glaser worked with senior executives to get them to go more into a discovery mode instead of their usual top-down approach. She took them through 5 steps: 1) be transparent about the problem; 2) focus on building rapport and respect before taking on talking about the task; 3) listen to understand different perspectives; 4) focus on shared success rather than self-interest; and 5) test assumptions about reality gaps in people's versions of the problem and discuss them.

Glaser created communication newsletters to get everyone aware of all the conversations and perspectives, and they began to merge onto the same path forward, focused on customer feedback. Over time, they started to ask questions they had no answers for and began to discover the knowledge they needed to climb to the front of their industry.

As the conversations shifted, their sales went from $250 million to $4.5 billion in less than a decade. Furthermore, by applying these strategies to other companies, Glaser was able to help many companies create powerful problem-solving cultures by cultivating these higher-level discussions.[202]

Dynamic Facilitation® is another powerful tool for tapping into a group's collaborative intelligence. New opportunities emerge when people come together with a desire to merge their understandings of a problem from various vantage points and seek consensus on the best way forward. This approach allows groups to improve their collective problem-solving capacity.

### DYNAMIC FACILITATION

It's incredible how often little things can trigger significant events. My friend Susan came to visit from Ashville, North Carolina, and we had a discussion probably neither of us expected. Both of us were thinking about how contentious everything was getting in the political climate and how disappointed we were about people's behavior, so it probably shouldn't have surprised us when the talk turned to problem-solving. We researched Jim Rough's Dynamic Facilitation technique (DF) and decided to give him a call.

Jim's workshops are designed to bring people together and teach a technique for finding solutions to problems in a way that brings out the group's collective intelligence. Usually, these events involve people with dramatically different viewpoints. Our spontaneous call led to some not-so-short hours of planning a workshop. We invited friends and other facilitators and had our first training.

When Susan and I first invited Jim Rough and his wife Jean to give a Dynamic Facilitation training seminar, I wasn't sure how people would respond. While Jim described the process to us, I had yet to learn what it would be like to undergo a three-day workshop. Sitting through three days of talks could be exhausting. Yet, when they came, I found it exhilarating to watch how the group came alive, and people began to connect intimately in very short order.

Our workshop was in an old, chilly church. In fact, some of the participants left with colds in addition to a new way of working together. Reverend Gumbo from Zimbabwe was the minister at the church, and he gave us a good deal. The attendees were a diverse group in our first DF workshop. One woman worked on food policy councils to help create a better local food network, and another woman was head of the city neighborhood improvement office. Yet, over time, all their stories became mixed into a sense of camaraderie as we tackled various problems together. What I had yet to anticipate was how inspiring and transformative the experience would be.

Later, after some instruction, we all broke into small groups to discuss the issues we cared the most about and applied the facilitation techniques we were learning. The subjects covered a wide range of topics, from how to finance Food Policy Councils to how to fund third-world projects in Zimbabwe. We got together in a vibrant way around problems we wanted to solve. Everyone felt empowered from working in a group with such a strong sense of solidarity around an issue at the end of the conversations.

The minister was excited and impressed with what we'd done, so he brokered my first facilitated event. I partnered with a friend who had taken the workshop with me. The topic focused on sending money back to Zimbabwe through a newly formed non-governmental organization (NGO). The audience was a bunch of Zimbabwe ex-patriots, and the head of the NGO had flown in from Washington, D.C., to persuade them to donate to it. Before the presenter even got up to speak, the crowd started complaining about how much corruption there was in Zimbabwe. Of course, that set us up perfectly for the use of Dynamic Facilitation because it is a process that allows people to delve deeply into their concerns.

The speaker was planning on a walk in the park. He was upset that the audience didn't immediately support his cause. Instead, they wanted to know how he was going to prove to them their money was going to go to those he claimed would be the recipients. They had a long history of seeing their money intended for the needy intercepted by greedy individuals.

At my first facilitation, I realized immediately that the people in the room needed more information and time to develop trust in the new NGO. It felt like training under fire. In the end, the featured speaker appreciated what we had done. Our efforts not only had people contributing immediately but resulted in many later gifts from people who reflected on the event and got their concerns addressed at a different time. My fellow facilitator and I were proud that we could stick to our commitment to reflect the group's sentiments and resist the temptation to let the presenter talk them into something before they were ready.

Peggy Holman, the co-author of *The Change Handbook*, which outlines many facilitation techniques, recognizes that DF offers some unique tools for engagement practices. I am not alone in recognizing its profound power to stimulate deep problem-solving and enthusiastic experiences within groups. In Rosa Zubizarreta's manual on DF, Holman wrote in the Forward about her experiences as a group participant using the technique. She explains that the charm of it lies in its ability to help us get underneath dysfunctional outbursts and tap into the deep angst underneath all our clamoring. The conversation helps uncover what is at the heart of our concerns, and in the process, we also map out a vast, more complex picture of the whole problem. It emerges, to our surprise, as a coherent deep response that has been enhanced by examining many different perspectives.[203]

 We came to appreciate that the most divergent voices often brought the best ideas into the room. While most of us are uncomfortable with the tension associated with opposing views, those unique perspectives proved to be valuable in transforming the group's thinking within this welcoming space.

Holman explains that she and others shifted attitudes in response to the simple act of being deeply heard as the facilitator reflected back the words of all the contributors. It became easier to see the humanity of her fellow participants. She felt more tolerance and compassion for divergent points of view as personal stories became linked to those perspectives.[204]

The next chapter describes how Vorarlberg, Austria, used DF to facilitate Citizen Councils. These were so successful that they became institutionalized by the state of Vorarlberg to bring a coherent civic voice into the national discourse to foster change. So often, these conversations, which have so much power and vibrancy, need to be given the authority and capacity to influence our politics. These examples show how government agencies can respond with better policies through more meaningful, inspired civic engagement.

# 8

## GENERATING A COHERENT CIVIC VOICE

*Examples of how Citizen Councils bring the voice of the people into government*

The Dynamic Facilitation technique (DF) was created by Jim Rough and derived from his experiences working in a sawmill on the Pacific Coast. He began by working with the employees only because management didn't want to be involved. They just wanted more harmony and efficiency in their workplace.[205]

### THE BIRTH OF DF

The discussion started with the men describing how much they hated their boss and how all their problems would be solved if he was fired. As they began to tap into a deeper level of group functioning, they realized that the boss was just symptomatic of the low trust level at the sawmill. People had little autonomy or respect. Throughout working with these groups, Rough was able to help participants develop more trust in one another; as they became more confident in advocating for themselves, the workers obtained more autonomy.

In his work, Rough created a safe space for a people to feel deeply heard, and perceptual breakthroughs would occur through his work. New decisions spontaneously arose as a consequence of their shifts in understanding. As a caveat, this is not to say that they all go into a "group think" mode and become like the Borg of Star Trek fame. People can maintain their individual differences but also work with the group to find points of convergence. Rough describes it as a process where people dip into their shared humanity and think from that more universal level.

Through working with the men in the sawmill and other venues, Rough found that he could reliably help groups create conversations where they would have breakthroughs and achieve consensus around a set of solutions. He discovered that his technique allowed people to engage in a process he calls choice-creating, where new options emerge because the conversation is open and honest, and people are learning together, all invested in increasing the group's problem-solving capacity.[206] Psychologists have found that if someone puts a puzzle in a chimpanzee's cage, the chimp will naturally try to solve it without any rewards.[207] Humans, too, are natural problem solvers and can be charmed into collaboratively working on finding a solution because of the intrinsic rewards.

## THE PROCESS

The process is really like a long conversation that is captured on charts. There are four charts to separate the information into categories as it arises. The first chart holds the problem statement. A second one captures the solutions given, while a third one captures data related to the issues. (Data include observations, details about the context of the problems, beliefs, perspectives, etc.) The final chart captures the concerns of the group that come up often when a solution is presented. These comments encourage the group to seek a solution that addresses the additional issues that are captured on the concerns chart.

This chart encourages people to hold the tension between different approaches until the end, when new ways of resolving these tensions may emerge. The conversation flows spontaneously, similar to a gathering of friends, and is captured on the charts. At first, it seems chaotic, but in the end, an underlying order emerges over time.

The facilitator's job is to listen deeply to each contribution and record it, often inviting a deeper description of what the person is trying to say. This keeps the process open for a long time and allows the group to digest many different points of view. The facilitator also encourages divergent thinking to maximize everyone's input and to avoid premature closure before the group comes to a more profound understanding of the issue.

Rosa Zubizarreta, who wrote *From Conflict to Creative Collaboration*, a complete manual that details the process even further, explains that there is a flow that has its own pace and allows breakthroughs to shift the conversation and move it to deeper levels. People are also invited to bring their passions and emotions into the room, which adds juice to the process. Zubizarreta says the role of the facilitator is to welcome with warmth and curiosity all opinions that are offered into the mix. She or he holds diverse perspectives and listens empathetically to everyone's contributions. The facilitator also creates a sense of safety so that anything can be said without negative judgments.[208]

DF differs from more traditional dialogue approaches—although information is shared, solutions are invited whenever they come up. Often, throughout the conversation, the problem is restated in a way that gets closer to the core of the issue, and the group starts exploring things from a new angle on a more profound level. It is not the usual linear approach. The conversations weave in and out around different aspects of the issue as participants voice multiple concerns.

Many solutions come up along the way, but the deepening of the conversation leads to the most provocative ideas. The facilitator's role is to hold the tensions between diverse solutions as more nuanced solutions emerge or even be open to a complete reconceptualization of the problem—which often happens—taking the conversation to a much more fundamental level.

As Rough gave more and more seminars in Dynamic Facilitation and asked groups to address major unsolvable problems, they came up repeatedly with the observation that the system we were living in was the real problem. He describes the system as a game with rules that we live by, but the rules do not reflect reality. For example, our systems are treated like football games. Everyone intends to score, and things get pretty competitive. But if someone gets injured, we realize it's just a game and attend cooperatively to the player's injuries.

On the other hand, in our systems, we need to remember that the designs are just agreements we have constructed to organize the rules of our culture, and we have gotten stuck inside them. We live our lives as though everything is a competitive game, but the truth is that we are interdependent. This structure only sometimes addresses that aspect of our reality.

Rough points out that people say it is just the nature of humans to act selfishly. Still, he suggests that if you put them inside a different structure, they act differently and favor other values. We have become trapped in a system that no longer works for us. Our rugged individualism used to work when people took responsibility for their actions. Now greed has replaced that ethos, Rough explains in *Society's Breakthrough*.[209] What is necessary is to put new structures in place that bring out our collective intelligence and wisdom. drawing on the increased capacity of a high-functioning group.

Rough suggests that we must move to a more interdependent system that brings groups together more practically and allows for examining issues from multiple perspectives. This new system will be more like a circle that allows decisions to be made from a new kind of conversation that comes from the group's collective wisdom.[210] These groups will then reflect the common-sense voice of the people that emerges once they have explored critical issues in a more nuanced way. Rough created the idea of having citizen groups come together in Councils to dispense the group's collective wisdom and develop recommendations for problems the government wants citizen input on.

## CITIZEN COUNCILS

Citizen Councils were an excellent theory, but when a state in Austria picked up the idea, it became more than a theory. The results achieved in Vorarlberg, Austria, prove their effectiveness with various systems in place that we can emulate for initiatives in the United States. For example, they have a whole ecosystem set up so they can include community input from their Citizen Councils. (Their Citizen Councils are 2 -3-day sessions using DF to address a particular social problem.) Manfred Hellrigl, head of the Office of Future Related Issues, has spearheaded Citizen Councils there since 2005.

Dynamic Facilitation combined with Citizen Councils is a fantastic process. It's hard to capture on film or even in verbal or written communications. The results, however, are life-changing. Some shifts go on inside the audience, leaving everyone with a sense of solidarity. Because of how tensions are held between different points of view, participants can keep going deeper, hearing differing perspectives until a united resolution emerges from integrating many ideas.

Few will dispute today's political system in the United States is broken. Most will argue there's nothing a mere mortal citizen can do. That's not true. Small community groups across the globe are accomplishing remarkable things.

This book is designed to help community residents and change agents have a more significant impact on regional and, ultimately, national government decisions. Most won't be able to stand up as a federal legislators to argue a point but might be amazed at how much can be accomplished at the grassroots level. After all, elected officials are supposed to be sharing the voices of the people they represent. Isn't it time we called them to task together?

Using a combination of Dynamic Facilitation and a random selection process, local public administrators in Vorarlberg, Austria, developed a system for bringing the people's voice into policymaking at the local, regional, and state level.[211] They have been able to do that by first structuring Citizen Councils that come together to discuss an issue and then the council's explorations and suggestions are then shared with larger groups, who give feedback on these recommendations. This process has grown and spread throughout Vorarlberg.[212]

While it may sound like a grueling process, it's not. Participants love it because they come in as individuals and leave with a feeling of solidarity. One participant from Austria's Citizen Councils raved about the experience, saying in all his 65 years, he had never had such a good conversation about politics.

## LARGE-SCALE CONVERSATIONS

The organizers also used techniques for seeding large-scale conversations based on the findings of the Citizen Councils. For example, a modification of the World Café method that is propagated by the World Café Foundation is used to disseminate the results of the Citizen Councils.

The World Café often uses a format that enables groups to come together and engage in 3-4 rounds of conversations around small tables that accommodate 6-8 people. A topic is chosen for groups to focus on with a rotation system where participants move to different groups to discuss the issue. People are assigned various roles, such as scribe, timekeeper, and presenter. The ideas are then harvested and shared with the whole group. It creates a shared space for productive conversations while simultaneously creating a basis for a shared sense of trust and commitment.[213] In Vorarlberg, they use a modified version of this format for small groups to share their experiences working in Citizen Councils with a larger group and then get feedback from them about their recommendations.

The founders of the World Cafe technique, Juanita Brown and David Isaacs describe the process as remembering a world we have forgotten, where people gather to talk about things and are not afraid to share what matters to them. While it has been overlooked by many, it is still waiting for us to use.

The sense of community created in a World Café is something many people crave. We may have given up on it, but the desire to be part of a vibrant, engaged community is always there; it may be dormant, but the yearning remains, and it can be awakened. In those moments when that need is fulfilled, there is a feeling of excitement, increased vitality, and satisfaction, coupled with a sense that this is the real promise of community that we've all been hoping to experience.

I once had the opportunity to go with some friends to meet Juanita Brown and David Isaacs. We spent the day there, lingering late into the afternoon before we left. They greeted us with such a genuine interest in what we were doing that it was like going back in time to a place where there was always time for long, deep, and intimate conversations. It was as though no one wanted to leave the space created for such charming discussions. I still remember it with vividness as though it happened yesterday.

While people may hunger for deeper connections, there need to be more community venues that bring us together to find points of agreement. To restore a sense of camaraderie within our country, we need to do things differently and build a more robust capacity for safe spaces that can improve our connections and allow us to move forward more effectively in ways that speak to our deepest values, hopes, and dreams.

Manfred Helrigl, an organizer of the Citizen Councils in Vorarlberg, Austria, describes how these councils have been addressing the problem that political parties are failing to consider. He points out that throughout Europe, democracy is in crisis everywhere because politicians serve special interests. Reporters even talk about how sick and tired they are of the political grandstanding.

Citizen Councils can reinvigorate democracy by bringing the people's voices directly into the public discourse. In Vorarlberg, they invite politicians to respond to the statements from the Citizen Councils. Politicians are also amazed to see citizens handle these issues with friendliness and come up with such generous answers. Manfred describes how it is changing their culture; the young people want this new approach now to replace our broken system.[214]

## HOW THE CITIZEN COUNCILS ARE STRUCTURED

Vorarlberg has developed a six-step process for their Citizen Councils. First, the Office of Future Related Issues designs a question and compiles all the data related to the question. Then participants are sent letters and asked if they would like to volunteer in the Citizen Councils. In step three, the chosen question is presented to approximately 23 randomly selected people who have accepted the invitations to join the Citizen Council.

These people are not expected to represent the views of others but rather their own personal perspectives. The power of what comes out of the group is primarily due to the facilitation technique that enables people to go to a level where they appreciate their shared humanity and speak from that vantage point. Their final decision is then presented similarly to an advisory board.

The fifth step is to hold World Café style presentations where other community members can also add input into the points from the Citizen Council. At these meetings, the sponsors (local politicians and public administrators who have sponsored the Councils) are present to hear the Council's recommendations and to see how the more extensive public responds to them. They usually have from 50-150 participants at their World Cafés.[215]

Step six involves a responders' group composed of stakeholders, public administrators, and agency representatives who track how the recommendations are implemented. The various local government departments and agencies then implement their suggestions. This stage also entails a follow-up report describing the actions that were taken. Information about the follow-up is also publicly shared with the citizens, especially with the Citizen Council participants.

Through these types of discussions on issues, community members in Vorarlberg have consistently been able to come up with common-sense creative solutions to problems. Collective wisdom comes from people looking at issues from multiple vantage points and generating a resolution that takes into account all the concerns in the room.

When the Vorarlberg government first started using Councils, they did them at municipal and regional levels. In 2011, they tested the concept statewide, then conducted 32 in the subsequent three years. Topics covered concerns ranging from how to retain young people in rural communities to creating energy independence. The results have been so well received that Citizen Councils were added to the state constitution in 2013. So now citizens can create one on a particular topic of public concern when they want to give input by getting 1,000 signatures, and the government will finance it. The government, in turn, convenes one when it wants citizen input on a issue.[216]

Vorarlberg has found that these Councils can reliably represent the common-sense voice of the people. They have continuously evaluated the process and found that it consistently produces excellent results. Because the people are randomly selected, special interests are also not allowed to undermine the discussion as they are in many political events.[217] It inspires people to become more engaged in their communities because their ideas are being heard.[218]

The Councils can also be organized at the bequest of the parliament or other government offices. The Office for Future-Related Issues has helped spread the process throughout Austria, Germany, and Switzerland by offering information and assistance to others who are interested.[219] They have found that it costs 7,000 euros (or $8,500) per year to run a Citizen Councils process, including the Cafés. The Organization for Economic Cooperation & Development put out a report in June 2020 that showed that it was one of the most cost-effective democratic interventions. All the other interventions were in the double digits. Some of the topics covered in Citizen Councils include quality of life issues, young peoples' future opportunities, the future of agriculture, and land issues.[220]

### EXAMPLES OF CITIZEN COUNCILS

To illustrate how these councils work, I will take you through several of their Citizen Councils sessions. One of the most compelling examples of the productive use of Citizen Councils was in Bregenz, Austria. Over two years, some investors had spent 100 million Euros ($132 million) trying to develop a plan to access the beautiful waterfront that faces Lake Constance. The problem was that a train track and a roadway cut off peoples' direct access to the waterfront. The developers wanted to build a tunnel underneath the trains and the rails. The mayor decided to convene a Citizen Council to get ideas on how to develop this prime area.

So, the Citizen Council met for a day and a half (following the usual protocol). They came up with the idea that they wanted a bridge accompanied by grand steps like the famous Spanish Steps in Rome, so they could sit high up and see the sunset over the water from a better vantage point. The Citizen Council participants were so excited that they later created a visual model of what they wanted. In one and a half days, through the group's collective wisdom, they had made a better model than the one that had been under development by experts for several years and cost $132 million.[221]

The second example tackles the issue of what to do about refugees. The state sent out 500 letters soliciting help with an upcoming Citizen Council. The sponsors selected a random group of 23 people who had accepted the invitation to participate in the Citizen Council. The citizens' task was to address the situation of asylum and refugee seekers in Vorarlberg.

First, people talked about their concerns regarding the high number of refugees. Then, they were disturbed and said that the government needed to be more transparent about the numbers. Someone then pointed out they should see the people behind the numbers. That stirred people's compassion for the refugees. Another person suggested they should help them find jobs.

In the end, the council made three critical recommendations: 1) the government needed an open communication policy; 2) they should coordinate stakeholder's efforts to create a coordinating website for refugees and others to use; and 3) they should inform the public and enlist their help to do everything they could for these people. Jim Rough told me that one of the people who organized the event said: "These are things no politician would feel comfortable saying."[222]

The meeting led to 28 other events involving World Cafes around the state (where 30-80 people were in attendance at each one.) Citizens gathered to hear the recommendations of the Citizen Councils and to add their own comments to the brief summaries that participants provided regarding the scope of the conversation, the highlights, and insights gleaned from the process. Through this process, networks were established to help new refugees.[223]

Citizens then talked in small groups about their response to the Citizen Council findings, they added things they would like to have included, or they could flesh out a part of the solution in more detail. The results of this Citizen Council were also published in three different magazine articles. One of the promoters observed that the Citizen Councils are creating a culture of collaboration.[224] The government and the people have started to work together.

One of the most powerful Citizen Councils was in Mauthausen, Austria, and illustrates how even very hot topics can be handled. In the Mauthausen Citizen Council of 2013, they decided to address the issue of what to do with an empty Nazi concentration camp that was the largest concentration camp in Austria. It was in the middle of their town and had stood empty since the end of World War ll. The facilitator was told that the topic was too hot to handle; she should not even touch it because the community was very polarized about it.

Nevertheless, she bravely gathered a group of randomly selected people to address the issue. As the group talked, a tense moment occurred when one man said he didn't want the former camp used for immigrants because there were already too many. They cost the state too much money. The facilitator asked him why he felt that way. The man was stunned to have his statement received that way. He expected the facilitator to verbally slap him, and then he planned to walk out of the room in a rage.

Instead, she asked for more details about his feelings about this topic. He explained that his daughter had been looking for work for three years, and it didn't seem fair that they should have help accessing work while she had searched everywhere. The tension in the room shifted as he became humanized. This led to the idea that job listings could also be made available to others looking for work. Then a 15-year-old girl asked if people were thinking about immigrants in the same ways that the Jewish people had been seen by the Nazis? Since he had felt heard, that opened up a space for him to consider her perspective without acrimony.

In the conversation, older people said they were tired of talking about the Nazi period and didn't want to talk about it anymore. In contrast, younger participants said they felt like no one ever really talked about it. As they began to talk about it in the council, one person said she wished she had acted more courageously and done things differently. Everyone had tears as people expressed their anguish over the past. At the end of the session, someone said that now they felt like healing could begin for the first time.

In the end, two 15-year-olds said it was beautiful to talk to older people and have them listen. The older people commented about how wise and knowledgeable the young people were and how glad they were to speak to them. One of the results of that Citizen Council was that they later convened a Human Rights Symposium in the town.[225]

Manfred Helrigl points out that a substantial benefit of the Councils is the emotional learning that goes on as people think collectively about issues and comes to terms with their feelings more constructively. He said people commented on how there were lessons of the heart that they needed to learn.[226]

## THE EFFECT OF CITIZEN COUNCILS

If we think about the creation of our country, it started with a collective conversation that introduced the concept of democracy to the public. Thomas Paine's book *Common Sense* tried to make it accessible to the common man. When countries become stuck in dysfunctional patterns of interaction, it is helpful to shift our discourse. Interventions that restore goodwill and trust within society can effectively unleash a revitalizing and healing energy that enhances our capacity to empathize with each other and find points of consensus.

Jim Rough explains that in the beginning, our government rejected an autocracy and chose a contract-based system, where interpreting the contract became the critical basis for making decisions. He suggests that our system's next level of evolution should include a co-founder mentality, which means a Citizen Council is convened every year with 12-15 randomly chosen people to develop a series of statements about the state of the union. The council is then disbanded until the following year.

Our governing could be influenced by some civic representatives that can create a living conversation that moves us forward and truly represents us. The value of this is that the people's voices would be expressed yearly, along with our representatives voices. They would not subtract from any of the other processes, but they could add to them.[227]

There have now been 100 Citizen Councils convened using DF in Austria, Germany, and the U.S. Dr. Patricia Nanz, from the Institute for Advanced Sustainability Studies, said that the most exciting thing she observed through her research on Citizen Councils was how they had created an evolving culture of participation in the state of Vorarlberg, Austria. Others who had been involved also added that it is a positive way for citizens to be involved without being engaged in the dark side of politics.

One mayor commented on how it saved him hours to convene a Citizen Council to get their feedback, giving immediate legitimacy to a project he was starting. Politicians are more cautious than citizens because they worry about how their behavior will affect their ability to get elected. On the other hand, randomly selected people can make decisions that might be unpopular to a politician. People are sometimes more aware of certain on-the-ground aspects of an issue than experts and are more grounded in reality. Experts can be caught in their own bubbles, as well. Furthermore, they found that the hotter the topic, the better, because participants were eager to come to the event. Citizens could also take a big-picture perspective on complex subjects with DF.[228]

## CREATING A FOUNDATION FOR HEALING

These case studies illustrate how these conversations could be the foundation for creating a living democracy where the compassionate voice of collective wisdom is expressed. When doing evaluations of the Councils, they found that people are yearning for these types of authentic conversations. They enjoyed the creative energy built into the process and the diversity of opinions that enriched the experience.

It also illustrates how the space can be welcoming enough to hold all the diverse perspectives that arise and then focus on the most profound, most significant aspect—often the unspoken parts of the trauma associated with the situation. It also held the tension between the young people who felt there had never been much discussion about the war and the older people who didn't want to discuss it. The resolution was for the older people to finally come to terms with their regrets, and then everyone held the pain together.

Coming together in civic groups could catalyze the revitalization of our other potential partnerships. More coherent deep civic participation like this could revitalize our democratic sensibilities and—over time—move us towards a partnership model of democracy where diverse groups of citizens work with the government in many ways to keep it a vibrant system that changes and adapts as needed. These civic groups could also help push our representatives to work in a partnership way.

In this period where profound change is needed, we will want to become an extremely efficient learning society that helps everyone understand what is coming and what they can do to make the transition as smooth as possible. There are psychological, intellectual, and spiritual changes in our orientation that could make our modifications smoother. Game-changing civic conversations could help create narratives that help us make the powerful shifts needed to handle our modern challenges.

# 9

## WE GET THE FUTURE WE CAN IMAGINE

*Powerful techniques for
making visions come true*

Have you ever had a conversation that went amiss? You start talking with a friend, and suddenly the conversation gets confrontational, and a fight erupts that doesn't end well. It was your intention to connect with them, but something triggered an emotional reaction. You walk away feeling bewildered, and your whole day goes downhill as you think about that conversation.

Our hours and days are colored by the quality of our conversations. We crave connections that help give meaning and great joy to our lives. Yet we don't always know how to get the results we want in our conversations. Sometimes we randomly wander into discussions that are so charming that they leave a sweet nectar that coats the whole day with warmth and delight. Yet we are not sure how to get more of those conversations and fewer confrontational ones.

In their book *Conversations Worth Having*, Jackie Stavros and Cheri Torres give valuable advice on how to be more conscious about creating more satisfying connections. They suggest using techniques and approaches developed through their work using Appreciative Inquiry, a process that makes conversations richer and more emotionally satisfying while solving problems simultaneously.

Stavros and Torres highlight two central qualities that help us create more of the conversations we want: starting with a positive, supportive orientation rather than a critical one and listening and talking from the standpoint of curiosity and inquiry. Valuable conversations add something to the interchange on those two scales – we leave feeling uplifted emotionally and are made aware of new perspectives. Those conversations foster understanding, attachment, self-confidence, and enthusiasm about potential future encounters.[229]

However, you can still deal with thorny issues but with more of a focus on the positive. In fact, this approach is most useful when dealing with difficult situations. Here is a simple example of a conversation described in their book that uses these tools with a disgruntled employee. It's a story to which many women can probably relate.

Colleen was irritated because her ideas were ignored at meetings. When men presented ideas that she had previously mentioned, their input was more warmly received. Furthermore, men routinely interrupted her. She left a meeting furious because these patterns had been repeated yet again. Her assistant, Trevor, came to see Colleen after he overheard negative remarks about her outburst on the way out of a meeting.

Trevor asked her if she was all right and the answer was a resounding no. Trevor asked for more details, listening carefully and empathetically responding to her complaints. Colleen began to settle down as he listened to her. She mentioned the idea of resigning and working somewhere else where they would treat her with more respect.

Then Trevor asked her if she thought other women felt like she did. Colleen said, they probably did. He suggested that maybe there was a positive opportunity to change the organization's culture for all the women in it. Consequently, because of Trevor's questioning and adding value to the conversation, Colleen, instead of quitting, changed the whole organization's culture over the next two years. That was a conversation worth having! It shifted her course of action and uplifted her sentiments so she no longer felt so helpless.[230]

The value of this interchange is that it first dampened some of her frustration because she felt heard in an empathetic way. Secondly, it unearthed a possible underlying assumption that she was being ignored because of her personality. It also may have uncovered the presumption that her workplace experiences would be different in another setting. Trevor's comments helped her step outside of her personal frustration and see the problem in a more systemic way. He also stretched the conversation to include different action steps than the ones she was thinking about. Alternatively, this conversation could have degenerated into complaining and castigating blame, leaving Trevor and Colleen more depressed and discouraged.

This illustrates the power of Appreciative Inquiry (AI) in helping individuals reshape their conversations, even on complex topics. It is a positive way to examine what is working and change underlying assumptions, and systems in an organization. Organizations can learn to work even more effectively through this process and simultaneously strengthen employee commitment to a shared vision.[231] Unlike many organizational methods, AI starts with the assumption that every organization has strengths, and analyzing a group's strengths is an appropriate place to begin working on improving an organization.

Catherine Moore, a psychologist from the University of Melbourne, describes the history of AI and its underlying tenets. It is a technique that has been around since 1986, when David Cooperrider wrote his dissertation about it under his mentor, Suresh Srivastava.[232] Ron Fry also helped co-create the process.[233]

It arose because Cooperrider found himself in a very hostile organizational environment and had an exciting idea. He wondered what would happen if he shifted the energy in the room by talking about what was working. He realized that the questions you ask can orient the group's attention in a more positive direction.

Members of an organization could start by examining what is working right in an organization and use their strengths to address their challenges. From that vantage point, employees work cooperatively to create a shared positive vision for future improvements. It is both strengths-based and inquiry-oriented.[234]

AI started out as an action research approach to organizational development. (Action research identifies problems in an organization and then collects data to determine what is wrong and how to fix it.) Then in 1990, a group of consultants collaborated to create a methodology to support organizational change and planning from this perspective. This process was embraced by corporate development, and they developed the 4D model to take them through a four-step process: Discovery, Dream, Design, and Destiny.[235]

The process begins with defining the topic of interest – for example, excellent employee morale or high levels of customer satisfaction. (Notice the goal is always framed positively, though it reflects something they want to improve on.) AI is predicated on the idea that if you want more of something in your organization, e.g., enthusiasm, it is more effective and direct to ask people when they have felt enthusiastic about their work and then to examine the factors that went into those moments. Exploring low morale to get more enthusiasm is more indirect and less effective. Organizations tend to move in the direction of their inquiry. If they study problems, more and more issues become apparent.

The Discovery phase includes interviews to uncover an organization's strengths so those can be used to address the area they would like to improve. The goal is to highlight what is already working in the organization and allow people to escape the deficit orientation. They can then move into a more positive perspective that will open up a new outlook that engenders more growth possibilities. Unlike other organizational development formats, AI recommends involving the whole organization in the AI process to create a shared vision in the end.

The Dreaming stage allows people to start by imagining different possible ways forward. Employees are encouraged to dream about what the organization could look like. By shifting people out of their preconceived constructions of the organization's limits and shifting towards what is working, employees can be free to imagine a new way of operating. This builds on the strengths discovered already and can become the foundation for new creative ideas and beliefs about what is possible.

After sharing their conversations about their dreams, the Design phase unfolds as people start to put together their ideas of how their organization could move toward a shared vision. The key to making this part effective is to be deliberate about including multiple voices to enlarge the vision and increase employee excitement and commitment. The group agrees about the future they want to pursue through extensive dialogue and debate and is then inspired to bring it to fruition.

The final stage, Destiny, entails broadening the circles of dialogue as more voices are brought in, and innovations become more elaborate and more actionable through various refinements. They turn their ideas into plans and then shift their operations to align with the new roadmap.[236]

AI is driven by five central principles: 1) our truths are created often through our conversations, and they can evolve through them, as well; 2) inquiry itself can cause change, 3) people frame their experiences in terms of stories with different assumptions and different perspectives, 4) our expectations inform what we search for, see, and understand, and 5) the more positive and powerful the questions, the stronger the emotional effects and the actual outcome.[237]

This translates into the notion that positively framing things inspire people to act more enthusiastically and frees them up to ask hard questions without fear of being shamed. The inquiry also helps unearth hidden assumptions and can shift the group's thinking about the best approach. We all see things differently depending on our orientation and where we put our attention. The words we use can trigger feelings, images, and visions of our future, so we must use them carefully and be intentional as we construct the culture we want to create. Our expectations play a significant role in assessing whether we can move toward the things we imagine.[238]

These processes are enlivening and positively affect large and small groups. My friend Linda Bark, who has a well-developed coaching practice and is the author of *Wisdom of the Whole,* described her experiences with AI when she was a student at a small alternative graduate school. The school was having problems, and there was a concern that it might close. So, she returned from work abroad to finish in time to get all her credits.

When she got there, they hired an AI consultant to help them figure out how to handle their crisis. In the AI process, they interviewed a lot of students. Linda came to the interview with a list of all her complaints, but the interviewer started by asking what the school was doing right. She resisted focusing on that and continued to talk about the school's flaws. Then the interviewer asked about her initial hopes and dreams for their graduate program.

Those queries created a shift in mood as Linda refocused on her initial enthusiasm and she revitalized her excitement. From there, she joined various committees to help them get back on track and pursue their dream more effectively. In approximately six months, the school had solved its problems, and students felt the atmosphere had totally shifted.

Linda Bark became a firm advocate of AI and used it with nurses during the pandemic to help them imagine ways to get back in touch with their dreams of nursing. She uses it successfully in arenas like nursing homes where low morale is a perennial problem. At first, she wasn't sure if AI would address the depression and sense of overwhelm the nurses felt. They started with a focus group where they examined what was going well in nursing. They came up with things, and just as Linda had shifted herself when they followed up with interviews, they became reinvested in the dream of nursing and began to imagine ways to rekindle their enthusiasm. They left excited about the shifts they could make in their routines to address their problems.[239]

Appreciative Inquiry has a long and robust history of creating profound organizational shifts. An example of an impressive case study of AI is how it was used with an extensive Global Relief and Development Organization (GRDO) that had 120 partners in the developing world and was located in the United States. They had partners in East Africa, West Africa, Latin America, and North America. Their goal was to create a new assessment tool because the current one was unpopular, even though it was considered the gold standard for this type of work.[240]

The first problem was that the assessment tools were used every six months to evaluate the nongovernmental organizations (NGOs) they worked with. When the AI facilitators started to work with the organization, they noticed a lot of deficit-oriented language in their descriptions of the NGOs. Weaknesses were highlighted, and funding was contingent on their answers to the assessment.

The tools also encouraged a lot of negative blaming and an attitude of paternalism that their parent organization (GRDO) exhibited. Despite the many differences from one country to another, they used the same measures for every NGO. Administrators were rigid about controlling implementation and thought they knew better how to create capacity than the leaders of the Southern NGOs. The organization committed to a 3-year AI intervention using the 4D model described earlier.

They started by asking the GRDO what their deepest desires were for their organization. Participants said they wanted to build a wildfire of capacity that would lead to new NGOs spreading worldwide. Two goals surfaced: 1) learn from each other about making substantial, healthy NGOs, and 2) discover new ways to work with their partners more equitably.

At the end of the first year, each NGO switched to creating its own criteria and method for increasing its capacity. They inquired about what makes organizing possible and enables it to function successfully. At the end of the second year, the GRDO shifted its language towards partnership and away from the paternalistic orientation.

At the end of the AI intervention, there were many benefits, but three will give you a sense of the impressive gifts that come from fundamental shifts in perception. First, the GRDO started a new initiative that linked entrepreneurs with NGOs to increase the market for the entrepreneurs' products. This venture raised $3 million in two years and created productive relationships between the NGOs and the business community.

The dream of a wildfire of NGOs was realized when they embraced a more participatory approach to capacity building. They created more than 100 new NGOs. These new outposts serve thousands of additional communities.

GRDO leaders switched from the old assessment tool participants found off-putting to summits every three years where relationships were cultured. This enabled them to reinforce their shared vision for the future with a focus on strengths instead of the prior weakness emphasis.

These stories highlight the expanded possibilities and profound new orientations that can arise with simple shifts in inquiry. AI is also a powerful tool for increasing coherent civic engagement. Applying it to modern politics could generate a new vision for our democracy. Civic groups could start to talk about their dreams for America, seeding new possibilities into our discourse. These kinds of conversations should be modeled by our leaders to inspire more social progress.

One of the most robust features of AI is its capacity to build new relationships while expanding our sense of what is possible. Instead of intensifying our differences, we could work to re-enliven the initial underlining dream of America with an updated framework. Our conversations could shift and turn us toward solutions while simultaneously modeling better ways of talking and working together.

If the toxic effects of negativity in social media dull our connections, what would it be like to use tools that could reverse that trend? If we could instead lean into a more positive orientation like the approach AI uses, could we reverse that trend and become smarter instead by accentuating our strengths and building on our successes? We should work together to move our country closer to our unrealized potential by starting with dialogs emphasizing our strengths and generating positive visions for our future. Below is an interview I did that reflects one man's ideas about what is best about America and what his hopes and dreams are.

## AMERICA AT ITS BEST

I wanted to see what Americans think about our country by focusing on our best attributes and then asking them how we could use our strengths to help make us stronger. Some Appreciative Inquiry experts helped me craft a pilot interview to see what one person was thinking about the state of affairs in the United States and his ideas about how we could grow stronger.[241]

This interview was with Michael Levin, a retired lawyer from South Carolina. We started by examining a time when America was operating at its best. He said he thought that America was at its best "when John Kennedy was president and the country came together, both the private sector and the public, to accomplish the goal of going to the moon. At that time, the country was functioning cooperatively, and things were getting done."

When I asked him what qualities were present then in America? He responded: "people were talking to each other, trying to cooperatively address issues and come up with solutions that worked for everyone."

Next, I asked him what he thought were America's best qualities. He said that our generosity towards charities comes to mind when he thinks of the best of America. Other countries are less generous than we are in that regard. The other thing is that we are a welcoming country to immigrants; they made up the foundation of our country. "My father came from Russia, and his father, of course, too," he explained.

The most positive feature of America, he thought, was our ideal of equal treatment under the law and adherence to the Constitution. The country also tries to address the needs of all the people.

His concern is that our representatives and leaders across the board are not listening to the people. They take positions and then don't follow them. People should listen better to each other, too. Michael's highest hope is that our country will start working together cooperatively and profitably while advancing the concerns of everyone.

He thinks that people should express the biblical value that you treat everyone how you want to be treated, in a compassionate, charitable way. You should follow a moral compass that leads you to do the right thing, even when it may not be in your personal interests.

Then I asked him what his deepest longing for our country was. He said, "My greatest longing is for us to start talking and listening to each other." He explained concerns about speakers being chased off campuses because of their beliefs. He thought that an essential part of learning at college comes from taking courses in philosophy and getting many perspectives. Yet, at his alma mater, Tufts University, there are no speakers except extremely liberal ones.

I asked him: "What would a democracy that works for everyone look like?"

He said: "the quality of any organization is dictated by the leaders." Right now, the country is being divided, and leaders need to say that we can have different positions, but we still need to work things out. I don't see any of our leaders doing that at the present time.

But he added that it is hard to attract good people when potential candidates are attacked for something trivial that they did in the past. Leaders don't want protestors in front of their houses. We should be more civil to them. At the same time, leaders should listen to the people. Some school boards, for example, have not always been willing to listen to parents' legitimate concerns.

Next, we talked about his wishes for our country.

He explained, "I was talking to a congressional representative from Connecticut, and she said she had to start fundraising right after she was elected. One wish he has is that we take money out of politics. He said he knows that to be true."

It is like a treadmill. "It (this problem) could be addressed in a number of ways. There was $6 million spent in Arizona on one candidate. That's outrageous! They could limit the amount of money they spend on campaigning for various positions. A portion of their money could also come from federal funds. We have a problem attracting good people to Congress. If we had better candidates, we would get a better organization."

These are the sentiments of someone who leans Republican, but I thought this is an excellent example of the desires most of us have for our country. We also recognize the problems similarly – both groups see money as a significant political problem. While our concerns may be different, our yearnings are similar. I suspect both sides would find overlapping issues if they spent more time together. While we may be in a divided space right now, I think on a deeper level, many of us are eager to close the gap and embrace our similarities and differences in a more charitable fashion.

This is just one interview, so to imagine the whole experience of Appreciative Inquiry, it could start by picking a topic – say, we want to get money out of politics. Various ideas are merged in the subsequent design phase to generate a plan. The final stage would be to select actionable items that could bring new innovations into our current systems and imagine a way to implement them. It is not hard to see how such a group could create vibrant and robust discussions that could lead to innovations that could be implemented locally.

# 10

## CREATING A COMPASSIONATE CIVIL DISCOURSE

### *Meeting peoples' needs can reduce violence*

Have you ever been in a place where your mood suddenly switched, and you didn't know why? One minute you felt great, and then a little while later, you felt really sad or irritated, but you had no idea what caused the shift. Marshall Rosenberg, the founder of Nonviolent Communication (NVC), suggests that the cause of most conflict, even discomfort within ourselves, often comes from some unmet need. We don't always realize what is missing until we start to feel upset. For example, we notice we are hungry when we get grumpy or lonely when we get depressed.

The teachers of NVC created a needs inventory that is not exhaustive but helps people identify what need is not being satisfied. Their list covers our needs for connection, physical well-being, honesty, play, peace, autonomy, and meaning.[242] A friend of mine described how she went to an NVC workshop and became excited when she realized it was all right to have so many needs.

Yet their nonviolent techniques have been used most prominently in reducing conflict and healing trauma between warring tribes. Rosenberg was inspired by Gandhi's use of nonviolence and codified a language of nonviolence to help people express it more fully in their lives. As a clinical psychologist, Rosenberg started NVC as a conflict management tool and worked with universities to mediate between protesting students and the faculty in issues related to school integration in the 1960s.[243]

Empathy is a critical component of what makes it work so effectively. NVC is predicated on the following ideas: people want to feel heard, but they also want their needs met, and violence is often a  response to not having their basic desires met.

Rosenberg stresses that there is a possibility of going beyond right or wrong to a realm where groups can come together and address each other's unmet needs. When wars break out, it is because the unmet needs have become so severe that the situation is intolerable, and violence erupts. Conflicts can be resolved if both sides agree to meet each other's unfulfilled needs and share power with each other rather than trying to maintain control over each other.[244]

In his book *Living Nonviolent Communication,* Rosenberg discusses diffusing many kinds of conflict with these techniques. The key piece he focuses on is discovering the unmet needs of each party. The tricky thing was getting the other side to hear their opponent's desires. Once he could get the tribes to really understand the unmet needs of their opponent, the resolution became easier.

 NVC has been used in at least 60 conflict-torn countries worldwide since the Center for Nonviolent Communication began.[245] Rosenberg came up with a language of compassion that helps people focus on the kind of deep listening that is free of judgment and defensiveness and can keep people centered on a more compassionate way of being that can lead to healing. Rosenberg stresses that at the heart of any conflict is an unmet need – whether it is couples fighting, urban gangs, or warring tribes.

In the first chapter of his book *The Heart of Nonviolent Communication*, he describes a tense experience he had leading a workshop in a Refugee Camp in Palestine with 170 Muslim men. Rosenberg observed on the way into his talk that there were tear gas canisters near the gathering with the letters U.S.A written all over them. As he stood up to begin his presentation, someone yelled "murderer" when they realized he was an American. Quickly, fifteen other people joined in chanting murderer. It was a harrowing moment, but he immediately started using his NVC skills.

Rosenberg listened empathetically to the first man's words and reflected back his feelings with the same level of intensity that was being expressed. When he asked the refugee if he was angry that the U.S. was using its resources this way, the man emphatically exclaimed he was. Then Rosenberg switched from using the word mad to furious to reflect the intensity the man felt more accurately. When the conversation switched to the man's needs, he complained that his children went to a school without books and played around open sewage, which made them sick. Rosenberg responded that he sounded desperate and wondered if anyone could understand what he was going through.

This conversation continued for another twenty minutes, with Rosenberg acknowledging the feelings by using words that captured the intensity of the refugee's emotions and highlighted the needs behind each statement. Rosenberg didn't agree or disagree with anything the man was saying, and he didn't see them as attacks but instead as a situation where a man was sharing his pain and deep vulnerabilities with him. An hour later, the man who had called him a murderer invited him over for a Ramadan dinner – a festive holiday meal.[246] It takes training, though, to achieve this level of composure and focus when under attack.

These healing conversations highlight the power of empathetic listening and carefully chosen language to diffuse conflict and generate a more compassionate approach that can simultaneously consider the needs of multiple groups. They also demonstrate that attending to people's unmet needs is a powerful way to defuse conflict, something we could use in our country where violence seems to sprout up in many places.

In their book, *The Coddling of the American Mind,* Greg Lukianoff, and Jonathan Haidt describe a disturbing incident.[247] Fifty-three years after Mario Savio stood before a crowd of students on the campus square at Berkeley University in California, calling for free speech, another group gathered. These were masked Antifa demonstrators, a radical left group estimated at 1,500 strong. Their quest, though, wasn't about freedom of expression. It was to stop the speech of Milo Yiannopoulos, an alt-right provocateur who had been banned from Twitter for his abusive, racist behavior.[248]

Antifa destroyed an electric generator, shot off commercial-grade fireworks in the buildings, destroyed an ATM, and beat people with pipes and poles. The university and town property damage exceeded $500,000. On February 1, 2017, this riot underscored a trend in campus incidents, as conflicts over speakers more frequently turned to violence to protest hate speech.

UC Berkeley never did a formal investigation. No one was punished. In an op-ed piece, one student, who claimed involvement with Antifa, explained they wore black clothes to hide their identity. He suggested that behind the masks of participants, though, were many UC Berkeley students.[249]

These confrontations illustrate how our culture is regressing. Where the Free Speech Movement of the 1960s was organized against racism, current students are now fighting hate speech and white supremacy. Former nonviolent sit-ins and protests have been replaced by pipe-wielding assailants and firework explosives. This is unsustainable from both the violence and impunity standpoint. Our country also seems stuck; progress seems tenuous as we recycle the same issues. Yet violence doesn't serve us. Instead, it pushes us further apart, complicates the resolution, and keeps us stuck in an unsatisfying standoff.

More shaming and judgment also get in the way of creating the connections necessary for an effective national discourse that can be the basis for practical problem-solving. Within a climate of lost accountability and diminished morally responsible behavior, people have often decided they should become the arbitrators of justice, sometimes with disastrous consequences.

Cancel culture is one way that people can be censured. It is an organized boycott of a person on social media that can have devastating effects. People find a post they judge inappropriate, then draw increased attention to the person's past, searching for other potentially offensive incidents. The victim usually goes viral for a few hours and then is left with a diminished following, a tarnished reputation, and sometimes even employment termination. Here is an example of how these incidents evolve and spread deep anguish.

A man I call John, to protect his identity, was attending a conference for tech developers, and he started joking with his friend sitting next to him about a ridiculously large dongle with a phallic shape. (Dongles are the small devices that plug into a computer port and establish increased functionality.) A few moments later, a woman several rows in front of him turned around and took a quick photograph of him.

The photographer, whom I will call Sara, sent a text message with his picture saying his joke about big dongles was not cool to her 9,209 followers and got immediate results. John and his friend were taken to a quiet room at the conference and asked to explain themselves. A day later, his boss fired him. This was terrifying for him because he didn't know how he was going to support his three children.

John posted his story about losing his job on an online forum, and there was a backlash. Trolls bombarded Sara's workplace and sent her death threats on Twitter and Facebook that included revealing her home address. Fearing for her life, she left home and slept on a friend's couch for the rest of the year. Her employer's website went down, and the hackers responsible threatened to keep it down unless they fired Sara. She was fired that day. These stories are described by Jon Ronson in an article in The New York Times before the publication of his 2015 book, *So You've Been Publicly Shamed.* [250]

Let's rewind this story and re-imagine it before cell phones, Twitter, and Facebook. Instead of tweeting a message to her 9,000+ friends, Sara takes John aside and says she was offended by his remarks—or something like that—and they have a short conversation that resolves it. They part with more understanding. She gets to stay in her bed at night, and they both retain their jobs. The danger of this kind of behavior is that it creates trauma that hurts the lives of the people involved and undermines the trust and goodwill that makes societies cohesive. Should a five-minute slice of someone's private life be used to exact such punishment?

## THE PERILS OF SHAMING

Social science researcher and speaker Brené Brown highlighted the downsides of this kind of shaming in her "Shame and Account-ability" podcast. She discussed the false notion that shaming people is helpful. Instead of generating positive effects, it produces more humiliation and violence. Shaming is distinct from guilt or holding people accountable, which can sometimes be productive.[251]

Shame contributes to people's flawed self-perception and sense of being unworthy of belonging. Experiences where we feel unworthy, can be traumatic. This is intensely painful because our relationships with others are critical to our happiness. People flooded with shame cannot experience empathy because they are too focused on their pain.

Brown suggests there is a strong tendency to avoid responsibility in our society; we have a phobia about this. The courage to change is needed, yet often our response to being ashamed is not fear but withdrawal as we try to hide or avoid dealing with challenging situations. What establishes more strength is action. Brown explains that holding our leaders responsible, on the other hand, is what citizens are supposed to do.

Is this the society we want? It is as though we have become trapped in a wild new world that emerged overnight. In some ways, these events are like public floggings, only the results are more draconian; the shaming is intense, eroding a sense of safety while undermining our already tenuous basis for trust and giving power to mob rule. Furthermore, it damages civic engagement and discourse. Who wants to contribute to a public space fraught with such perils?

Culturing a commitment to restoring healthy norms is part of saving our democracy. The dysfunction in our system can be seen when political candidates often use trivial and contrafactual information to peddle outrage with great emotional gusto, making one emotional issue override attention to all others. Political grandstanding prevails over authentic problem-solving conversations that can lay a foundation for progress through compromise or a more nuanced approach. This is a cheap way to win an election. Other dysfunctional patterns we see in our discourse include battling narratives, false equivalencies, lying, deceit, and denial.

Battling narratives often try to cancel the other perspective: law and order vs. justice, Black Lives Matter vs. Blue Lives Matter, etc., stressing one side of the equation over the other. Of course, we need a justice system that values all lives, but Black lives are most under threat; therefore, that battling narrative creates a false equivalency. It rubs salt in the wound of a nation grieving from watching innocent Black people get killed repeatedly, despite all the protests. On the other hand, police work has become soul-crushing. Perverse incentives encourage and undermine justice, leaving police caught between a rock and a hard place. Deep reform is in the best interests of both the police and the Black communities pushing for it. Bringing groups together to discuss our challenges can help people understand each other better, enabling more positive problem solving.

A large-scale study by Larry Diamond, James Fishkin, and Alice Siu at the Center for Deliberative Democracy at Stanford University, called America in One Room, had very positive results. It was a massive project that brought together a representative sample of 500 people in one room in Dallas, Texas. The discussions were moderated by 14 students from Stanford University. The group of 500 was exposed to balanced briefings on five issues: the economy, immigration, health care, environment, and foreign policy. The Center for Deliberative Democracy has done more than two dozen events worldwide, using their Deliberative Polling Method, but this was the largest. The representative sample of voters was arranged by NORC (the National Opinion Research Center) at the University of Chicago.

The results were that many people moved closer to the middle after changing their minds through this encounter. Republicans were less hardline about immigration after hearing stories from immigrants, and Democrats were less wedded to a $15-an-hour wage after hearing how difficult that might be in certain parts of the country.[252] The moderators and participants left feeling more hope for America. They felt the more we realize that we don't have to have animosity toward each other if we disagree, the less polarization we will have.[253] The most stunning consequence was that participants felt differently about our democracy. Larry Diamond, a senior fellow at Stanford's Freeman Spogli's Institute for International Studies, said the most impressive thing was that peoples' belief that American democracy was doing "reasonably well" doubled after the event (from 30% to 60%).[254]

We need to seed new ways of interacting like that event, so we can create a foundation for more coherent public discourse based on more positive interactions and healthier norms. Citizens should consider the kind of conversational interactions we would like to predominate in our culture. Most rational residents would support returning to a place with more civil discourse and better listening.

∽᠗᠘᠙

The tools I have described in this section could help us learn together how to become a more compassionate and caring society. They could also create more effective narratives that could be the foundation for extensive changes. Often there is a kernel of truth in each perspective that gets lost when the grandstanding starts. It behooves everyone to move away from those conversations and towards more authentic interactions.

Powerful coalitions can result from coherent local interchanges at the grassroots level. Then we can build a more substantial consensus and lasting connections as the foundation for the large-scale reform that is necessary. We could also use healing conversations that bring us closer to each other, genuine problem-solving discussions, and dialogs that encourage us to dream together of the future we want to move towards in a united fashion.

A key step is to convince people that they deserve something more and to do that, sometimes we have to tell the story of how we got to where we are and remember what was possible in the past. Norms change over time; without another frame of reference, less functional patterns can take root. We could use new civic groups using these tools to model new ways of having discussions that can break us out of this stuck pattern we have been in for so long.

# PART IV.

## A POLITICAL SYSTEM THAT SERVES EVERYONE

These days it is easy to feel overwhelmed and hopeless about our politics, but citizens are now the most important secret ingredient to creating the changes we want. While the problems we see today may seem daunting, we have vast resources to bring us back into alignment with our principles. The most important thing is putting integrity back into our community discourse and decisions – something many constituents share but most elected officials seem to be lacking.

Once grassroots efforts gain traction, we can reform our system to hold politicians accountable to their constituents. After all, it's our vote that puts them in office and our tax dollars that keep them there. It's also what our political system was designed to do.

Modernizing our democracy is essential, too, so that we can have the tools we need to solve our 21st-century problems. We especially need bold new ideas to bring our society back into a more balanced place where extremism is not so compelling.

Examining the journey we took to get where we are is good preparation for imagining the next steps for taking us into the best future we can imagine. There were mistakes along the way and periods of impressive progress. Those are both parts of our legacy; we now have to hold on to the best lessons from those positive moments as we tackle some of our darkest moments. It is good to find hopeful moments in easy times, but it is an essential strategy in challenging times because it fends off the cynicism that leads to despair.

# 11

## How Politics Went Off the Rails

*Citizens need to work together to restore a healthy government*

I was excited to travel with my parents to Europe after finishing my first year at college. Their tales of the beauty of the palaces and the vast art museums in Paris had cast an aura of magic around the place. The enchanted city of Venice, with exquisite buildings that draped the canals and heralded back to a much grander time, seemed much more exotic than the south side of Chicago.

It had been a tough year, with the murder of Martin Luther King Jr. in April of 1968 and riots in more than a hundred cities. That was followed by the death of hopeful presidential candidate Robert Kennedy in June. Those assassinations had a chilling effect; I felt a sense of deep sorrow as we mourned the loss of those visionary leaders. It felt good to leave the country for a break from the upheaval of the times.

While waiting for our plane at the Chicago O'Hare airport, my parents and I watched TV footage of the protests at the 1968 Democratic Convention. There were 15,000 protestors amassed in Chicago's Grant Park. Police arrested a protester who had started to lower the flag. Activist Rennie Davis went up to the police and reminded them that they had a protest permit, hoping to prevent violence. In response, they beat Davis unconscious. Another leader, Tom Hayden, encouraged people to go to the nearby Conrad Hilton Hotel, a public space more accessible to reporters who might discourage further police violence by monitoring their actions. Protestors spread across the park to the front of the hotel where the delegates for the Democratic National Convention were staying.[255]

This strategy didn't seem to help. Police used heavy mace to attack reporters, protestors, and people walking through the hotel area. In the end, there were many days and nights of rioting; 650 people were arrested, some needing medical attention, including 100 who were hospitalized.[256] The media claimed Nixon won the 1968 election that night because the left seemed so chaotic. It was mayhem in the streets being broadcast to 89 million Americans on national TV for 17 minutes. Nixon campaigned on a "law and order" promise.[257] He also ran on a promise to end the Vietnam war by drawing down American troops and asking the South Vietnamese to take on more of the fighting.[258]

As we boarded the plane to London, we left behind the TV scenes of protestors being beaten and alarmed reporters under attack. It was a whirlwind tour for two weeks, a few days in each of the major cities of Europe. It was even more stunning than I'd imagined. My parents and I parted at the end, as I went on to a Danish folk school for a month.

While in Denmark, I learned the Transcendental Meditation® technique, joining the millions of other meditators who had embraced it that decade. The first time I meditated, I felt like some unclaimed part of myself that I hadn't even known existed was waking up. It was a striking contrast from the turbulence of the sixties. I felt more comfortably tapped into the universal and timeless elements of existence. In many ways, my meditation provided me with a sense of stability through the turbulence of the 1970s and beyond.

&#x223F;&#x25C8;&#x223F;

While meditating in Denmark, a political shift occurred in the United States. Republican party candidate Richard Nixon won the presidency. In his book, *Nixonland,* Historian Rick Perlstein notes that there were many voters who voted for Lyndon Johnson in 1964 because it seemed to invite social chaos to do anything different, who later voted for Richard Nixon for the same reasons.[259] The Republican party tapped into the fatigue with the continual unrest of the sixties and capitalized on the excesses, stressing the need for more law and order. They targeted messages to people whom Nixon called the "silent majority."

In Nixon's first victory speech in November of 1968, he described how a young teenage girl, dressed in red, white, and blue, held up a sign that said "Bring us together" as he vowed to try to do that.

Yet it was a difficult time, and it would have been challenging under the best of circumstances. It was a time of such upheaval that every summer since 1964 had brought conflict in urban centers. President Johnson left blank executive orders allowing Nixon to quickly impose martial law on any city in turmoil.[260] Three trends have been particularly damaging to our democracy ever since the culture wars began and expanded their influence: more divisive political discourse, the takeover of our government by special interests, and the neglect of the middle class.

### Divisive Discourse

Nixon delegated much of the public railing to his Vice President, Spiro Agnew, who pioneered the kind of destructive attack memes that we saw in Trump's speeches. Agnew made a well-received speech in 1969 asserting that the press was full of liberal "nattering nabobs of negativism." history professors Jerald Podair, Zachariah Messitte, and Charles Holden suggest that Agnew was the first politician to create appeals to conservative, populist politics that has remained central to Republican appeals ever since.[261] Some staffers privately worried that Agnew's attacks might be offensive to some of their educated voters. Yet, in late 1969 polls, he was America's third most admired man (behind Nixon and Billy Graham). Agnew called the political opposition elite snobs who looked down on the working class.[262]

After this, there was more political grandstanding and fewer attempts to compromise. This pattern continued from the 1970s to today, punctuated by Newt Gingrich's actions that upended traditional civil discourse in Congress in the 1990s.[263] Gingrich's appeals to the grassroots level spawned a new era of populist interest as he nationalized 435 local races and won many of them. He spent more than $8 million to identify challengers, provided governor and legislative candidates with talking points to use against Democratic candidates, and sent monthly tapes with tips and advice on election tactics. He developed "wedge issues" around Democratic party positions the public didn't support and "magnet issues" to attract voters to Republican party stances. However, despite his rhetoric, he tried to work with Clinton on legislative initiatives. Those who followed him failed to make that same distinction. [264]

Speaker of the House, Tip O'Neil, decried his immature tactics of name-calling and conspiracy-theory-mongering, saying his behavior was the lowest thing he'd seen in all his 32 years in Congress. Gingrich used fights to push his agenda and weaponize the legislature while refusing to vote on anything requiring a compromise.

While he was pushed out of Congress for his overreach, Gingrich's fingerprints remain on the Republican party strategy to this day. He counseled Senate Republican leader Mitch McConnell to become an obstructionist to Obama. Later, he encouraged Trump to use divisive strategies when he ran for president, a position usually thought too august for such antics.[265]

During Gingrich's reign, an already challenged political system became gridlocked. The 103rd Congress was considered one of the worst in 50 years because Gingrich blocked everything.[266] Our constitution is designed to force people to balance their differences in a way that invites honest dialogue and accommodations for many in the quest for solutions. If we are to unwind the effects of this approach, we need a sizeable bipartisan rejection of these tactics. The skill in leading well is to gracefully hold the tension between various perspectives, as Parker Palmer states in his book *Healing the Heart of Democracy*.[267]

As the nation focused on the battles between the right and the left, subterranean groups were also waging different wars to accrue more power and influence. Two of the most influential groups that infiltrated politics in this period were corporate lobbyists and the religious right.

## THE CORPORATE TAKEOVER OF POLITICS

Lewis Powell, an influential corporate lawyer who served on 11 corporate boards and later Nixon's Supreme Court, sent a memo to the US Chamber of Commerce in 1971.[268] It proposed that businesses work together to resist the rise of further regulations after a flurry of bills passed between 1969–1972 (including the Clean Air Act in 1970 and the Clean Water Act in 1972).[269]

The Powell Plan went into effect, and change happened rapidly. In 1971, only 175 firms had registered lobbyists in Washington, but by 1982, nearly 2,500 did.[270] By 2019, the number of lobbyists had catapulted to 11,891. That comes out to an average of 27 per congressman.[271] Businesses began to work in coalitions to fend off regulation in ways they never had before, and they became incredibly effective at it.[272]

 Once the unions were diminished in the 1980s, there was no other substantial funding source for political campaigns except corporations. The Democrats created the Democratic Leadership Council and began to endorse the neoliberal politics of the Republicans to secure corporate funding.[273] Consequently, by the time President Clinton came to power in 1992, the Democrats were also influenced by a large corporate base.[274] When the funding mechanisms shifted, so did the norms around donation streams.

In 1989, Senator John Stennis (D) turned down the opportunity to host a fundraiser for military contractors because he was serving on the Armed Services Committee and didn't think it would be proper. Over time, bribery became the standard operating procedure in Congress. In 2010, for example, Max Baucus (D) took $3.3 million from the healthcare and insurance industries while controlling healthcare in the Senate. Lieberman (D), Bayh (D), and Nelson (D) followed suit, opposing universal healthcare while taking millions from medical industry coffers.[275]

In a column for *The Nation,* Lawrence Lessig, a Harvard professor committed to getting money out of politics, underscores that while corruption is present in all societies, dangerous breakdown occurs when there is no longer any sense of dishonor associated with it. Lessig suggests there is no conscience left in Washington.[276]

Corporations took on writing laws and regulations to create legislation during the 1980s through ALEC (the American Executive Legislative Council). Many regressive and anti-democratic bills have been introduced in legislatures by their members. Model laws promoted by ALEC include attempts to thwart laws like Virginia's energy policies and regulations estimated by the EPA to prevent 150,000 asthma attacks and up to 6,600 premature deaths annually. Their impact goal is modest compared to nearby states.[277]

Corporate forces even intervened in the realm of science. Scientific historians Naomi Oreskes and Erik M. Conway reveal in their book *Merchants of Doubt* how some scientists pedaled false doubt about issues for decades. Industries paid expert scientists to muddy the waters so companies could continue unthwarted by regulations for years. A small group of scientists channeled industry money through think tanks and foundations—stalling action on concerns such as smoking, acid rain, the ozone hole, and climate change. This ecosystem of deception just moved seamlessly from one issue to another, protecting different industries.[278] These tactics also convinced George W. Bush to not join the Kyoto global climate change treaty in 2001, making us one of only three United Nations members to reject it.[279]

When attacking the science didn't work, the final strategy was to claim climate change prevention interfered with free market economics. The Americans for Prosperity sidelined the science in favor of touting free, unregulated markets' economic and social benefits.[280] Exxon Mobile spent $8 million encouraging the dissemination of doubt by funneling money to 60 different organizations.[281] Along with the rise of corporate power, the religious right strengthened its control over time.

## THE RISE OF THE RELIGIOUS RIGHT

In 1971, the South created religious private schools to avoid integration. From 1965- 1975, Christian day schools grew tenfold. In 1978, the IRS commissioner, Jerome Kutz, decided to enforce the law that required that all schools have at least one-fifth minority students to be able to maintain tax-exempt status. Since many of the private schools in the South were created to avoid integration, Catholics and evangelicals joined forces in a fight to resist this.

There were also a series of hearings both in Congress and at the IRS, where they complained the ruling was undermining religious freedom. As historian Stephen Prothero points out in his book *Why Liberals Always Win*, the religious right pivoted the argument away from the IRS enforcing integration to it denying religious freedom. Pastors and parents sent 500,000 letters claiming they were not segregation academies but "Christian academies." This was too much pressure. The IRS caved in and agreed to examine each case individually, leading to ineffective enforcement.[282]

This taste of success inspired the Christian Coalition to go further; over time, many things became political for the first time. Abortion, for example, was the law of the land in 1973, with the Roe vs. Wade Supreme Court decision, but it took another five years before it became a political issue. It only became an issue when the religious right saw it as a way to galvanize Catholics and fundamentalists, and over time, they came to take on the culture as a whole.[283]

Historian Stephen Prothero points out that the religious right worked throughout this period to frame their goals in different terms that expanded over time. First, they talked about restoring traditional religious values, then conventional family values, and finally, they stressed the need to return to a Christian society to restore moral integrity in America.[284] By the 1994 midterm elections, the religious right comprised 60% of the 600 Republican contenders for local, state, and national elections.[285]

Former Republican aide Michael Lofgren wrote a book titled *The Party is Over: How the Republicans Went Crazy, the Democrats Became Useless, and the Middleclass Got Shafted*.[286] He points out that the Republicans invited the reactionary ideas of the religious right into the public square and normalized them. The Democrats, on the other hand, could not call out the Republicans because they were also pandering to corporate interests. The title of Lofgren's book is a good summary of how our politics became so dysfunctional. In the meantime, we went from having a thriving middle class to a diminished one.

## THE STAGNATION OF THE MIDDLE CLASS

The political commentator, Thom Hartmann, points out in a Salon article titled, *How Reaganomics Killed America's Middle Class,* that Reagan's economic policies that undermined the middle class are still with us today. Hartman points out that French economist Thomas Piketty has made a strong case for the idea that having a vibrant middle class is always a choice, and it is dependent on high-income taxes on the wealthy, inheritance taxes, and strong unions with good labor laws. Left to its own devices and without regulations, capitalism leads to high levels of inequality. The post-WWII economic boom was due to the decrease in inherited wealth from the war, and increased taxes on the wealthy helped pay for the war. Progressive taxation, if done correctly, discourages company executives from extracting excess money from their companies or giving lower wages to their workers because their taxes are so high that they don't gain much.

During the birth of our strong middle class described in Chapter 1, our income taxes for the highest earners were in the upper regions to pay off our war expenses (between 74% and 91%). From Roosevelt to Reagan, we had the lowest levels of inequality. When Reagan cut income taxes on the wealthy from 74% to 28%, inequality increased. Conservatives Russell Kirk and William F. Buckley, Jr. complained that when money is spread more equally among all parts of society, people want more from their country and start demanding more rights. This is true; the civil rights movement came at a period when income tax rates were the highest.[287] Of course, a solid middle class demanding rights is the very definition of a robust democracy.

This economic trend of undermining the middle class has continued so that by 2021, new data from the Federal Reserve shows that the top 1% (1.3 million households) own 27% of our wealth, while the middle class, which constitutes the middle 60% of the population (77.5 million households), own only 26.6% percent of our wealth. This is the first time since collecting this data in 1989 that the middle class has had less wealth than the wealthiest class.[288]

## UNDERCUTTING SOCIAL SERVICES

Under Reagan's presidency, federal spending on housing was cut from $26 billion to $8 billion, barely enough to maintain their current stock of buildings. Federal funding to cities decreased from 22% to 6% during Reagan's presidency. Discrimination increased as he cut the department of Housing and Urban Development's regulatory branch. He reduced low-income housing so that by 1985, 3.3 million people needing low-cost housing couldn't get it, whereas, in 1970, there had been a surplus of low-income housing available. This was the end of adequate federally funded housing that had kept homelessness at bay. Since then, we have never returned to a level that could end it. The National Low Income Housing Coalition wrote in 2002 that if we had provided 500,000 low-income units every year since 1976, we would have 14 million families in federally subsidized housing by now. [289]

The result of the underfunding was that by 1982 there was a considerable upswing in homelessness so that every major city like San Francisco, New York, and other metropolitan areas combined had approximately 36,000 people homeless.[290] Before that time, there was no long-term homelessness issue. The housing budget has never been restored to a level that would prevent homelessness. For example, in 2019, with a low unemployment rate, San Francisco had 8,035 homeless. This figure came from a comprehensive count that is done every two years.[291]

There were, however, some bright spots after this period. Economists Alan Blinder and Janet Yellin call Clinton's administration a good decade where everyone fared better. Our country experienced the most extended continuous economic growth in our history under his two terms, with a federal government surplus for the first time in three decades. Our gross domestic product (GDP) grew by 35% overall, median household incomes increased by 14%, 22.7 million jobs were added, and unemployment fell to a 30-year low. They attribute these results to vigorous investments in the middle class, education, technology, infrastructure, inner-city communities, and rural areas.

These investments also led to 40 new empowerment zones, adding $800 billion in assets to low-wealth communities. The federal poverty rate decreased for the first time in 30 years as Clinton created federal programs to aid with health insurance for children, adding tax cuts for low-income workers and funds to make Americans more food secure.[292]

Clinton's economic policies balanced the concerns of the right with those of the left by incentivizing work and using housing vouchers to increase upward mobility. Welfare dependency was decreased by 60% due to these strategies. Tax breaks for companies hiring former welfare recipients removed 8.4 million people from welfare.

Despite all that, it was not a fabulous decade for everyone, as United States workers lost 4.5 million manufacturing jobs between 2000 and 2016, resulting in a 5% reduction in the US share of global manufacturing. This was unique to our country; no other industrialized country suffered such losses. In the European Union, they maintained their share of global industries while simultaneously avoiding overdependence on foreign suppliers.[293]

## LESSONS LEARNED

Today we need bold moves to strengthen our democracy, ones that unravel these trends. Civic leaders should encourage local municipalities to restrict money in politics, discouraging the bribery that occurs under our current system.

 Policies that favor the middle class and uplift the lower classes offer the biggest benefits to our society. Otherwise, inequality breeds crime as people struggle to survive, and everyone's quality of life decreases. A strong society also depends on a well-educated middle class with leisure time so they can be stewards of the government.

Finally, if we want to live in a first-world country, we must invest in it; send needed money to our cities, reduce inequality, strengthen our institutions, and have the wealthy pay their fair share. Otherwise, we will continue the trajectory we are on and end up like Russia, where 3% of the country owns 90% of the country's assets, according to the Moscow Times.[294] There are other challenges we will have to address simultaneously.

# 12

## THE DANGERS OF POPULISM

### *We need to strengthen our democracy to weaken the appeal of tyranny*

Trump fed the culture wars, ramping them up new ways, drawing out our differences. He did, however, appeal to broadly shared desires with promises to end wars and bring manufacturing jobs back. He tapped into the nostalgia for a time when a job could last a lifetime with good pay and benefits—even unskilled workers in an auto assembly line had decent salaries.

He promised to drain the swamp in Washington, and people hoped he would. Confidence in the government had dropped sharply over time. In 1958, 75% of the Democrats and Republicans had faith in the government that it was doing the right things always, or most of the time. Since 2007, the number of people who said they trust the government always, or most of the time, has not surpassed 30%.[295]

Since Americans knew their government had become less functional over time, the promise of bringing back effective operations had enormous appeal. Once the Republicans saw the charisma Trump had with their base, they one-by-one fell into line behind him, along with their vast media resources, especially Fox News.

While Trump was not an attractive character, many people felt desperate from decades of stagnant wages, rising inequality, and increasing political corruption. (Bandy X. Lee, psychiatrist and world health expert on violence, author of *Profile of a Nation: Trump's Mind, America's Soul,* makes the point that only a dysfunctional society would choose Trump.)[296] After he won, Trump played up our differences to stir resentment toward those who disagreed with him and were not part of his tribe.

Social psychologist Jonathan Haidt explains that the strong desire to be part of a tribe runs deep in our blood. It stems from our ancestral past, where being excluded from the protection of your tribe could have deadly consequences as you become prey for predators. On the other hand, if you were a valued member of the tribe, you had stature, prestige, safety, and comfort. This feeling of being part of a community taps into our deep desire to be part of something bigger than ourselves.[297]

A happiness survey found that the 400 wealthiest Americans on Forbes' list scored 5.8 on a happiness scale, with the highest mark of 7.0. Groups of people who belong to clans rank equally well. For example, the Pennsylvania Amish—who favor horses over cars and tractors—tied the rating of the ultra-rich. The Inuit of northern Greenland also scored 5.8; they are an indigenous tribe who survive by hunting and fishing. Also, the Masai, a traditional herding people in East Africa who live in mud huts without running water, nearly tied with America's wealthiest by scoring 5.7 on the happiness scale.[298] Tribal identities provide a strong sense of belonging and connection; it is prominent in our list of needs, surpassed only by food and shelter, according to the psychologist Abraham Maslow of Maslow's Hierarchy fame.[299]

From the start, people connected to President Trump in different ways. To his supporters, he was incredibly charismatic. To many on

the right, Trump was the epitome of the "American dream." Bandy
X. Lee explains that 50% believed God chose him to be president,
according to a Fox News poll.[300]

Many underestimated him—even when he became the nominee of
his party. Yet this yearning to be part of a tribe can also become so
extreme that it breeds anger and resentment, undercutting the essential bonds of citizenship.

Trump promoted himself as a strong, influential, confident, wealthy
entrepreneur who could do anything. In one boast, he bragged he
was so powerful that he could shoot a man on Fifth Avenue and get
away with it. Trump ran as a populist leader because he promised to
represent the forgotten men and women. A populist leader can come
from either the left or the right, but their main message is that they
represent the neglected needs of the people versus serving the elite.
He promised to bring back jobs, coal would even make a comeback,
and America would be great again. Initial perceptions of Trump
depended on which way you leaned.

Trump was an American nightmare for the left, and he was not
sent by God but from the other side. He brought out the worst in
America. Beneath the veneer of the celebrity cult figure was a man
without a soul. He was not about making America Great Again but
about making America Hate Again and amplifying that hatred from
the largest platform in the world.

For example, at a rally in Wilmington, North Carolina, Trump told
the crowd that if Hillary won, she could pick judges without voter
consent while suggesting second amendment advocates could do
something about it. At another rally, Trump incited his followers to
punch a protestor in the mouth and promised to pay their legal fees.
A former CIA head, General Hayden, told CNN that if someone
else had suggested using guns to influence political outcomes, he'd be

in the back of a police wagon now with the secret service questioning him.[301]

Cities that hosted Trump rallies experienced a 226% spike in hate crimes in their counties.[302] By 2019, there were also 55% more hate groups in the country than there were in 2017, according to the Southern Poverty Law Center.[303] His attempts to incite violence were working, yet when the FBI advised white supremacist oversight, he discouraged it.[304]

In the Politico article "How Everything Became the Culture War," Michael Grunwald points out that Trump whipped up his supporters by demonizing the political opposition. He ramped the culture wars up into overdrive, freezing the pay of federal employees who were a big part of the democratic constituency. He battled with California over fuel-efficiency standards, net neutrality, and water policy. Then farmers, who tend to vote in a Republican bloc, got a $12 billion bailout.[305]

As a result of his divisiveness, the left and right also ramped up their battles, each side demonizing the other without trying to understand the motivations behind their different stances. Some on the right were labeled deplorables, not a term that would inspire more communication. The right derisively called the left who disliked his policies "Never Trumpers." Liberals weren't insulted because, of course, why would they ever want to endorse what they perceived as a vicious, cruel man to rule the country?

As the pandemic raged, Trump defied recommended measures by encouraging his base to "liberate their cities" from wearing masks. Some did it, the faithful got sick, and some died.[306] Throughout Trump's presidency, his ratings remained constant despite the 500,000 plus COVID-related deaths by February of 2021.[307]

This was strange considering the experiences of other administrations. For example, Bush's ratings went up after 9/11 but went down as a result of the Iraq War. A November 2019 Monmouth University poll showed that 62% of Trump's base said they would support him no matter what.[308] After inspiring the January 6, 2021 insurrection at the Capitol, in a bid to reverse the election results, 61% of the Republicans said the president did nothing wrong, according to an ABC/Ipsos poll. That same poll found that 58% of Americans favored his removal.[309]

Two pieces of the puzzle explain this unusual dedication to a leader—the charisma of a populist who then turns towards authoritarianism and its effect on their followers. Though it isn't just their charm, there's a playbook, a well-worn plan that Yale professor Jason Stanley discussed in his book *How Fascism Works*.[310] There are multiple factors that Stanley links together to explain the way fascism spins its web.

First, it relies on the idea of a mythic past, a time when things were purer (religiously, racially, or culturally). The leader attaches an emotional sense of nostalgia to the myth, such as a location, in this case, America, was better in the past because it bonds followers to this person and his ideology. It also creates an "us versus them" paradigm where one group is virtuous, and the other is responsible for the decline.[311]

Hitler accused the Jewish people of polluting the culture and the so-called Aryan race. In Trump's America, immigrants and African American protestors broke the natural hierarchy with their demands for equal treatment. Trump said protestors "were carried out on a stretcher" in the good old days at one rally where a Black man was complaining.[312]

"We need to fight those who are taking our country away from us," Trump says.[313] These phrases imply a natural hierarchy where the country belongs to certain people and others are intruders, which is another tactic that autocrats use. A demagogue makes classes in a culture more rigid and heightens the myth that hierarchies are natural and good.[314] Previous leaders already set some of this up for Trump. Racism and xenophobia have been around for a long time; he just exacerbated citizens' fears by using these old tropes. For example, Trump called Mexican immigrants drug dealers and rapists.[315]

Propaganda amplifies and legitimizes the message, and Fox News worked to reinforce Trump's rhetoric.[316] His speeches used language that served to dehumanize his opponents, stoking fear, hatred, and resentment in the hearts of his listeners. This dehumanization works to limit his followers' capacity for empathy.[317] At the same time, he soothed his followers' worries by promising he had their back. Most demagogues rely on emotional bonding to connect their listeners to their goals and animate the irrational to undermine the power of the intellect.[318]

Another aim of despots is to build up a sense of deprivation. Many of Trump's white followers (45%) believed they were being discriminated against more than African Americans.[319] The fact that African Americans have $5 for every $100 the average white family has doesn't matter because charged emotions are undercutting rationality.[320] The majority (54%) of Trump's supporters also believe that Christians are the most persecuted religious group in America.[321] Since they had already embraced their victimhood when Trump showed up and fed into it, they were receptive.

Tyrants also strive to create an anti-intellectual climate as a basis for destroying their opposition. Of course, some of this was also set up by others too. The late right-wing talk show host Rush Limbaugh claimed that many of our institutions deceive us. The deception is rampant in all areas, including people in government, universities, and the media. Science, he said, is filled with socialists and communists.[322] Curiously, Stanley points out that fascism, by design, undermines public discourse by undervaluing education, expertise, and news.[323] When political groups present one ideology as right and everything else as deceit, it creates a hostile environment for authentic discussions. Anti-intellectualism can be used as a tool to help undermine the opposition. The ultimate goal is to demonize, dehumanize and intimidate non-followers. This rhetoric also made violence more acceptable.

Steve Bannon tweeted Anthony Fauci, a CDC expert working on the pandemic, should be murdered. He said we should replicate the old times of Tudor England, where people had their heads put on pikes. Bannon suggested putting Fauci's head on a corner of the White House to warn federal bureaucrats to follow the rules or suffer dire consequences.[324]

During Trump's administration, scientists' recommendations were ignored and ridiculed, prompting some followers to make death threats against medical advisors.[325] This is how tyranny works; leaders undermine the opposition by belittling their ideas. Then when the strongman expresses his disapproval, his minions make death threats to silence detractors.

Multiple scientific associations came out in opposition to Trump. For the first time in its 175-year history, Scientific American endorsed a political candidate (Biden), and eight other major medical societies followed their lead, including many medical journals like the Journal of the American Medical Association, Lancet, and the British Medical Journal. The New England Journal of Medicine, the most prestigious medical journal in the world, took a political stand for the first time in its 208-year history, stating Trump's response to the pandemic was so inadequate that he made what was a crisis, a catastrophe.

The truth is undermined when the scientific method is not respected and legitimate media commentary is discredited. When the public is barraged by lies, and all information is deemed false, people are forced to rely on their leader's words.[326] An autocrat's ultimate goal is to create confusion about information, so followers rely on him to sort out the truth in a chaotic world.

Finally, through this gaslighting, the only thing that retains credibility is what is repeated over and over again by the leader. Objective truth becomes a casualty of these dynamics. Stanley states by the time people start using conspiracy thinking, reason in political consider-ations has already been lost. A fascist leader's goal is to make power more important than truth.[327]

In the midst of this confusion about the truth, demagogues find a particularly potent myth or lie to galvanize their base. In Germany, Hitler persuaded the public that they were winning WWI until Jew-ish people and socialists betrayed the country. This lie was used to justify the slaughter of approximately six million Jewish people in the holocaust during WWII.[328]

Many Americans believed Trump's assertion—that election fraud occurred during his reelection bid. No amount of reason would shift their beliefs. This fallacy was perpetuated by much of the right-wing media.[329] It is so pervasive that 17% of the Democrats, 28% of the unaffiliated, and a solid 62% of the Republicans believed the claims, according to a Rasmussen poll in December 2020.[330] Fascist tactics transform the news from a platform for information and reasonable debate into a continual performance where the tyrant always stars as the main attraction, Stanley explains.[331]

Tyrants do not necessarily aspire to world domination or the geno-cide of a whole population segment, as Hitler did. They can be narrower in their goals, perhaps just wanting to secure their own country's rule without opposition. Yet, their desires for complete domination are incompatible with democracy and a far cry from a conservative vantage point. The traditional conservative wants to conserve the good things about the past, rejects violence, and discourages radical change. They also want to reduce government interference in their lives—the opposite of what an autocrat wants.

The trouble is that the image of a mythic past is vague enough that people can read anything they want into it. Paul Jackson, a lecturer in history at the University of North Hampton, points out that Trump's approach is like a Rorschach inkblot test where people can see Trump's appeal in many different ways.[332] (A Rorschach test is a series of abstract inkblot pictures that psychologists show clients and ask them what they see. The images are very abstract and could be seen as many different things. What they see is construed to reflect their inner psychology.) Some people admired Trump because he was so straightforward and didn't try to sugarcoat things or go along with the political correctness that was annoying to many on the right. Others admired him for breaking from the traditional Republican rules when he suggested stopping wars and instituting tariffs.

Consequently, many people didn't see the violent side of Trump's nature, and if they listened to the right media stations, they also didn't hear much about it. They became attached to Trump, like a child in a parent-child relationship,[333] and believed he was a victim because that was what they heard all the time. Yet what is particularly dangerous is his followers, who turned towards threats and violence to support him.

Stanley's work helps us understand *how* fascism works. However, there's a psychology that makes it work. Trump's demagogic qualities include pathological lying, manipulation, lack of compassion, and limited emotional affect, according to Bandy X. Lee, an academic psychiatrist who studies the rise of violence around the world. She edited a report on Trump titled *Profile of a Nation: Trump's Mind, America's Soul.*[334] A shorter and more direct observation of Trump's lack of empathy was offered by his former lawyer Roy Cohn, who observed that he pisses ice water.[335]

 Bandy X. Lee explains that the relationship between Trump and his followers who seek violence evolved through various stages identified by Lee to create a cult-like following. Michael Cohen, his former "fixer," and others described leaving the cult of Trumpworld after they woke up to the subtler dynamics of Trump's behavior. Loyalty, though, becomes an obsession in cult thinking and many followers have their reason diminished because of that emotional bond.[336]

Another stage consists of what Lee describes as the "battered nation syndrome," where followers become too invested to leave. They then have a hard time admitting that they made a mistake. The sort of die-hard support that comes from a sense of shame and feelings of low self-worth can make it hard for people to admit the error of their ways. Others are attracted to him because he seems untouchable, criticism fails to stop him, and his followers would like that level of impunity.[337]

During the final stage, followers experience a state of shared psychosis or mass hysteria, falling susceptible to false claims and conspiracy theories. Many people don't understand the contagious effect of mental illness, but it can be quite overwhelming, as we're seeing. When the leader espousing false beliefs really believes them himself, the psychological pressure for his followers to agree increases due to their intense emotional connections. They now start to live in an altered reality where "mass hysteria" overrides reason.[338]

Our country is now suffering from this battered nation syndrome that Lee described, and we must find a way back to restoring better norms. She underscores the need to counter Trump's false messages with the truth, and we should continue to hold others accountable for unlawful behavior. The important thing is to do everything to counter the normalization of this type of interaction among leaders and followers. Removing such leaders from the limelight is the best antidote to undo these effects. Over time, without this continual false messaging, people can return to normal. The sooner the intervention, the quicker the recovery. It helps to limit their exposure to propaganda as well. Then, they also need support to address their trauma from the experience.[339]

Using toxic rhetoric to create a shared psychosis has been thoroughly studied since WWII. Trump used it masterfully. There is another critical component of the formula for fascism: the destruction of the individual, rational mind. The totalitarian leader sets off an ongoing tension between the mature and the immature self, continuing until one or the other is destroyed. Joost A. M. Meerloo, the author of *The Rape of the Mind*, a Dutch psychiatrist who studied totalitarianism during WWII, explains how fascism takes over by bending peoples' minds. This explains why perfectly normal people became wildly irresponsible and started fighting like children about wearing masks while believing whatever conspiracy theory was in vogue. The appeal of fascism is to the helpless part of ourselves, Meerloo explains. The followers then become part of the irresponsible mob. [340]

Lee says it is critical to not normalize the abusive behavior of Trump and his violent followers.[341] This is hard to do because once someone has created a map for achieving this level of power, others will try to chart a similar path forward. Wannabes have already stepped into the role. In the end, demagogues wreak havoc through their rule because they undermine the norms of acceptable, humane behavior and destroy the minds of perfectly normal people who become caught in their spell.

Fascist exploits are prevalent throughout history. A million were killed outright, and another 3-5 million people died of starvation in Russia under Stalin. The genocides in Rwanda, Cambodia, Darfur, and Bosnia all illustrate the damage a demagogue can do. Ordinary people are moved to do horrific things when their anger toward an enemy is stoked through toxic rhetoric.[342] Many of these culture wars ended in terrible violence between two clashing ideologies. We should try to avoid replicating that mistake.

The final question is, how did we get where we are, and how can we return to normal? What makes a country susceptible to this sort of predatory attack, and what can we do to discourage it? Lee suggests that our high levels of inequality breed a sense of humiliation and resentment, as well as a sense of helplessness. This pervasive malaise has fueled the old tensions between whites and Black people, as both groups experience the shrinking of the pie as wealth continues to rise within the top tier. Furthermore, indoctrination with the idea of white victimhood through right-wing media talk shows also helped pave the way for the rise of Trump and the expansion of the alt-right.[343] Tamping down the sense of them or us could create a new narrative that we can all rise or fall together – which is, in fact, the truth.

We also have to generate comfortable off-ramps for people to reject these trends that have been so toxic for our country. This has been a potent elixir for many people, and they need support and compassion as they transition away from this trap. Shaming and blaming work against the end result we want, which is a society with healthy norms again. Central to shifting away from relying on a strongman, is to meet the underlying concerns that made him appear so appealing. This means we must stop neglecting so many peoples' needs and begin listening more honestly to them.

## REJECTING AUTHORITARIANISM

Trump illustrated both how easy it is to damage our national discourse and how critical it is to maintain healthy norms. Damaging our information space created mass confusion and enflamed our sense of distrust. The conservative columnist, David Brooks, was prescient and courageous enough to predict on January 31, 2017, the Republicans had made a deal with the devil, and it would cost them their soul. [344]

The problems we face are deeper than Trump, though. People must see another choice besides returning to the status quo or re-electing the strongman. We have been on a long slide away from democracy. What is called for is a reform effort that goes to the roots of our dysfunction and casts a new inspiring vision of the future we want and moves us towards it.

Civic leaders have powerful tools to bring people together to restore rational and compassionate discourse if they choose to use them. These group conversations could provide opportunities for people to reconnect and revitalize healthier norms. Grassroots efforts that bring citizens together in cooperative settings with local government could do this.

The next chapter examines the despair that permeates our country and ways to come together to address our emotional malaise and broken systems. Strengthening our connections is where our healing must begin because it will amplify our sense of hope and belonging that has been damaged by our divisiveness. Then we can come together and attend to our deteriorating social safety net and other concerns.

# 13

## A HIGHER QUALITY OF LIFE

### *Healing broken hearts, broken promises, and broken systems*

These unusual times also bring opportunities for significant change and we need to draw on our greatest strengths to create new possibilities. Let's start by asking what kind of country we want.

Educator, activist, and writer Parker Palmer, author of *Healing the Heart of Democracy*, claims we should have a politics that is worthy of us, that serves the common good, and satisfies the spirit. What could more effective politics do for us? It could inspire a culture of empathy, and compassion, weaving together a more caring culture, and an effective democracy, one that truly reflects the depth and wisdom of the human heart. It could meet these seven aspirations. Our dream is to have a thriving country aligned with our greatest ideals.[345]

1. **We could commit to creating healthier communities** by reducing income inequality and violence while providing the resources needed to design thriving communities for everyone.

2. **Strengthen our social safety net** to the level of other industrialized nations (where homelessness and food insecurity have been reduced).

3. **Restore the middle class to 75% of the population** (pre-1980 levels) by bringing back manufacturing jobs, creating green jobs, and providing progressive taxation.

4. **Modernize our governance systems**, so they support democratic values more accurately (Congress, the Supreme Court, social media, etc.).

5. **Design a world in harmony with the laws of nature** so that our sacred Earth can flourish for future generations (see Chapter 17).

6. **Repair race disparities** through reparations that eliminate multi-generational poverty, support criminal justice system reform, and foster integration (covered in Chapter 2).

7. **Reform the universities** to make college affordable, eliminate student debt, strengthen teaching resources, and reduce bureaucracies (see Chapter 15).

After determining our aspirations, the next question is, what strengths could we use to open up new possibilities? Some of our assets are 1) great universities, 2) wealth, 3) extensive diversity, and 4) our constitution is based on powerful principles (liberty, freedom, justice, and equality). We should use these resources to create the country we want. I focus on the top four issues in this chapter because the other issues are discussed in different chapters.

## HEALING BROKEN HEARTS BY DECREASING INEQUALITY

Income inequality is a problem that reduces our quality of life and builds resentment and a sense of despair because the gaps are so significant between what a small percentage of people have and what the rest of us experience. Washington State University spearheaded a study published in *Nature Magazine* that looked at the effects of inequality throughout the history of civilization. The results of increasing inequality are increased social unrest, decreased health, less solidarity, and more violence. The study, supported by 13 other universities besides Washington State, found that countries with a high Gini coefficient can reach a tipping point where revolution or the destruction of the state becomes inevitable.

Revolution happens once other mechanisms for reestablishing income balance have been exhausted. Scientists use a measure called the Gini coefficient to measure levels of inequality that goes from 0 to 1.0, with zero being no inequality. The United States currently has a Gini coefficient of .81, one of the highest in the world, according to the 2016 Allianz Global Health Report.[346]

The United States isn't fated to this future. We can still demand change to avert these dangers. Our wealth doesn't have to be so unequally distributed. In 2018, U.S. households had, $113 trillion in assets. If that total of all our household wealth was equally divided among the U.S. population of 329 million, it would give each individual over $343,000 according to the Brookings Institute.[347]

A 2018 United Nations report by Philip Alston, UN Rapporteur, revealed that 40 million people live in poverty in the United States, 18.5 million are in extreme poverty, and 5.3 million live in Third World conditions. He states that the United States is the only industrialized country that doesn't provide food and healthcare as part of people's human rights.[348] Just to put those numbers in perspective, the entire population of Canada consists of 38 million people.[349]

These numbers show how inequality levels play out in individuals' lives. These problems can only be solved by returning to a "we are all in this together" mindset, versus every man, woman, and child is on their own. Universities and other thought leaders could amplify this message. Our goal should be to have a high quality of life with higher levels of economic well-being for more people and reliable social services for all, equivalent to other highly functional industrialized countries.

Throughout the ages, our communities and the federal government conspired to keep people healthy, fed, and housed. Watching more people become food insecure and homeless highlights the failures of our contemporary society to meet a government's historical obligations and responsibilities.

Eric Lui, and Nick Hanauer, authors of *The Gardens of Democracy*, point out that there is no strong and wealthy democracy in the world that does not powerfully regulate its government. The tools they use to maintain a high-quality of life are regulation and high levels of progressive taxation.[350] These are the tools we could use to revive a more functional system.

Part of the malaise is seen in our high use of drugs. Our neglected rural towns where decent paying jobs have disappeared and opioid addiction is surging are evidence of peoples' dissatisfaction. Overdose deaths involving opioid use increased by 519% from 1999 to 2019, according to the National Center for Drug Abuse Statistics.[351]

Many Americans had similar experiences where a short-term opioid prescription for pain turned their everyday lives into a nightmare that sometimes ended in overdoses and premature deaths. These deaths were also due to abusive and predatory behavior by pharmaceutical companies and distributors, who ignored the telltale signs of drug abuse. The abuse was often brought on innocently by doctors unwittingly prescribing opioids to patients, with both parties unaware of their addictive properties.[352] Other problems arose when regulators ignored telltale signs of misuse of the drugs. For example, Miami-Luken delivered 2.3 million oxycodone pills to a single pharmacy in a town with a 1,400 population.[353] They're now out of business with a blatant disregard for the law. The damage to communities left in their wake continues, though.

Although we're seeing headlines now around corporate entities manufacturing and distributing legal drugs being taken to task, these unhealthy addictive patterns in our country have been around for decades. Drug use rose exponentially between 1979 to 2016, doubling approximately every nine years. During that period, the death rate from drug overdoses was 600,000. Easier accessibility has contributed to the drug abuse problem. So has a lack of economic mobility and social disconnection, according to Donald Burke, the senior author at the University of Pittsburg Graduate School of Public Health, who helped uncover these trends.

People have lost their sense of purpose, feel trapped in an economic caste system, and are isolated, says Burke. He also suggested we develop robust and more accurate behavioral benchmarks that draw attention to the social causes of these high levels of addiction.[354] We should recommit to a promise to advocate for each other's needs while directing our leaders to reinvigorate our commitments to caring for the economic well-being of all citizens.

## RESTORING OUR BROKEN PROMISES

Historically, we have been committed to the middle class, but we have neglected their needs for a while. Andrew Yang, a Democratic candidate for president in 2020, highlighted the issue of job loss due to automation when he was interviewed on Fox News. The conservative journalists agreed with all his points. Yang was an example of a leader trying to break the rules.

There was something refreshing about his campaign as he talked about cross-over issues that no one else was addressing. When he spoke to truck drivers about the upcoming automation of their jobs, their first response was, your party doesn't care about us.[355] Yang reiterated these sentiments publicly as he criticized the Democratic Party for appealing to coastal elites, ignoring significant issues that need to be dealt with in other population segments.[356]

This kind of job loss is a huge problem. Future green energy jobs will help, but we also have to consider that truckers may not always be good candidates for green jobs. Many could use alternative choices. The issue of automation will affect even more workers in the future. Since few unions represent workers, politicians have no incentive to attend to these issues. Communities, however, can work to bring back unions, create more co-ops where workers own their wages because the business is cooperatively owned, or develop local organizations to lobby for the working class. Anticipating the challenges of automation and rising up to meet them is a much more effective approach than being unprepared and trying to come up with solutions after the fact.

Non-college-educated whites are desperate for change. Working-class families feel they're falling behind in their ability to access the American dream, and their children are too. Three main factors diminished their quality of life: the loss of manufacturing jobs due to globalization and automation, the opioid epidemic, and the high cost of college.

Millennials especially need help. They have been financially crippled by the high costs of college, the 2008 recession, and the pandemic. They have only managed to accrue 4.2% of our national wealth,[357] yet account for almost 22% of the total U.S. population.[358] Between 1999 and 2017, synthetic opioid use increased by 6000% among millennials.[359] The millennials have also been hit by the high price of education more than any other generation.[360]

Yet the alternative to not getting a college education is often even bleaker. Millennials without a college degree were four times more likely to die from drug use-related causes than college graduates born in the same year.[361]  In addition to neglecting our previous commitment to the middle class, our systems have become so dysfunctional and corrupt that they no longer serve the majority well. We should create new pathways for the middle class by not only bringing manufacturing jobs back; but eliminating college tuition at state schools. Apprenticeship programs and free community college would also be a great boon for this population.

## FIXING OUR BROKEN SYSTEMS

Our broken social safety net also adds to the neglect of peoples' needs. We live in the world's wealthiest country, yet our quality of life has deteriorated drastically because our systems are not serving us. Instead, we are serving them. Our bodies are fodder for a healthcare system that makes money off our diseases. Criminal justice has become a revenue-generating system that funds our cities off the backs of the most vulnerable Black people. The violence in our country puts us second in the world for gun deaths.[362]

Our healthcare costs are overly expensive; we pay twice as much as other industrialized countries for health insurance. We pay more not because we use more insurance but because each interaction costs more.[363] Our most troubled systems, though, are the ones that are so neglected that people stop even thinking about them altogether. No one notices until problems are so pervasive that damage control is difficult. By devaluing people's emotional well-being, we've lowered the bar on what's acceptable and understood relative to mental health.

Focusing on mental health, we can see that concerns are largely ignored in our national discourse and society. It's hard to talk about some of our culture's most critical and troubling aspects because so much has been deemed political.

Now, when a significant national mental health emergency emerges as people begin to believe conspiracy theories and other false rumors, there is no context for discussing these issues in a nonpartisan way. We end up unable to talk about the obvious mental derangements embedded in our everyday lives. When our neglected rural towns' domestic product is opioid addicts, we must also consider how this impacts our psychology as a nation.

Mental health expert Bandy X. Lee notes other countries have experts that helps guide the president, legislature, and courts. They are independent but have the authority to share their knowledge with government actors. Lee also points out that when a two-party political system makes it difficult for people to tell the difference between what is partisan and pathological, expertise can help clarify these things through standardized, neutral methods.[364] We should address the diseases of the body and the mind that undermine our health. We have long neglected our country's mental health and social well-being.

Our conflict resolution skills are also too primitive. Too many people reach for their weapons to resolve conflicts. In this climate where desirable norms have been lost, these patterns get exacerbated while our systems deteriorate. Attending to mental health would reduce some of the burdens on our criminal justice system and strengthen the lives of people suffering from mental health issues. It would also reduce the amount of gun violence and accidental deaths by police who are ill-equipped to deal with these problems.

Mental health professionals are ideally situated to create a plan to achieve these aspirations cost-effectively. Experts could put together a plan based on what they think would be the most effective way to deal with these trends in our country, and local areas could start by adopting parts of it. Other countries provide template examples for a better healthcare system. Too often, special interests get in the way, and costs skyrocket because the consumer's needs are minimized against the desires of profiteers.

Our political parties are also broken; they are not as transparent as they should be in a modern democracy, and there is often a gap between their claims and reality. A more effective way to design change is to take it out of the political arena until the citizens, and the universities have tested and proven solutions.

The funding relationship between corporate financial sponsors and Congress is so strong that it leads to broken promises to constituents on both sides of the aisle. For example, the Democratic Party wants housing for everyone, progressive income taxes, and education for all. Yet when you examine the cities run by Democrats, homelessness is often rampant, and tax breaks are skewed towards the wealthy. Educational funding also supports affluent neighborhoods with more resources, while poor communities suffer from substandard schools.

Binyamin Applebaum of the New York Times editorial board explains how this liberal hypocrisy plays out in various blue states and cities. Starting in California, he points out that bad neighborhoods put children at a permanent disadvantage with poor-quality schools and a lack of public services. Yet the median cost for a house in San Diego County is $830,000. This keeps many families out of healthy neighborhoods. When less expensive housing is proposed, there is a NIMBY (not in my backyard) response. People say they want to address homelessness in theory, but no one is willing to make any sacrifices that might bring their housing values down. For example, Palo Alto created 677,000 new jobs but only had 176,000 new housing units. When a 60-unit affordable housing project was suggested for the elderly, however, it was rejected.[365]

Many liberal states have regressive income tax rates. For example, liberal Washington State is even more regressive than the red state of Texas. School funding in Cook County, Illinois, where Chicago is located, gerrymandered their districts to give the wealthiest neighborhoods significant funding sources and poorer ones much less.[366]

San Francisco is one of the most discouraging sites, a city with tremendous wealth, yet 8,024 people are unsheltered every night. That translates to one out of every hundred residents. With the rising housing costs, homelessness has doubled in the last five years. Lack of federal assistance and affordable state housing funding has led to this situation, according to Wes Enzinna, a contributing editor of Harper's Magazine.[367] In some cities like San Francisco and Seattle homelessness and crime have increased without enough intervention so that the vitality of the city is undermined while the needs of the homeless go unattended too. It is a complicated problem but research suggests that the first key is to provide permanent supportive housing. Rohit Naimpally a senior researcher at J-Pal (a poverty action lab) examines the policies that are working around the world to address homelessness. A housing-first strategy has been rigorously studied and it demonstrates that it is more cost-effective than other interventions.[368] It is clear, in any case, what we are currently doing is not working, The U.N. special rapporteur observed in 2018, when he went to San Francisco, that the scenes there revealed a level of cruelty that he hadn't seen in any other country, and he had traveled to every continent.[369]

Vienna started building luxury complexes after WWII that were so inexpensive 60% of the city's residents now live there. They spent more than $700 million to create existing units and have additional land to expand. Helsinki, Finland, took a similarly radical approach of eliminating all temporary shelters and providing housing with no preconditions. After housing the homeless, they addressed other problems like joblessness, alcohol, and drug addiction. This housing-first approach has been successful in significantly reducing homelessness there and in other places, as well.[370]

Both parties are failing us in different ways. There are more home-less people in blue states, but in the red states, people are more likely to die from the pandemic. Of the 18 states with the highest pan-demic mortality rate, 14 were red.[371] Both parties have blind spots and are constrained by a system corrupted by money and slowed by bureaucracy.

While autocracy from the right is not very attractive to the major-ity, neither is socialism from the left with a government that is not transparent and willing to sell out to corporate interests. Our politics would be better served by civic groups working together to balance the partisan extremes and create an agenda that focuses on the roots of our problems.

While the constitution is a powerful guide, it is old, and our country has yet to be able to adapt to the times by just adhering to it. There are no rules for handling social media, for example, or how to react when one party stops playing by the rules. There are also modern methods to determine what the majority wants that could be used instead of relying on corrupt politicians.

Furthermore, institutions like the electoral college have become antiquated and undemocratic, allowing the person with a lower popular vote to gain the presidency. The last time we passed a substantive amendment was in 1971, when we passed a law giving 18-year-olds the right to vote. We need a more modern and agile government that can adapt quickly to changes and hold people accountable.

We especially need a modern conservative party. The GOP has appealed to reactionaries for a long time now. Trump's message, "We need to take back our country," meant to many on the far right that the government would advocate for their religious beliefs.[372] These are narratives that reflect a feeling of losing a sense of belonging.

Fear is what drives these emotions. Instead of helping people adapt to a modern world, the Republican Party has pulled the whole country back in time to pander to their desires. Their hope was that by resurrecting the past—or clinging to it—they could secure a more prominent place in the social fabric of our nation. A modern GOP could instead embrace going forward, rather than resurrecting the past; and focus on conserving our best values in a rapidly changing world.

They pulled the country further to the right, promising things would improve by slowing down the pace of change and reverting to older values and lifestyles. Instead, the extreme factions of the Republican Party now deny science, expertise, and truth itself to please reactionary elements of their base. While there is a lot of truth to their observation that our morals and values have been corrupted, the rejection of scientific facts is pandering to the least functional aspects of our society.

No society can resist change altogether. It can slow it down or modify it, but adaptation and change are a vital part of the natural evolution of life that allows a culture to adapt and survive. How we manage the change makes all the difference in the world.

The Manifesto Project analyzed 1,000 political parties and their manifestos in 50 countries from 1945-2018, examining their right/left characteristics. They found the U.S. Republican Party is unusually far to the right compared to other mainstream conservative parties. Thomas Greven, a political scientist at the Free University of Berlin, suggests that is the tragedy of the two-party system because extremists don't have to be part of a bigger tent as they do in Europe with their multi-party systems. Greven says democracy can't work with this level of dysfunction.[373]

We also must acknowledge that if we ignore science, as we saw in the pandemic, we just die in more significant numbers. Furthermore, the pandemic was just a small dress rehearsal for what will happen if we fail to meet the correct numbers to avoid climate change. The Republican Party should become a modern party that acknowledges climate change, the need for racial justice, and universal healthcare.

Many left the Republican Party when it became seen as anti-intellectual. From 2010 to 2018, college-educated Republicans decreased from 40% to 29%, as whites without college degrees increased from 50-59% of the Republican Party.[374] A modern conservative party could attract more followers if it appealed to the quality-of-life concerns of uneducated whites and those in Black communities. This would free them from having to appeal to the most reactionary elements of their base. Less education often is coupled with less exposure to diversity, so this group is more likely to have racial resentment.

Author Parker Palmer suggests that society can break in two different ways from the tension created by brokenheartedness—despair or greater understanding. It can break into despair and destruction when it can no longer stand the strain from the pain like Germany did in the years after World War I. Humiliated and exhausted by war, reeling from multiple social crises, their wounded pride made them susceptible to the myth of Aryan supremacy.[375]

Another way to shift is to break open a heart so that deeper insights and understandings can emerge. It doesn't end the tension, but it reduces it and allows progress, at least temporarily. Frustrated and discouraged by centuries of racism, Dr. Martin Luther King Jr. decided to bring attention to the shocking, brutal treatment of Black people in America. T.V. was a factor in the awakening; when people saw the horrors of beatings, murders, bombings, and police attacks on nonviolent protesters, Congress responded positively when President Lyndon Johnson sent over civil rights legislation.

Now again, we face a similar moment where we can either go towards the heartbroken path of fascism or towards a brighter future that comes with strengthening our democracy and recommitting to creating a healthy multicultural society. If we can recommit to these goals, we can step out of the divisive rhetoric and resume our role as stewards working together to revitalize our fragile democracy and improve everyone's quality of life.

## LEANING TOWARDS THE FUTURE TO CREATE A MORE FUNCTIONAL SOCIETY

New narratives should focus on how we are all better off when our systems care for everyone. Our capacity for maintaining a healthy society rests on several vital shifts: decreasing inequality, improving our social safety net, and modernizing our political and governing systems. Our universities and thought leaders could help affirm these needs and suggest the most efficient way to attend to them quickly.

As we reimagine and redesign our broken systems, we need to be cognizant of the broader changes happening in these times. Then we can use emerging ideas to help create more sustainable modern systems capable of handling the complexity of the 21st century. An entirely new worldview is emerging, one based on new scientific understandings that can address the failure of old systems. One of the crucial assets we should bring to this time is a new attractive sense of the possibilities that we could move towards. Ultimately, the future should be imagined as more alluring than the past; otherwise, people will continue to resist it.

# PART V.

## INSPIRING A NEW VISION FOR A 21<sup>ST</sup> CENTURY DEMOCRACY

When you look around, everything is changing. The Earth is warming, our democracy is a mess, and the old ways of doing things don't seem to work anymore. We need to change many things but can't agree on anything. We are stuck. It is like we are on the edge of a cliff, and going down looks dangerous, but we can't stay where we are because doing nothing is even more problematic. Yet we are too busy fighting about going forwards or backward to ask where we are and how we might get to where we want to go. This section focuses on what we need to understand and do to meet our future challenges in the most proactive way.

To create a better future, we need to understand the past and discriminate between the things that are worth preserving and those we should unravel. That way we can encourage the right kind of change and rise to meet the future in a way that diminishes our fear. Together, we can develop a better map of a way forward that will give us the capacity to meet our challenges through a new inspiring vision that will also give us practical solutions for our times.

# 14

## EMBRACING THE DANCE OF CHANGE

### *The more we lean into the future, the better it will be*

In their book *Abundance,* Peter Diamandis and Steven Kotler envision an enhanced future world where nine billion people have water, healthy food, affordable housing, and plenty of energy.[376] This abundance created by all the advanced technological tools that are on the horizon could create a world where everyone is busy creating and playing, not scrimping and fighting.[377] This is a more compelling and accurate narrative about a new era that's inviting and more attractive than the present. The challenge will be for humans to evolve in concert with the technology so they will have the social capacity to collaborate in a way that guarantees that we use these newly developed resources equitably to bring about their vision.

The friction from our culture wars is just a smaller subset of a broader struggle though to shift to a new worldview. It involves dying systems, emerging new ones, and cultivating new learnings simultaneously. Sally Goerner, engineer and system analyst, describes our current period in her book *The New Science of Sustainability*. She explains that it is a time of "great change" where many systems need to be completely redesigned simultaneously. As one system changes, another will need to be altered, causing cascading changes through-out the whole structure of our civilization.[378]

Perspectives, as well, will shift. Historically, humans have been oriented toward the conquest of nature and the development of empires. These have served as testaments to our outstanding accom-plishments in the world. Yet climate scientists tell us we must leave 60% of the oil and gas where it is and 90% of the coal if we are to avert ecological disaster.[379] Furthermore, cooperation, not conquest, will be necessary to tackle climate change adequately.

Goerner also suggests it will require a combination of conserving past societal lessons and embracing new ideas simultaneously to help us learn how to overcome the limitations of our present time. She asserts that we will have to learn many new things in order to quickly transform our society into a more functional one and avoid collapse and its associated chaos.[380]

Another problematic aspect of today's challenges is that things are crumbling around us before the new systems have not yet emerged. Too often, the future is portrayed as a fearful and austere place where we will have less material wealth and personal power rather than an advanced technological wonderland as previously described. The lat-ter is likely a more accurate prediction.

It's important to reconsider our place in the universe, our relation-ships with others, how we organize our society, and how we make sense of the world. This perspective shift towards a more optimistic future involves re-imagining systems. While new ways of envisioning our relationship to the Earth are emerging to assist us in re-framing our place in the universe, these narratives still need to become a part of our accepted national discourse.

My focus here is on three aspects of this process. One, how an old worldview is becoming outmoded and why a new worldview is emerging. Two, an examination of what this new worldview will look like and how it will affect us. Finally, I describe the evolving new orientation and why we should embrace the future in order to make the transition smoother.

## THE TRANSITION

What is it that propels people toward a new worldview? Goerner suggests that old worldviews are sticky and can exert a constraining effect until we are freed from them by a new spiritual impetus. The desire to switch from a society run by an elite class to a partnership model, where power is shared more equitably, is pushing us towards a major shift.[381] New worldviews arise out of a need, and as new visions emerge, a tipping point occurs, and the new replaces the old, obsolete view.

Sometimes, it is not that a new ideology prevails, as much as the old one fails. For example, in 1999, the city of Cochabamba, in Bolivia, privatized its water system and sold it to a company called Bechtel, with a 40-year monopoly on it and the right to 30-40% of its profits. In January 2000, they raised water rates by 400%, making water and food inaccessible to many. In February that year, Bechtel was driven out of the city by massive riots. The people then went on to oust another water privatization company and multinational companies in oil and gas. In 2005, Evo Morales won the presidency on a platform that included nationalizing the oil and gas industry. Oligarchy had failed to address their needs, and control by the state seemed more promising.[382]

Political philosopher Steven Pepper suggested that societies organize their worldview around a "world hypothesis" that explains how the world works, and that perspective is organized around a central metaphor. When a model is shifted, everything shifts. For example, a significant shift similar to ours, Goerner suggests, occurred when we went from the Middle Ages to the Renaissance, progressed to the

Reformation, and on to the Scientific Revolution and Enlightenment. The Scientific Revolution then set the stage for the Industrial Revolution. Leaving the Middle Ages, we shifted from the "God's design" metaphor to our current "machine" metaphor within a mental worldview. During the Middle Ages, society was organized around the church and service to God. The church established guidelines for life as prescribed in the Bible, and the nobles were to uphold God's rules and care for the serfs. When the priests and nobles became corrupt, the system became increasingly dysfunctional, and the serfs struggled. When the old systems become ineffective, new ideas emerge.

In addition, the rise of new understandings, inventions, and theories help propel society toward a new frame of reference. These major modifications lead to a switch in values, social and political arrangements, and critical institutions, all within a few short decades. Historically, crises also precipitate a failure within the old system, revealing the inadequacy of outdated theories.[383]

We have seen catastrophic events arise in the 20th century as world wars, depression, and environmental devastation displayed our contentious and destructive relationship with other countries and the natural world. Changes are now sprouting as a new root metaphor is arising around the idea that we are part of a large, interconnected web of ecosystems and that we must learn new ways to cooperate globally to repair the environment if are to survive. The shift we are going through takes us from the machine metaphor towards a web metaphor where systems are all seen as interlinked and interconnected nodes embedded into an increasingly complex and expanding network.[384]

Jean Gebser explored the shift we are going through in his epic book: *The Ever-Present Origin,* published in 1949. Gebser studied the evolution of human structures of thought or consciousness, and he concluded that humans have progressed through four different phases. We are now on the cusp of entering a fifth stage called the integral phase.

 The Integral era will also make transparent all the previous eras (Archaic → Magical → Mythical → Mental). The first phase, the Archaic, carries a sense of oneness with the whole and an immersion into the world without differentiation. Through the increased use of meditation, people are becoming more in touch with the timeless nature of reality that was part of the archaic era. In the archaic time, there was no dimensionality.

The second era, or magical stage, is where consciousness separates itself from the world in a dream-like way. Humans experience the realm of their emotions and experience awe and wonder in this phase. This level of life is one-dimensional, where humans first differentiate themselves from the natural world and become conscious of their own will.

The mythical stage is where language emerges, and timeless stories are born that allows humans to experience the life of the imagination. This stage introduces the second dimension of life, where a recollection of the origins of the world is born through myths and stories.

The mental stage emerges as causality is introduced, and humans start to use their minds to understand why things happen. From there, people began to work to master the world around them. Perspective emerges through the three-dimensional paintings of the Renaissance. The individual ego becomes fully differentiated, and a logical, rational worldview evolves into existence.

This is the era we are in now, but there are signs of an emerging new era, the integral stage, arising. For example, now we are uncovering new insights that highlight the limits of our old models of causality.

[385] What is unique about the integral phase is that it not only introduces new perspectives but also makes the other previous stages more transparent for the first time.

We also can see the world of magic being revived in the popularity of movies like Harry Potter, where a whole hidden realm comes alive. The turning of our attention to these inner realms of awareness rekindles a sense of the wonder of the magical era. The increased popularity of meditation brings more people back to the experience of the archaic time when we were deeply connected to the oneness of existence. From 2012 to 2017, the Centers for Disease Control found that the rates of people practicing meditation more than tripled, going from 4.1% to 14.2%.[386]

The impersonal nature of this fast-paced outer-driven worldview is also being changed as people focus more on the stories in their lives. Postings on Facebook focus on sharing our internal worlds with each other in a bigger arena. Bringing awareness back to all these elements from earlier epochs will enrich our appreciation of life in new ways and restore our sense of the timeless continuum we have lost in the mental era. The new dimension of the integral period is a broader sense of time. The transition from the mental to the integral stage involves shifts on many levels.

## QUALITIES OF THE MENTAL ERA

The mental era led to an excessive emphasis on materialism and fragmentation of the connection between people and nature. Machines created a loss of freedom as people became tied to them. Time became divided. The present became separate from the past or future, so the continuity of time became torn apart. Guilt over lost time and conquest over space became features of this mental perspective.

As this era comes towards its end, humans experience more anxiety, intolerance for others, and a desire to flee from the constraints of the narrow mental world. The constant search for entertainment is part of our quest to escape the limitations of our routinized mechanistic mental lives. The search for something outside of oneself—something greater to be part of—leads to a search for something objective to fill that void. This perspective is subject to what Gebser calls deficient magical thinking, where institutions such as the military create a sense of false unity that can counteract the isolation that predominates in contemporary life.[387]

We are currently in the last phases of the mental period, and we see the worst parts of our culture blossoming as part of the last stand for this crumbling worldview. Corruption and autocracy are rampant in our society. According to the International Institute for Counter-Terrorism, our trends toward fanaticism are also part of a worldwide trend that has increased by 320% from 2014-2019.[388] Usually, new perspectives arise because the old systems have become increasingly unable to deal with emerging threats and challenges. Yet there are always groups clinging to the past, as well.

Some of the limitations of the mental perspective are that it tends to make us less attentive to the psychological, spiritual, and experiential aspects of life, so we are often driven by our unsatisfied emotional needs. While the mental perspective has brought excellent knowledge to us, there are also huge components of life that have been neglected.

According to Gebser, just as the mental structure of consciousness was characterized by a deeper appreciation of the capacities of the mind, the next phase, integral consciousness, will integrate the experiential components of life and include a broader sense of time.[389] As this new worldview gains prominence, the old mechanistic view of reality diminishes its hold on our society.

## THE MEASURES OF SUCCESS IN THE MENTAL ERA

Our current mental worldview revolves around the machine metaphor, which evolved from the industrial revolution, a natural consequence of the scientific age. This view turned us toward a more materialistic, mechanistic approach with similar organizing principles interwoven into many of our systems.[390] For example, our systems are designed around a mechanical model of repeated inputs that produce predictable uniform outputs.

Central organizing principles include control and uniformity. Schools, for example, are structured around the factory model where every child is supposed to receive the same information. The outputs (measured through timed tests) should be uniform. The guiding principles of this machine model are speed, efficiency, uniformity, and low costs. These parameters are constantly controlled and monitored throughout our social systems. Even something as individualistic as eating has been reduced to a search for a meal cooked quickly, and inexpensively, one that satiates our taste buds, in the same way, every time. Already prepared cheap meals that you can buy, and eat soon, became popular: the factory-like fast food formula for success.

Yet over time, these systems have become wracked with problems that make them time-consuming, inefficient, and expensive. Our fast-food lifestyle has produced alarming rates of obesity which require additional time in and out of doctor's offices and costly investments in healthcare to counter the adverse effects it produces.[391]

Our schools are failing to teach children effectively. For example, 25% of high school graduates take non-credit remedial courses in college, according to research from the College Board in 2019. Furthermore, only 30% of college students will earn their desired degree, according to the California Public Policy Institute.[392] This seemingly large-scale efficient machine model for learning through age grouping in large high schools doesn't appear as efficient as we'd hoped.

All around us, we see the limitations in using these mechanistic matrixes for determining the effectiveness of a system. School settings that recognize the diversity of needs and provide more customized education produce better learning results. It shouldn't surprise us that efficient, impersonal schooling designed as one-size-fits-all, is costly if calculated per college graduate.[393] Also, it is becoming clear that nutritious, customized meals that take longer to prepare and are more costly are better because they don't lead to expensive healthcare problems that can persist throughout a lifetime.

The Indian philosopher and sage Aurobindo points out that we have created a civilization that is too complex to manage with our inflated egos, small spiritual sensibilities, and diminished ethical capacity. Our systems that are organized with an extensive complex machine-like orientation also use the wrong metrics. Too often, our enterprises are geared towards high levels of productivity without considering the consequences of large-scale production on our fragile ecosystems.[394]

The rise of new scientific theories and the demonstration of the world's increasing complexity has highlighted the shortcomings of the machine metaphor. It is creating the foundation for a new integral perspective that emphasizes the interrelated aspects of systems. Not only will our institutions change, but our internal perspectives will also shift.

This is a time that requires cultivating and expanding our ability to go beyond our egos and think collectively in a way that brings out our best emotional sensibilities. As contemporary scientific theories have shown us broader connections between systems, we also see more clearly the limits of our mechanistic worldview. Things are more intricately interconnected than we imagined. Two theories highlight the limitations of our linear causal orientation, where we search for one thing to cause a result in a linear and predictable way.

## A New Worldview is Emerging

Two new major theories have been especially challenging to the machine metaphor's sense of causality: Chaos theory and the Dynamic theory of evolution.[395] Chaos theory has its roots in mathematics, with the discovery that small changes in the initial conditions behind an event can result in significant, unpredictable differences in the eventual outcome. Newtonian physics thought there was a rational order to everything—that we could predict the events of any system if we could plug in enough variables. The idea behind "chaos theory" is that we can predict what systems might do, but we cannot be sure. The new science of chaos centers around two points: exploring the hidden order within chaotic systems and studying how self-organization emerges from chaos.[396]

The study of schools is an excellent example of how chaotic systems work. These systems are so complex it is hard to predict which variables will have which effects in any given incidence, much less see a pattern. It is challenging to determine which variables add the most to a school system's success, but it is also challenging to know how these differences will play out over time and place. For example, in one school, veteran teachers may outperform others; in another, young, vibrant inexperienced teachers may be super achievers. [397]

Not only do many systems behave unpredictably, but the parts also have an interactive relationship. The biologist Lynn Margulis explains life does not exist on Earth. Instead, life is interwoven and embedded in the whole planet itself. Margulis points out that it makes no more sense to think of the Earth as a chunk of dirt inhabited by life than to think of our bodies as made up of bones infested with cells. She proposed a shift from the Darwinian notion of life as a passive phenomenon to considering it an ongoing adaptation to a changing environment.[398]

## THE DYNAMIC THEORY OF EVOLUTION

Tiny organisms create the conditions for life, while others respond and evolve in reaction to the changing environment. These theories have begun to move us away from the machine metaphor toward envisioning systems in terms of large interactive webs. Another result is that fields that used to be studied separately, like economics and ecology, are now seen as inextricably interwoven. We must be aware of the ecological health of an area in order to really think accurately about the economic well-being of a country. Communities with no water because of the effects of global warming, for example, are economically devastated and ecologically damaged.[399]

The view that emerges from a deeper analysis of the patterns of evolution demonstrates how energy drives evolution as simpler forms of life combine and work cooperatively to create an intricately balanced web of existence. Collaboration of individuals simultaneously created the capacity for more complexity and specialization. The tribes that can both serve the individual and the whole simultaneously have the best staying power. If a group serves individuals at the expense of the eco -system that the whole group depends on, this signals disaster for the survival of the tribe.[400]

Finding the right balance between the needs of the individual and the eco-system is the key challenge of our time. An important part of solving it, will depend on culturing our collective intelligence so that groups experience and feel their intimate connection with their fellow humans, particularly those that live near them.

## NEW RELATIONSHIPS

As a result of these new theories, we are also shifting our view from one of trying to control nature to a more complex interface. Instead of manipulating our environment, we realize we must redesign our systems to work in conjunction with the delicate ecosystems of the natural world. A new eco-logic is emerging as biologists help specialists design systems that reflect the laws of nature. For example, our rules could include building redundancies into our systems. Building systems with multiple safeguards makes them more resilient. We have two kidneys because the other can take over if one fails.[401]

Our current shift into the integral stage will involve not just attending to the rational or doing level of life but also more attention to the actual experiential underlying "being" level of life, the inner aspects of our thinking that influence our activities. The characteristics of integral awareness are:

- keener awareness of the unity of time and space,
- understanding that the relationships between things are as important as the things,
- transcending duality,
- more attention to the intensity of experiential knowing, and
- valuing contact with the state of being (as in a meditative state).[402]

## A New Orientation

The current switch from a hierarchical organizational model to a more organic web-like team orientation is also a shift away from the mental era. It has energized workers to be more self-sufficient. It is also moving us towards a more distributed leadership model where some decisions will be made closer to the source of the problem by self-organizing teams. As the world becomes increasingly complex, teams have become imperative in more and more areas of life. Effective teams require new social skills, such as greater cooperation, and more agility and flexibility, so that decisions can be made quickly by teams on the front lines who know what needs to happen next. These new groups also require new organizational styles.

## NEW MODELS FOR TEAMS

Leadership patterns are shifting as executives use their authority to inspire initiative and leadership within their teams rather than trying to control and dominate them. In some businesses, catalysts direct and manage teams less conspicuously. Companies now compete worldwide to find the most talented people who can catalyze the most creative actions. The leader sets the parameters of an organization's culture and then works behind the scenes. He differs in the following ways from a traditional CEO. He is a peer, not a boss; he is inspirational instead of imposing; and collaborative instead of controlling. He often works behind the scenes instead of operating directly, managing, and commandingly.

This indirect approach spawned the development of Wikipedia in 2001, essentially the brainchild of Jimmy Wales and implemented by Larry Sanger. Before Wikipedia, the team created an organization called Nupedia, a business dedicated to creating an online encyclopedia.

After spending $250,000 over 18 months, Nupedia had 20 articles completed due to the snail's pace of content production that was based on their elaborate editorial process.[403] Then Wales decided to launch Wikipedia in 2001 with guidelines for writing articles and opened it up to anyone wanting to make submissions. By 2002, they had 20,000 articles; by September 2012, they had 23 million articles in 285 languages.[404] The rest is history. This story illustrates that we are just beginning to unfold what is possible under the right conditions once we escape some of the parameters of the past.

## ISSUES TO ADDRESS: CHANGING NATURE OF WORK

Futurist Buckminster Fuller made the point that we should stop thinking everyone should earn a living through jobs when a collection of people can create breakthroughs to support everyone. However, one of our biggest challenges is not old forms of leadership but the changing structure of the world of work itself. The challenge will be reconsidering our current wage-based system to provide another way of distributing finances.[405]

Fuller suggested that people should be encouraged to go back to pursuing their dreams before someone told them they have to get a job. He also claims we could make the lives of everyone as abundant as the lives of the wealthy.[406]

After conquering so many of the debilitating diseases of the past and creating a global communications network, we could rise to the challenge of re-imagining work. This is our opportunity to restore a more balanced approach with a healthy work-life arrangement and a more equitable distribution of resources.

## OVERCOMING OUR FEAR OF THE FUTURE

Imagining the promises of the future can help mitigate people's fear of change. The information/computer revolution is already moving us to smaller and more mobile devices, making implant accessories in the body possible soon. Such additions will enhance our capacities in unimaginable ways. To smoothly change our society, we must learn new perspectives, deepen our moral sensibilities, and expand our collective intelligence.

With this new worldview, our perspective will shift from a human-centric materialistic view of the cosmos to a more nature-centered and broader view of the cosmos. We will reconnect more

authentically with our subtler nature and ground ourselves in the
new tenets of this emerging worldview.

- Governments are shifting: Oligarchy → Partnership
  Relationships.
- Economic System under scrutiny: exploit the Earth → nurture
  its abundance
- Education System: same input → more customization of
  learning
- Organizing teams: a controlling leader → an inspiring leader
  who sets the initial conditions for self-organizing teams (a
  Wikipedia world)
- Work relationships shifting: control and command people →
  empower and inspire

The future can be better if we make it that way. Massive changes
are coming, and we must all work together to make them as smooth
as possible. It is our legacy to usually bring the future to the world.
When President Kennedy said we would go to the moon, no one
knew how we would do that. We had to invent new alloys to get
there. Now is not the time to get squeamish about the future: instead,
we should focus on the more pristine and stunning world we will be
creating and the more wise and expansive sensibilities we will develop
in the process.

# 15

## DESIGNING A LEARNING SOCIETY

*We need to expand the dimensions of learning to prepare us for the future*

The first evening I attended Dr. Maxine Greene's course, I was surprised by the range of disciplines she covered, her rich choice of language, the depth and breadth of her knowledge, the provocative questions she threw out to the audience, and her ability to be so entertaining in a large lecture hall packed full of students stuck there for three hours. During all my years getting a Ph.D., I never encountered another teacher who gave such elaborate and fascinating lectures.

The lectures themselves were works of art; they were amusing, multidisciplinary, and packed with stories and deep questions skillfully woven together. When someone answered a question, her deep interest and enthusiasm around their responses led to heavily interactive discussions. She was a brilliant and lyrical speaker, too. Even though it was a long evening class, it was the most riveting part of my week.

I was becoming a certified teacher during the day and taking classes at night, so I could get worn out by the time I entered her class. However, her questions always woke me up and inspired me to ponder new dilemmas and make novel connections between disparate ideas. She was also an original renaissance woman; every night, strands of philosophy, literature, history, and art were woven into a fantastic tapestry of knowledge, yielding new insights.

Her college degree was in American history with a minor in philosophy, but she also knew literature. Her Ph.D. was in Educational Philosophy, but there were barriers to women becoming faculty members in specific fields. They eventually admitted her into the field of educational philosophy after she reached such acclaim that they could no longer refuse her. [407]

She had us reading literature interspersed with educational philosophy articles. I distinctly remember one class discussion of *Portrait of a Lady* by Henry James. In the novel, a young woman inherits a large sum of money and then has to choose which of several earnest suitors she will marry. They all seem relatively attractive except the one she chooses, who turns out to be interested entirely in her money.

Greene asked us: "What kind of education would have prepared her to make a better choice?" Her lectures were always accompanied by intriguing questions like that. How do you teach someone to be a more accurate judge of character?

In our utilitarian view of education, we rarely think of how powerful education can be in shifting our thinking and giving people intellectual tools for analyzing some of the most significant decisions in their lives. Life is one long continuous, integrated learning experience that can be enhanced by different perspectives and critical lenses. In some ways, this reflects an old philosophy that suggests that a good education should also develop character through an association with principled, analytical big thinkers who also helped students hone their own skills of analysis.

The class gave Greene a standing ovation at the end of our semester. She had clearly earned it. She was touched and said something like:

"Thank you, that means a lot because if you hadn't done that, this would have been my first class where I didn't get one."

After she died, the New York Times proclaimed that Greene's work at expanding educators' perspectives made her one of the most revered education philosophers of the past 50 years and a hero to thousands of educators. Greene was regarded by many as the spiritual heir to John Dewey. He was one of the most influential twentieth-century educational and political philosophers who reformed education by suggesting that children learn best by engaging in activities that require solving real-world problems. He also attributed the success or failure of democracy to the habits students acquire in the educational system.

Dewey claimed that education should build on the child's natural interests and prepare the student to participate fully in a democratic society. He thought that the education system should develop habits of inquiry that allow students to alter their opinions when presented with different perspectives or new information. Developing effective communication skills should be part of the curriculum as well, so students learn to speak openly about their differences, modifying their opinions based on shared learning.[408]

Teacher's College announced that Greene's work remains a touchstone for generations of students at Columbia University, including faculty, alumni, students, scholars, and artists worldwide.[409] Greene stressed the need to teach literature and the arts to inspire peoples' imaginations. She encouraged teachers to have children formulate their own questions and projects to find purpose in their lives. This enabled individuals to look beyond their current circumstances to design their most meaningful life.[410] Greene suggested that art could allow children to understand and imagine what could be brought into creation. Literature, for example, can bring whole new worlds into existence. Furthermore, all our constructs and social values come from thoughts that become a reality in our lives. We must envision new values and narratives to support them for social values to change.[411]

Maxine Greene could bring stories and iconic images together, showing the natural richness of weaving art and story together in a learning experience. She also showed how greater understanding could come from integrating different disciplines' perceptions around an issue. These lectures brought ideas to life. People were eager to participate in the dialogues that emerged.

This kind of dynamic and personalized education that Greene advocated, one where people designed questions to make their lives meaningful, is needed now in our society, which is on the brink of major change. The university can play a vital role in preparing us for needed changes and help us design the required new systems. Of course, they will also need to train the leaders who will bring us into these new perspectives and run the new institutions.

In order to make the transition smooth, there should be a sense that we are all shifting toward this new era together. If we make that "we" as inclusive as possible, there will be less resistance. Our society benefits by moving towards a more interactive civic education. One that continually engages the public in conversations that invite their participation in bringing in this new worldview.

These changes will prompt radical changes in everything—from how we grow our food to how we do business. As a foundation for initiating these changes, we could teach people by introducing them to emerging new concepts while inviting them to participate in bringing those changes to fruition.

Finally, our universities can discourage violence and demonization on each side by demonstrating how differences on major issues can be debated in a civil way on their campuses. Our diversity of opinions should not be seen as a liability but an asset, and the broader the range of rich ideas that students are exposed to, the better.

 Humanizing our fellow citizens is the first step toward strengthening our democracy. Moving toward each other, listening, and attending to the pain and anxiety underneath the anger will also reduce the concern that people are experiencing in this tumultuous period. While that may be the kind of university culture we need, it isn't what we have now. A student's odds of being taught by someone who was a tenured professor with brilliant ideas, like Maxine Greene, has been diminished dramatically since the 1970s as the corporatization of the university has taken hold.

## RECONCEPTUALIZING THE ROLE OF THE UNIVERSITY

The corporatization of the universities has meant that most administrators run the university with the idea of maximizing profit: schools have become a business enterprise, and students are treated like consumers buying a costly gourmet education. Only what makes it expensive is not the knowledge being conveyed but the quality of the food and lodgings. To maximize their profit, administrators have cut back on tenured professors by half since 1970, according to Marshall Sahlins, an anthropology professor who organized the first teach-in at the University of Michigan and then went on to teach anthropology at the University of Chicago.[412]

Sahlins explains that they mainly use graduate students as teaching assistants and adjunct faculty and pay substandard wages of $22,000 for non-tenured faculty. On the other hand, the bureaucracy has increased at four times the rate of faculty, with well-paid staff. Half of the school budget is spent on non-educational purposes. They create 5-star dorm rooms, gyms, recreation centers, and food courts. This is done to satisfy the consumers, who are taking on enormous debt, even though 75% of them come from the top 25% of the economic scale.

The consequences of this takeover are that students major mostly in business because that gives them a chance to repay their loans. The trouble is we don't need to only develop more green companies. We also need more people to solve other problems. In the 1960s and 1970s, the differences between the number of social science and business school graduates were less.[413] In 2019-21, there were 387,900 BAs in Business and 161,200 in the social sciences and history. [414] Furthermore, the price tag for this cheaper quality education with less tenured faculty members is much higher.

In this era, our society needs high-quality professors and eager students to take on some of the most complex social challenges of all time. Universities could and do generate new ideas to prepare us for the future. Still, they must return to their original mission of preparing talented future leaders in many fields. We need more graduates from the social sciences and high-quality tenured professors to steer us toward the new era described in the previous chapter.

But most importantly, we need affordable tuition so that more people can be educated, as they were after WWII. The average annual cost for full tuition and room and board was $1,405 in 1971 for public schools and $2,979 for private colleges. That ballooned in 2016 to $20,000 for public schools and $45,000 for private schools. Graduates end up with so much debt that they are forced to acquire high-paying jobs to repay their student loans.[415]

College debt for 44.7 million students in 2020 was $1.56 trillion. According to Forbes magazine, the average student carries $32,731 in student loan balances with $393.00 monthly payments. The default rate of this nondischargeable debt is 10.8%; 5.5 million borrowers are in default.[416] Comparing the costs of education in the United States to other countries reveals how exorbitant our rates are in comparison. Free college tuition is available in one-third of all developed countries, and another third keeps the student costs for education at less than $2,400 per year.[417]

Does it seem like a good idea to strap our future leaders with such crippling debt? Other countries realize this is counterproductive. Isn't it enough that we are leaving them a damaged planet, a crumbling democracy, and so many other problems to solve?

While Biden recently forgave some of that debt, what we should also do is return to less expensive colleges that are regulated to reduce the bureaucratic overhead and abandon the resort model for college. They should also return to hiring tenured faculty, especially in the social sciences, who can help prepare students to lead us through redesigning our society. The public should reduce the costs of this overpriced education before it picks up the tab.

Beyond eliminating such high fees, we could also offer a broader curriculum. Topics designed to help deepen students' self-awareness about their talents is an excellent place to start. Historically, jobs were about applying for a position and convincing an employer of one's talent. This can be painful. As work becomes more fluid, our orientation should shift from fitting people into existing jobs toward developing the skills that people already have. Helping students draw out their innate talents and sensibilities would help them design meaningful lives. Also, wouldn't it be great if we could also prepare students for life in a world where work, as we know it, may disappear?

Cultures shape people through shared beliefs passed on and assimilated by the next generation. As opinions change through this time, we will need to collectively shift our understandings to pave a road for the journey into the subsequent worldview. Building communities of thought leaders who inspire us to work together to redesign the systems will make these large-scale changes less daunting, more interesting, and more acceptable. Envisioning a collective blueprint for the next era is a way to engage people in cooperatively designing the future. Rather than just managing the transition, we could also develop a more collective, caring sensibility.

Some theorists have erroneously used Darwin's theory of survival of the fittest to give philosophical credence to, and amplify the idea, that competition for survival is the best way to organize society. This has contributed to an over-emphasis on aggressive dominating tendencies and devalued the qualities of caring and collaboration. Yet this approach actually contradicts what Darwin really observed. He discovered that humans, as a social species, have a natural tendency towards empathy.

Except for psychopaths, we are programmed to reach out to others in distress, move in protective circles, and express anguish when members of our social clan are injured. While we compete within groups to "look good," the most cohesive group has the best adaptive capacity over time and lives longer.

Humans combine competitiveness and empathy, competing for food, mates, and territory. But we are also mutually interdependent and seek a workable middle ground. While independence and self-sufficiency serve a function, they are not enough. Social connection is both necessary for socialization and our most significant source of joy. We need human contact; otherwise, we become depressed and fail to thrive.[418]

Social Darwinism has emphasized competition rather than our communal nature. This approach has spawned perspectives that applaud overly competitive and self-sufficient behavior rather than recognizing our mutual interdependence. If there isn't enough to go around, the important thing is to position yourself to look out for number one, to be one of the survivors, and to get the most you can. This orientation requires winners and losers. It does not instill compassion or encourage a sense of community and shared responsibility. Instead, it divides people and pits them against each other.

As a result, we celebrate callousness, selfishness, and greed as part of the human condition, giving legitimacy to a perspective that is entirely opposite to our true nature. It negates the very essence of what constitutes a civilized society. It ignores our deep capacity to care, culture love, act cooperatively, and seek spiritual fulfillment.

Instead, we could gain more satisfaction from generating a collective mindset that encourages people to work together globally on issues like climate change, income inequality, and poverty. Our culture has allowed this dynamic to develop because people hope they will be among the declining few heroes in this cultural myth that glorifies the rich. As a learning society, the challenge before us is to pivot in the other direction and create new narratives that encourage and manifest more cooperation and compassion.

Influential civic leadership is essential, but so is empowering citizens to see themselves as stewards of our democracy and our planet, critical caretakers that can stir up more compassion and involvement around vital concerns. Six or so 21st-century learning hubs in various regions around the country could be designed to provide civic education and help solicit local involvement. These units could be connected to universities and each other and grow with hubs in different countries over time.

There are five crucial national conversations these hubs could address:

1. What are the most efficient ways to revitalize our planet and create energy self - sufficiency?
2. What is the easiest way to quickly strengthen our democracy?

3. What is the most effective way to heal and end our culture wars?

4. How can we create a healthy, inclusive, multicultural society?

5. What is the best way to catalyze a more righteous society that is law-abiding and just?

What is needed is not only more knowledge about these issues but shifts in related attitudes, as well. We ought to try to inspire a sense of excitement, not anxiety, about our future and welcome the promises inherent in major shifts.

I worked with a small community center in Durham for many years, giving and attending lectures. I realized how hungry people are for conversations about these problems. The discussions we had went on for hours as people tried to grapple with these issues that seemed so wicked and intractable. A lot of pent-up energy could be focused on problem-solving instead of blaming the other political side or the politicians. Unleashing civic power is our best approach to use as we lean into becoming an effective learning society that can help people make this transition smoothly.

## ENHANCED STEWARDSHIP PREPARATION

Citizens could be better prepared from the very beginning of their education to take on their role as stewards of our democracy and caretakers of the Earth. Not only should they have a decent level of understanding about how our government works and the needs of the Earth, but they should also gain a sense of how they might get involved. Citizens need more opportunities to experience making choices to help the collective, not just themselves. If we want to try to inspire a sense of commitment to maintaining and revitalizing our democracy and the ecology of the planet, we need to create more opportunities for civic involvement. Early on, students should grow up with a sense of obligation and preparation for those roles.

I once talked to an environmental sustainability director from Copenhagen at a sustainability conference. She described how neighborhoods in Copenhagen compete to see who could get the lowest carbon footprint. This is the kind of civic involvement we should be striving for. Education in the 21st century should give citizens direct exposure, input, and the power to affect local issues. Copenhagen achieves its high level of climate education through its folk schools, the country's state-funded continuing education program.

Finally, citizens need critical thinking skills to discern fact from fiction. While knowledge has expanded exponentially with the birth of the Internet, false narratives are also quickly spread. People need well-developed problem-solving abilities to make good choices.

Finland has successfully created a culture that can resist the seduction of false information on the Internet by stressing these discrimination skills throughout its whole educational system.[419] We also need to encourage, throughout our educational institutions, a public information space that demonstrates and rewards reasonable discourse and the cultivation of wisdom. Knowledge may come and go through one's education, but wisdom stays with you as you progress and helps people grow and increase their capacity to fulfill their dreams and goals.

**UNIVERSITY EDUCATION FOR THE 21ST CENTURY — CULTIVATING WISDOM.**

Modernizing our culture requires enlarging our perspective and seeing things from a broader, global perspective. For example, we will have to handle the effects of global warming, so we ought to prime people to think more globally. Universities should create teach-ins about the global changes that are occurring so that citizens can become more knowledgeable about our circumstances.

A college education is also a place to explore many different areas and establish lifelong hobbies and interests, preparing students for life. Students should discover ways to explore the kinds of questions that Greene presented in her classes, existential questions such as: *What are my talents? What makes me come alive? What goals should I have in my life? How can I create a support network to help me achieve my goals? What does true love look like? How do I create a fulfilled and happy life? What does a moral life entail?* These could be questions asked and explored as we extend our sense of education to include preparation for life with a deepened understanding of responsibility.

Exposure to more significant ideas, and a more global perspective, could bring our citizens closer to the modern world. Knowing more about how other countries have handled our current challenges could spread the notion that we also deserve better systems, and all we have to do is replicate some of the successes of other countries. Healthcare is a good example. We could learn from different countries about what has worked and what hasn't since we are one of the few countries to not have universal affordable healthcare.

Universities can also model ways to have a civil discourse that handles the tensions between opposing ideas. Political correctness has seeped into colleges, making conversations more difficult. Political correctness has been defined as giving guidelines about what language to avoid offending people on race, gender, and sexual orientation. George W. H. Bush said at a 1991 University of Michigan graduation ceremony, "The notion of political correctness has ignited controversy across the land. It declares certain topics off-limits, certain expressions off-limits, and even certain gestures off-limits.". However, the movement arises from the laudable desire to sweep away the debris of racism, sexism, and hatred; it replaces old prejudice with new ones.[420]

The whole college experience is predicated on the notion that young people will explore new ideas, share their own backgrounds, and feel open to new ways of looking at the world. These sensibilities have had a stifling effect on the school climate. Not only has this cramped the style of students, but professors have been forced to change their lesson content to be less provocative due to today's environment.

Jonathan Haidt, a professor at NYU, explains that if he accidentally offends a student, he can get written up. He has modified his curriculum because of this threat. These extensive rules around political correctness make it hard for students to feel comfortable with the critical conversations that should be a central part of the college experience on campuses and other online places. It makes it more difficult for people to feel safe to explore the crucial issues we need to examine to become more connected to each other, despite our differences.

Another troubling development on college campuses is the rise of people promoting hate speech. Speakers who advocate white supremacy have been invited to college campuses by Republican factions, and legally, state universities cannot deny speakers access to the university based on differences of opinion.

Auburn University was sued and lost in Federal Court when the white supremacist, Richard Spencer, was not allowed to speak at their university.[421] Mob action from the liberal factions has also impacted universities like Berkeley, Middlebury, and other campuses. Speakers have been uninvited to avoid the potential violence, expense, and liability.[422] Free speech is no longer what our founders intended.

By 2017, at least 17 states had enacted free speech laws.[423] Many state legislatures have passed laws to expel students who have disrupted speakers three times.[424] We do not want students to be afraid of diverse ideas because the political party they identify with prevents them from considering differing opinions.

In a New York Times article, journalist Jeremy W. Peters raises the question, what do you do when one person's ideas sound like hate speech to another person?[425] Suppose colleges disinvite speakers who don't add intellectual rigor to a topic but instead come to incite hate. In that case, Peters suggests that denying a college platform access isn't a free speech matter. There are plenty of other avenues for such talks.[426] It's not productive to encourage our campuses to become scenes for political food fights where people lob abusive language out without substance. This doesn't warrant the expense or time wasted, especially if they provoke violence.

Aaron R. Hanlon, writer and assistant professor of English at Colby College, pursues the same logic in his article in the New Republic titled *Why Colleges Have a Right to Reject Hateful Speakers Like Ann Coulter.* He argues that there are plenty of good reasons for avoiding low-value speakers, and while people are guaranteed freedom of speech, that doesn't mean they deserve a college platform. He suggests free speech activists could limit their definition of censorship, recognizing that free speech should be interpreted to mean something other than that colleges are obligated to invite such speakers to campus.[427]

These incidents, though, send a chilling wind across campuses where university administrators have become hesitant to invite controversy because it may result in violent and expensive demonstrations that would require police action. When conservative talk show host Ben Shapiro spoke at Berkeley, it cost the school $600,000 to protect his ability to speak on campus. These talks create an inhospitable and prohibitively expensive climate for debate and compromise.[428]

Hate is an old idea that contracts peoples' awareness. It plays on peoples' emotions and drives them to act in ways that are counterproductive to a healthy society. Through two world wars in the last century, we have seen the global power of unmitigated hate. It is not new or exciting; in fact, it must be discouraged as we move toward the worldwide collaboration needed to address climate change.

If these hate speakers began saying such abusive things about white people, would they be allowed a college platform? Doubtful.

Instead, universities could create campus debate opportunities to discuss the pros and cons of allowing hate speech. This would hold the tensions in a civil way and would enable the debate to be open. This also negates the practice of one side arming to destroy provocateurs while the other side becomes more eager to provoke them. Universities could band together and create higher standards for speakers. Radical political groups have pressured universities to provide their speakers with a platform no matter how bankrupt their ideas are. Instead, colleges should consider inviting more moderate conservatives who could begin to spread less reactionary and offensive views, illustrating how a modern conservative ideology might contribute to our society rather than tear it apart.

A well-educated populace is especially critical in these tumultuous times. The United States did the first experiments to see what happens when you invest in educating large numbers of people. It is time to go back to our roots and beyond. Now more than ever, we need a more involved and engaged public that can represent the voice of the citizens coherently. Furthermore, we need a new vision for what a modern America could look like. While profound adaptations are necessary to support those changes, they will also require value shifts and a robust democratic sensibility.

The next chapter builds on our understanding of how to use our power effectively to create a vision that entices us through a renewed commitment to generating a society with more integrity. People can then work to bring the country more aligned with what the public wants, deserves, and knows is possible.

# 16

## Empowering Citizens

## *From cultural warriors to influential reformers*

Francis Morre Lappe, in her book *Democracy's Edge,* suggests that our democracy is too thin, and because of that, it doesn't address our needs.[429] A deeper, more dynamic system would demand more from our representatives. It should also be agile and able to adapt to the changing times, alive, and responsive to citizens' needs.

Three shifts could empower large groups of citizens to have a more substantial influence. First, we should focus on persuading people to pivot away from fighting with each other to working together and finding consensus around the critical reforms that could make a significant difference in our system. The second task is to create a shared vision and new narratives to promote the necessary transformations. Finally, activists should understand how power works so they can build broad coalitions that shift our interactions from battling cultural warriors to collaborative reformers.

### Finding Consensus

The good news is that in this populist age, there are already high levels of citizen engagement. Some of that engagement is focused on changing the wrong things, like our democratic traditions, and blaming the wrong people. The bad news is that it tends to be incoherent.

Currently, each political side blames the other for our problems rather than recognizing that we are all held back by our broken system. We could use an alternative approach that appeals broadly to people and works towards painting dissatisfied civic activists as potential allies instead of enemies - turning our attention to another way of framing the situation.

Our fates are interwoven through our shared citizenship and the desire to strengthen our institutions and quality of life across the country. Furthermore, even though we are told to blame the other side, many people from both parties tend to have similar complaints about our government–get money out of politics and return more power to the people. While there are various concerns we have less consensus on, our fundamental agreements could be a starting point for the kinds of civic conversations that should happen. The urgency now is that we are in a crisis of legitimacy, where large segments of people don't trust the government and are working to undermine it. Empowered activists could remind people that we are the ultimate stewards of our democracy, so in the end, we are the ones who should solve these problems.

## A New Vision for Our Democracy

We could advocate for a resilient, flexible, modern democracy strengthened by strong leaders and a powerful movement, with a clear rejection of autocracy and a vision that gives more power to citizens. Instead of battling narratives, it would be exciting for diverse groups to generate interactions that could pull the majority towards a promising story about the future we all want.

A new vision could ignite a spark in our hearts that rekindles our commitment to living in accord with our nobler values. FDR used his fireside chats on the radio to introduce new ideas and bring out greater equality in a country devastated by an economic depression.

He created a deep bond with them by speaking directly and candidly to the American people about his goals. Obama demonstrated how to soothe us in our broken moments, talk about our difficult stalemates, and still hold on to the promise of our country. Most importantly, we could use leaders who help us rebuild a shared commitment to our historic values and aspirations.

We could also use a democracy movement that reclaims the power of citizens, restores balance to our national discourse, and inspires people to talk authentically about what they need and deserve. One that deploys new mechanisms to bring a more coherent civic voice into the center of our national discourse. It should build on the work of past visionaries and modernize our systems so that a 21st-century democracy comes of age.

The descent towards autocracy results from years of festering corruption that made the last step seem like a way out when it really dug us in further. The counter-offensive should be to create a system that is so strong that it will be impossible for future dysfunction to set in. That will, of course, depend on us, the citizens.

Ultimately, our vision of the country we want to live in should have strands from the past and present and embrace the future. From the past, we deserve to live in a country with a higher quality of life for all by restoring our commitments to the middle class and extending loans and benefits to eliminate multigenerational poverty. From the present, we should institute modern changes that bring the people's voice directly into a place of authority through propositions that people can vote on. To ensure we have the best possible future, we should rise up to address the challenges on the horizon – like work lost through automation.

Our vision could include elements of these ideas, which are my visions for the future country I want for my children and their children. However, my ideas are only a part of the story; what is essential is that we come together and begin to dream collectively about these issues. That way, we can generate a commitment to our goals and find a way forward to make the bold, game-changing reforms that will close the gaps between our ideal scenario and our reality. To do that, we also must lean into the partnership model of power.

Our system of government was designed to be a model where compromise was required to accomplish big things; it was built on a collaborative model. It goes most smoothly when parties come together and use the tensions between their differences as a way to pass more effective legislation. Our system works better when the civic sector collaborates with the government. It is strengthened when the elite work to push for reforms like the more enlightened robber barons did during the Progressive Era. It can function when only some of these alliances are working, but it becomes problematic when they all fall apart. These alliances can be the foundation that can spread more connections throughout our society. A central part of our vision should include strengthening all these partnerships, beginning with the civic sector.

Another important aspect of deepening our democracy should be enhancing our encounters with diverse perspectives so we can expand our imagination. A robust democracy has high levels of civic engagement and compelling narratives that align with their actions. A living democracy connects people from the grassroots directly through the ranks of government to the top, strengthening partnerships along the way.

Drucilla Cornell, a professor of political science at Rutgers University, explains how we can expand the collective imagination by experiencing different perspectives. Democracy ideally maximizes peoples' exposure to novel ideas, which also expands our collective imagination.[430] Cornell suggests that it is the only way to effectively confront our crisis. We must begin to see our fellow citizens in new ways. Engaging the broadest levels of diversity stretches peoples' imaginations; once you stretch their imaginations, you can start to design something new. Once the collective imagination stretches, expectations grow as well.[431] Diversity is not a liability; it is our greatest asset. It can stretch our imagination, unleash more of our collective intelligence, and make us better problem-solvers. Working with diverse groups can also produce more compelling stories of how to bring changes that appeal more broadly to most Americans. The key is that we must hold the tension between our differences in a respectful way.

## New Narratives

A central part of shifting the culture is to switch out of the corrupt slogans that stir fear and resentment instead of inspiring more connection and a broader sense of unity. The current narrative that justifies our power arrangements suggests that the wealthy deserve their excessive riches because they are more brilliant and have made better choices. We should appreciate them and not over-tax them (both literally and figuratively), and eventually, their benefits will trickle down to the rest of us. Eric Lui, author of *You're More powerful than You Think, A Citizen's Guide to Making Change Happen,* points out that this story was made up by the wealthy and their political operatives, but it is starting to wear thin. People are now less convinced that it is accurate.

This awakening to the falseness of this narrative also carries a lot of pain. Lui suggests it can go one of two ways – towards cynicism or action.[432] Empowering citizens with the knowledge and understanding they need to acquire power and create change could help weigh the balance in favor of action and interrupt the cycle of more power accruing at the top. It also opens the possibility of a new narrative that says we are all better off when we share our wealth and care for each other in a way that creates a high quality of life for all. (A narrative that many industrialized nations accept.)

Part of enhancing our democracy entails changing the operating assumptions that drive our system today because people who create the underlying stories define the direction of politics, Lui suggests. For example, Jefferson wrote in the Declaration of Independence that we hold these truths to be self-evident, but they were only really self-evident after Jefferson wrote them down.[433] It would be helpful to make it equally apparent that democracy depends on caring for each other through collectively strengthening our politics and sharing our total wealth more equitably.

There is also the issue of demanding what we deserve; part of the argument against universal healthcare is that healthcare is not a human right. We get rights by claiming them, and the fact that every other industrialized nation thinks that healthcare is a human right might convince us to update our conception of what people deserve. Now, as an aside, didn't people think free education was a right for veterans before they passed the GI Bill? [434]

Today we could use a Citizens' Bill of Rights and Responsibilities that could serve as a basis for demanding that our society reflect a higher quality of life at the same level as other industrialized countries. In Massachusetts, progressives from the Green-Rainbow Coalition proposed an Economic Bill of Rights endorsed by the Massachusetts Democratic Party. It is taken from Bernie Sanders' 2020 platform but harkens back to an earlier time.

FDR announced his ideas for a similar bill in his 1944 State of the Union address, where he claimed that people who were not economically secure could never be free. The Sanders version suggests that we should guarantee people the right to a job, a living wage, affordable healthcare, complete education, affordable housing, a clean environment, and a secure retirement. So, it is an idea that has echoed down through the years.[435]

One of the problems is that the right thinks the government has all the power, and the left believes that the corporations have all the power. They tend to be blind to the validity of the other side's complaints.[436] (Of course, it should be clear that corporations invaded the government in the early 80s, so both statements are factual, they are just looking at different aspects of the same phenomenon.)

These perspectives have led to a fatalism where we have stopped thinking we can have any control over our government. Power has been subcontracted out to professionals who create slogans and expensive ways to sell us politics we don't want. The result is a diminished level of civic knowledge and an inability to use power effectively to generate significant change.

## UNDERSTANDING THE DYNAMICS OF POWER

Eric Lui created a citizens' university to teach activists how to generate change. His goal is a revival of civic empowerment by teaching activists how to assert their power effectively.[437] Democratic systems require faith, not in a demagogue or a religion, but in each other, he claims. Groups long to be part of something with a transcendent purpose. It is just a question of being able to create results. He also explains that values drive culture, and reform must start by creating a narrative that suggests we change our values – for example, we end the corruption in our institutions.[438]

There are three rules around power that Lui highlights. First, strength concentrates over time. Yet concentrated power has a shorter lifespan than cooperative and inclusive coalitions, so that is one advantage large, diverse groups have. Secondly, it justifies itself; it has a narrative that gives it legitimacy because, without citizen buy-in, the system is unsustainable. Finally, power is infinite. Anyone can acquire it; they just need to use the right strategies to interrupt the existing arrangements.

Activists also need to find the most appropriate message that can move people. In his book, *You Are More Powerful Than You Think*, Lui stresses the approaches that advocates should try to create profound changes: 1) shift the rules, 2) change the prevailing narrative, and 3) redistribute power.[439] Shifting the rules means changing the parameters around a system or attacking a plan.

He gives the example of the Frisco Five, who went into action after several killings of people of color in San Francisco in the spring of 2016. They went on a hunger strike at City Hall and called for the removal of the chief of police. The strike lasted 17 days; they were so weak they had to be hospitalized. After the strike ended, hundreds organized more protests, and with another innocent killing, the chief resigned. None of these five people were well known. They were armed with nothing other than a powerful story and a high level of commitment.[440]

First, they altered the rules by asserting their desires into the chain of command. Instead of having a debate and setting up a pro and con narrative, they changed the story by just taking action, so their demands became non-negotiable. Their moral commitment inspired others to join them, and when another killing came, the pressure was too much to maintain the status quo.

It is also essential to define your sphere of influence – the arena where you can have the most power. You can expand it to spread your message or contract it, so there is less opportunity for the opposition to undermine you. These considerations are critical in deciding how to wage a confrontation. The tactics you use are also crucial. The event can backfire if you overplay your hand and ask for more than people think is reasonable. Movements need to also build on successes to generate momentum.[441]

The first step in creating influential groups is to connect deeply and create an ambiance that feeds people in the groups in many ways. Deep roots and small wins are necessary to keep groups functioning well over the long haul. As Linda Stout, a long-term and highly successful activist, says, we are inspired to participate through our relationships with others in the movement. A winning campaign should focus on both what's wrong and a vision of what is possible.[442]

Activism has always been the tool for progress. FDR, arguably one of the most progressive presidents, told labor leader Philip Randolph that if he wanted segregation to stop in the defense industries, he would have to make Roosevelt do it — presumably, by making it a popular cause. So, Randolph planned a march on Washington to pressure FDR. When FDR heard about it, he asked him to cancel it. Randolph refused, and the president signed an executive order prohibiting employment segregation in the defense industries. Then the march was called off because Randolph had achieved his objective.[443] This was a strategy that King also used to get LBJ to do things he didn't want to do initially, such as the Voting Rights Act. Civic leaders should heed that advice, even now.

Sometimes, however, even an individual person can also dramatically alter the dynamics around a problem, finding secret maneuvers that can outsmart a failing system. In Summit County, Colorado, in 2019, Tamara Drangstveit, the executive director of the Family and Intercultural Center in Silverthorne, which helps people find health coverage, decided to take things into her own hands.

She analyzed premium rates for health insurance in Summit County and found that they had the highest rates in the country. Sometimes the premiums were even higher than people's mortgage payments. Drangstveit went to Denver to get help from the state and federal legislators, but she hit a dead end. Next, she reached out to her insurance commissioner, and he found an arcane law that allowed her to create a purchasing entity. This was a novel idea that no one in the country had ever tried before, and other counties started considering replicating the model. Just by continuing to ask questions, she was able to find a way to dynamically shift the situation. If she had stopped earlier, she would have missed this hidden opportunity.

Then she began negotiating with hospitals and consumers to find a price range that worked for both groups. After she created a pricing scale, she offered her proposals to healthcare insurance agencies, and they were asked to bid on them.[444] Through these strategies, she reduced their premiums by 50% from 2019 to 2020 due to a new state reimbursement program and negotiated lower prices. This story illustrates how her initiative paid off in spades, as it had ripple effects.[445] In 2023, Colorado is about to become the first state in the country to have a state-generated health insurance option. After ten years of negotiating to reduce costs, the state will be able to offer a lower rate to consumers, making Colorado a leader in healthcare reform.[446]

Our society could also generate more ways for civic engagement to occur for brief periods. This would give citizens an experience of thinking with a collective sensibility instead of the current mindset where personal matters or tribal desires are paramount. Generating a more coherent civic voice based on the use of citizen councils could be integrated into many levels of our government. There are various ways to bring citizen input into our decision-making.

### CITIZEN OVERSIGHT AND ACTIVISM

A living democracy would integrate the voice of the people directly into various aspects of running the government. A simple example of how that works is in Citizen Initiative Reviews (CIR), where a randomly selected panel of 24 citizens reviews a proposed ballot initiative. Then they give voters a summation of its ramifications before citizens vote on the proposition. The process effectively highlights the hidden or unintended consequences of a bill. This approach was initiated in 2009 in Oregon and was so effective that it became state law in 2012 that every new ballot initiative would be reviewed for voters prior to the election.[447]

This citizen review is helpful in many cases where the public needs to be more informed about the ballot initiative downsides or politicians are misrepresenting the downsides. An excellent example is something like Brexit, where people In England were asked to vote on something they needed help understanding. Ultimately, though, people will have to also come together to demand more responsiveness for our democracy to thrive.

Protests are part of the answer, but not enough; powerful strategies, profound narratives, and new visions are part of the tools that can generate strong demands for a different future. Cultivating new habits of the mind and heart is a prerequisite for a more robust democracy, habits that could be modeled by influential citizens stewarding us boldly forward.

Beyond learning new skills and ideas, we also should awaken unique spiritual sensibilities that inspire new values within our society. It's time for a more meaningful discourse about the spiritual level of life obscured by our crass, commercialized ecosystem. Our fast-paced society tends to turn our attention away from the revitalizing influences of the more subtle and charming aspects of existence. In the end, it will be from this level that change must come. We will have to go to a place where we revitalize our best moral instincts to re-establish a society in accord with our most noble values and emotional sensibilities.

# 17

## AWAKENING A SPIRITUAL RENAISSANCE

## *We need a moral awakening to stir up a more compassionate and honest society*

Drucilla Cornell, an emeritus professor of political science at Rutgers University, observes that our society suffers because it lacks a robust moral threshold that can discourage negative behaviors.[448] Destructive values like greed, cruelty, and deception become normalized in a culture without a strong principled sensibility.

As John Adams said in 1798, the Constitution was designed to be used by ethical leaders. It is too fragile to withstand unscrupulous ones.[449] Lately, we are experiencing vulnerabilities in that regard. Our system cannot survive without reviving a shared commitment to better norms. Democracy doesn't work when each side plays by a different set of rules and politically feasible behavior has become dangerously detached from what is morally appropriate.

How do we restore an ethical horizon, and what does that even look like? Don Lansky, a Unity Church International minister, described his personal spiritual journey in a book called *Peeling an Artichoke*. He explains how having a spiritual awakening is similar to peeling an artichoke; you must take off the hard and rough outer layers that protect the delicate heart to experience your own spiritual essence.[450]

Much like the individual spiritual journey that he describes in his book, countries too can have soul-searching conversations that help them peel back the false facade of corruption and take them back to their core essential values. Restoring a deeper compassionate, ethical center is a process of peeling back the wrong values, the hard, obsolete, and dying parts of our culture. It is not that we have to reach an agreement on the best policy choices, but we should come together and reconnect, agreeing on the need to restore our best values. Attributes like a strong sense of personal responsibility, generosity, openness, acceptance of differences, and strong ideals are the positive qualities that allowed us to attract people from around the world to our shores. In some ways, what is needed now is that we have to remember our commitments to our best values and to each other. It is a process of coming back to our best selves after a long slumber in a dark alley.

When spiritual housecleaning is in order, the first thing is to discriminate between the suitable values from the past and the bad ones that we have more recently acquired – ones that should be replaced. Corruption, greed, cruelty, and the lust for power and wealth have transported us toward decay rather than growth. These things should be discarded, so there is room for new development that allows the seeds of a better future to unfold. Spiritual leaders could help move us along this process.

Transformative changes and new values are necessary to bring about a spiritual renaissance that takes us out of the darkness and into a realm of healing. Mother Teresa said our problem is that we have lost sight of the fact that we are all connected to each other.[451] Our journey must take us back to remembering that what we do affects others and that we are all inextricably interconnected. Negative or positive feelings are contagious, like germs; they can make us sicker or pull us toward our better selves.

Counteracting the power of hate that has been summoned up lately can only be done by contacting the opposite force. Love is an expansive force; deepening it in ourselves and our groups naturally allows it to flow out toward others. It is a profound and soothing energy that can bind us back together, taking us to heights that the mind cannot scale.

Now, as a caveat, part of our neglect of these spiritual values is because religion has often been used to control and repress, even kill, people in the past and present. In the United States, we have not always seen effective spiritual leadership. My three-year-old grandson's favorite song is Bon Jovi's "You give love a bad name."[452] (I am not sure why; I think it's the resounding chorus since the lyrics about an abusive lover are clearly over his head.)

Following that theme, some religious leaders give spirituality a bad name. They appear more interested in accruing power and controlling others than promoting compassion and expanding and deepening our connections. Yet, just as we shouldn't give up on love because some people abuse us, we shouldn't abandon attention to these deeper sensibilities because of some leaders' shortcomings.

We need to also distinguish the difference between religion and spirituality. My father, for example, was a doctor who never believed in God and said if he died and found out there was a God, he would give him a piece of his mind. When I think of my father, who passed away more than ten years ago, up in heaven giving God a part of his mind, I am pretty confident that, if God exists, He has heard it all before. Yet, I think of my father as a deeply spiritual man. His compassionate, tender heart made it hard for him to imagine how a loving God could create such a painful world.

Theocracy is not what I am advocating, either. The separation of Church and State was one of the most valuable things that our founders gave us. Freedom of religion is a profound approach that spawned many of the other freedoms we cherish today in our culturally diverse society. Our freedoms have established a basis for our rich and varied population, making our country so creative, intellectually rich, and unique.

Critical to our success in tackling issues like climate change will entail new framings across the country, designed and tried out on participants. Religious communities are suitable venues for these activities because they have a long history of bringing people together around shared beliefs and finding ways to sustain their commitment. However, our disconnection from the spiritual foundations of life also makes it difficult to culture the wisdom necessary to take on some of these most demanding tasks.[453]

There are three challenges that spiritual leaders could particularly help with. First, they could advocate caring for the Earth as an essential ethical obligation to the next generation. Secondly, they could help us reduce distrust and divisiveness and return to caring for each other. Finally, people should be encouraged to take more personal responsibility for their own happiness and resist blaming others.

People within religious communities are often better at framing issues in a way that makes sense to their fellow parishioners. One common problem in framing climate change is that it doesn't support the usual narratives with clear protagonists and villains. It is more accurately a heroic quest that demands we overcome our internal weaknesses.[454]

## CULTIVATING THE WISDOM NEEDED TO CARE FOR THE PLANET

The other exciting aspect of these different perspectives on climate change is that both sides' beliefs mirror each other. Environmentalists and climate deniers believe the other side has false information and limited critical thinking skills. This reflects the different bubbles people live in, reflecting confirmation bias, which means we will seek out information that confirms what we believe to be true. Each side distrusts the other side's knowledge. Our different media sources are a real problem because they set up these separate spheres of information, focusing on diverse issues and solutions. It is like living in a country where people speak two different languages.[455]

We need a translator. Someone who asks difficult questions like how do you know when to trust a source? Different conversations where curiosity is present without judgment could help unveil some opportunities for affecting change. The important thing is that the sooner we can create a collective frame on this issue, the more cohesive our society will be as we go into the climate disasters happening more frequently. We can use other values to reach a collective sensibility. Finding a way to also generate more consensus would make us more effective at rising up to adapt to the devastating effects of climate change.

This shift is essential to making a smoother transition in this period. One of the problems is that people are still locked into old ways of viewing our relationship with the Earth. It has also been falsely presented in a black-and-white way – you are either with us or against us, instead of seeing it as a journey that we are all on together. There has been a lot of guilt, shaming, and defensiveness. Instead, I think we could frame it as a journey that we are all navigating in different ways, as we try to become more spiritually connected with the needs of the Earth. Individually changing our habits is good, but we should understand that the big payoffs will come with significant systemic changes.

Furthermore, we should emphasize that we will be fine if we do less. In fact, we will likely be less stressed and even more content. The data suggest that, by all measures, happiness was at its highest point in developed nations in the early 1970s, when Americans used their cars 60 percent less and traveled 80 percent less by plane, as climate activist George Marshall points out in his book *Don't Even Talk About it, Why Our Brains Are Wired to Ignore Climate Change.*[456]

The cultural historian, Thomas Berry, highlights the charm of having a more powerful connection with the Earth. He points out that we appreciate the Earth through our revelatory experiences of it and that we experience the sacred through our participation in all the wonderous aspects of our sublime creation.[457] Becoming more attuned to our connections to the planet will bring its own psychological rewards.

While we sometimes lose sight of the natural world's magic, life on a degraded planet will become significantly more difficult if we continue as usual. The Earth, also, is only on loan to us; we are just guests for a brief sojourn in its history. Our responsibility must be to care for it and pass it on in better shape than we received it, especially now that we know how damaged it is.

Humans have had constructs that framed their relationship to the natural world based on different mental maps. Fidel Xinico, a Kaqchikel Mayan at the Center for Global Education director, explains how the Mayan view of nature differs from ours. The Mayan culture values life—life internally, as they call it. The right to life includes the right to have healthy relationships with other people, plants, animals, minerals, and the whole world. They don't see land as an object to own. Instead, it is intricately connected with their own well-being. They feel that if they are not living in accordance with nature, they lose their health and sense of well-being.[458]

When we look at these older civilizations, there is a sense that there were reservoirs of wisdom in those societies that modern humans need to appreciate. Of course, the Native Americans are also trying to turn us in this direction. They carry this wisdom in their cultures, as well as in their hearts. They have been some of the fiercest fighters for climate change, and we need their wisdom, courage, and guidance right now. Being more attuned to the Earth's needs and becoming her protector will bring its own rewards.

There are also examples of visionaries trying to create experiences that take us toward that new perspective. Michael Reynolds is a pioneer architect trying to help people imagine a new approach that fuses technology with an old reverence for the natural world through his Earthship houses. He uses his Earthships to try to guide people towards a new notion of houses as being places where, he says, we make sanctuaries for plants instead of thinking of designing houses for the wealthy elite or royalty.[459]

In his 630-acre Taos, New Mexico, Earthship community, he has designed beautiful homes out of recycled tin, old tires for insulation, and recycled glass bottles (essentially what we call garbage). On the long southside of the rectangular homes are layers of plants that can produce 25-50% of the owner's food. A cistern collects water and recycles it through four phases of use before sending it through a plant purification system. The house has solar panels and used tires as thermal bricks for insulation. It is an off-grid house designed to be self-sufficient, integrating the lushness of plants into the hallways and creating a comfortable temperature year-round.[460]

Reynolds' goal was to create a concept that is flexible enough to honor present-day mindsets yet strong enough to evolve that mindset.[461] The way we live now is making the planet worse for ourselves and other plants and animals. He wants to reverse that by creating a house that uses recycled glass to mimic elements of the gorgeous mosaics of Spanish Architect Antoni Gaudi, who is responsible for many of the famous buildings in Barcelona.[462]

Reynolds' work unifies utility with beauty and offers low-end costs that could allow someone to escape the traditional housing paradigm where people are shackled for many decades by long-term mortgages. My experience staying in an Earthship for a few days convinced me that there is something soothing about being surrounded by plants on that scale. Integrating the beauty of large-scale plants into the house made me more aware, daily, of the vital nurturing interdependence we have with the natural world.

 Bringing the flowers inside, in addition to creating an ambiance of beauty and an oasis of peace, fused the indoors with the charm of the outdoors. These interconnections between the natural and human worlds will generate a more prosperous future in both arenas, illustrating that being more attentive to plants and animals could enrich our lives in ways we can't even imagine.

Our country should reach back and hold on to our deepest values and redesign our society more in line with them, using approaches like the design of Earthships. We could also use our love of the natural environment, which led to the creation of 62 national parks, to lean towards preserving our lands and avoiding the worst consequences of climate change.[463] This will entail designing new practices and institutions, some grounded in our oldest and best values but shaped into new systems and structures that better tackle our new requirements. While we need to reconnect with the sacred aspects of the Earth, we also need to reconnect with our fellow citizens in new ways.

## COMING BACK TOGETHER

Our country's two significant divides are the political and racial divides. We have created a collection of warring tribes that battle within and outside their own groups. Of course, there are divides within those groups and generational divides. Our news focus exacerbates these tendencies. All these tensions could benefit from spiritual leaders working to bridge the rifts in our society.

The first goal to connect people more tightly must start by bringing diverse groups together. People getting to know each other better is a prerequisite for change. Our tribalized living situation encourages polarization. We live with people who tend to think and look like us, and we bond around fighting other groups outside our sphere of influence.

The Gottmans, renowned marriage therapists, found that there are two kinds of marriage problems: those couples can solve and those they can't. Furthermore, they've found through extensive research that most issues fall into the second category. Yet, they still encourage people to talk about the problems they can't solve because talking can generate the empathy needed to build a foundation for deeper understanding and love. Then if the couple can feel more connected from their conversations, they will have more patience around their differences.[464]

As tribalism has grown, it has had the disastrous consequence of making everything more contentious. People stop thinking for themselves, become less effective stewards of our democracy, and become pumped, tribal warriors. We could use fewer fighters and more ambassadors for peace in our search for learning how to bridge our differences and journey into a place of greater compassion.

### FINDING BALANCE BETWEEN DIFFERENT MORAL ORIENTATIONS

In *The Left-Hand Side of God*, Rabbi Michael Lerner said there are two views of the Christian God, one associated with the left and the other with the right. The left-hand side of God stresses generosity, compassion, and hope. The right-hand side of God emphasizes the need for discipline, punishment, and dominance over evil and fear. While this is a generalization, it broadly captures the different shades of prevalent morality in each political orientation. We hold both perspectives within our minds, but each group tends to put more weight on one side. Each side feels like the other side is out of balance. The right thinks the left is unrealistic and naïve about what is needed, and the left thinks the right is harsh and judgmental.[465]

I had lunch once a month for many years with a small group of politically diverse women. It became clear that we all have things to learn from each other. I found from those conversations that we often described the same problem from different perspectives. It is like the Indian parable where five blind men represent an elephant to each other based on examining only a part of the animal. The man touching the tusk imagines that the elephant is complex and boney, whereas the man investigating his ears describes a leathery creature with significant, pliable parts.

Through private discussions with my conservative friends, I began to think about the essential obligations that underlie a functional society. I also began to think about the precious aspects of our connections as citizens. My friend Marianne observed that as an evangelical, she thought marriage was a sacred covenant under God and should be treated with a high level of reverence.

The conservative evangelical women talked about how it was necessary to not let people take advantage of you, while the liberals stressed generosity. Yet we all struggled to create the right balance in our personal lives. As a collection of women, we were extraordinarily generous with our time and gifts to people. In fact, we discussed our need to create appropriate boundaries and not feel taken for granted. In these moments, our ideological differences seemed to melt away; we were all searching for a generous middle ground where no one felt taken for granted or taken advantage of. Our differences are not as great as they seem when viewed through the lens of partisan media clips.

## A Politics of Meaning

Rabbi Michael Lerner explains that religious conservatives search for what he calls a politics of meaning. He interviewed middle-income working conservatives for 29 years in Canada, the U.S., England, and Israel to understand why conservatives voted for people whose economic policies were against their self-interests. He found that the conservatives were concerned about living in a society where values are corrupted, families are insecure, sexuality is promiscuous, and self-centered behavior is in vogue. Lerner asserts America is indeed experiencing a deep spiritual crisis which the right has capitalized on in its platform. They believed the right was the only party interested in addressing this crisis.

The left has never really advocated an alternative that addresses our spiritual crisis.[466] There is both a need and a possibility to put more attention on things valued by all of us: caring for the common good, strengthening our integrity, honesty, and compassion, and recognizing that our democracy is precious, too.

The covenants that we make as citizens to each other are also profoundly important. We could turn toward each other, just as we would towards our spouses, when trying to save our marriages. We might tend to each other, discussing and finding connections again while taking as much personal responsibility as we can for our own mistakes and prejudices.

After all, how can it be that many of our churches preach a gospel about loving your enemy while our culture is divided into rebel tribes that can't even talk to each other? Isn't it time we revisited this idea of loving our neighbor or at least trying to stop hating him? Most people agree about the redemptive power of love regardless of your religious or spiritual beliefs. We know many of these things in our heads, but we must also come to know them in our hearts. Much of our learning now is heart-centered; shifts must occur on that deep level.

Part of the problem, Rabbi Lerner says, is that we believe it is naïve and unrealistic to imagine that others also want a kinder, more generous world. This fearful view of others keeps us apart, as we stick to the belief that others might not respond to our overtures. That keeps people stuck inside these negative assumptions that other people will not see us as fellow human beings.[467] Our fear of humiliation, rejection, or any number of worries keeps us stuck in this shallow, dysfunctional space where authentic discourse unveils too much vulnerability.

Many of us want a more collective sensibility to emerge, where the concerns of everyone matter, instead of the self-centered view of looking out for number one or the endless political fighting. Yet there is a third way to achieve that without pursuing theocracy or continuing the status quo.

Freedom should not extend to undermining other peoples' individual rights in the name of religion. We have seen the consequences of that approach throughout history, and it doesn't go well. A narrative that discourages both the rise of corruption and greed and the temptation to go towards a fundamentalist society would be helpful. Instead, what is needed is a third narrative that begins to pull our culture back towards a more honest approach where people are inspired to think collectively again about the well-being of all.

## A Third Way

For example, suppose people are really concerned about women aborting their pregnancies. In that case, they could join with other women's groups to create a better quality of life for children to be brought up in – one with safe neighborhoods, safe schools, subsidized high-quality daycare, maternity leave, and other programs. They could also support better family-friendly policies, including maternity leave, working from home, equal pay for women, and more vacation time. Instead of trying to repress individual rights and forcing people into following a prescribed ideology, they could become leaders in a movement to create a society where women have the support they need so that our communities become more comfortable places to raise children in.

Spiritual leaders could advocate a more profound message that stresses more revitalization of universal values, like love, compassion, concern for the collective good, nonviolence, and peace. Building a healthier society will depend on our ability to enliven more of our shared core values by cultivating them in our personal lives and our communities.

The power of spiritual leaders, individual citizens, and groups to pull us back toward our more functional patterns of interaction will determine the possibility of creating a moral awakening. Another breach that could use attention is discussing race in a way that opens the conversation to more nuance and helps us determine the best way forward to form a more functional diverse society.

## CONVERSATIONS ABOUT RACE

One of our biggest challenges is addressing white resentment. Dr. David Campt, who the comedian Trevor Noah calls the "white people whisperer," makes the point that white progressives are the ones especially equipped to talk about issues around race with conservatives.[468] They have the most contact with conservative whites in our culture. When they talk to racist skeptics (deniers or minimizers), they don't have to revisit all the trauma of dealing with the historical effects of racism that Black people would experience.[469] Furthermore, white conservatives might be more comfortable talking to other whites about their concerns in a space without judgment. They could also discuss practices and policies that would reduce white resentment and anxiety, expanding our understanding of racial resentment, provided discussions were held in a space designed to promote deeper learning.

Progressives often express a lack of compassion towards conservatives by creating a simple either/or mentality around racism, and sexuality issues, or turning to political correctness to police speech in a way that shuts down discourse. This contempt towards others blocks opportunities for empathetic conversations. Campt explains that people are moved by stories, not facts. To illustrate the effectiveness of an anecdotal approach, he tells an authentic story showing his own biases to prove how insights and compassion can envelop a room instead of judgment and condemnation.[470]

Ian Haney Lopez has been analyzing the kinds of messages about race that resonate with conservatives. He is a law professor at Berkeley and the author of *Merge Left*. Lopez's research highlights a more nuanced understanding of beliefs. He concludes from his extensive research on racial tension that most whites hold liberal views, though they can be coaxed back towards reactionary ideas. He suggests our goal, therefore, as a society, should be to encourage whites to promote the anti-racist values that most already hold.[471] Finally, individuals also need to take more responsibility for creating their own happiness.

### SEEKING AN INTERNAL STATE OF FULFILLMENT

At the center of our society is a general sense of malaise and discomfort; some of it is legitimate due to circumstances beyond our control. For others who are not engulfed in poverty or other problems from our broken systems, happiness is an inside job. There is no amount of wealth that can bring you a rich life. That's an inside job. To experience contentment, sometimes our first job is to change ourselves, to create more meaning in our lives through work that brings out our talents, and to create a life that brings us satisfying connections with others. Religious and spiritual practices also satisfy a yearning to tap into the subtler realms of being that brings a fuller sense of satisfaction.

There are expansive spiritual practices that can generate more joy so the trials of life become less gripping. When we experience ourselves connected to the eternal and settling rhythms of the natural world, we understand that we are part of a much bigger story and that our limitations are primarily self-imposed. Through such experiences, we come to appreciate that we are powerful spiritual beings, and the longing to feel connected to that transcendent part of life constantly nags at us in one way or another.

Research studies demonstrate that the best antidote to drug use is more happiness. An analysis of 70 studies using the T.M. technique® to reduce drug abuse found a more positive effect than the standard approaches to dealing with abuse. Many people began meditation to reduce stress and experience increased stability, yet they found that it also answers to deeper yearnings.[472]

Ultimately, improving all three arenas (caring more for the Earth and each other and attending to our own needs) could contribute to a healthier culture. It could also generate a more robust sense of connection throughout our society. Creating a more healthy society will rest on our ability to generate new conversations that increase our capacity to revitalize a commitment to our past shared values and aspirations.

Robert Putnam and Shaylyn Garrett, in their book *Upswing*, suggest that a moral awakening is already happening, as evidenced by the rise of multiple movements, including the #MeToo movement, the Poor People's Campaign by Reverend Barber, and the 2018 March for Our Lives, where 1.2 million people attended over 880 events in the U.S. and around the world to protest gun violence.[473]

In these times, we need a new vision to crystalize around the positive elements of our culture and carry us toward the future we want. The next chapter examines what a spiritual revival might look like by examining a time in our past when we transitioned from a corrupt climate towards a period of extensive change. It was partly driven by soul-searching conversations that were encouraged by a group of Christians who generated a social gospel movement where they applied the principles of Christianity to social reform.

As industrialization marched along at the end of the 19th century, some social gospel ministers saw the social problems as due to the spread of greed and a failure to safeguard the plight of the workers. These leaders suggested that it was the job of Christians to build the Kingdom of God on Earth. As you'll see in the next chapter, this spirit became quite animated in the Progressive Era.[474]

# 18

## Revitalizing the Soul of America

### *Restoring healthy norms will bring out our better impulses*

Our divisiveness increases our feelings of anxiety, helplessness, or anger, at a critical time when our best option is to actually confront our most wicked conflicts. Many citizens would like us to shift to a more ethical society, for example, but they don't even know where to begin.

So, while it is all well and good in theory, the question remains, how could a shift to more moral attitudes even begin? This is where the lessons from history become helpful. In their book Upswing, Robert Putnam and Shaylyn Garrett do an excellent job of pointing out the things we could learn from examining the shift from the first Gilded Age (historians date it roughly 1870 – 1896) to the Progressive Era (1896 – 1916). The Gilded Age was a time similar to ours, where there was a significant disparity in wealth, and communities were dealing with some of the same issues that haunt us today: increasing urbanization, immigration, racism, and political corruption. The Progressive Era, on the other hand, became a period where massive reform switched the culture and mores of the time to a more compassionate and caring culture, moving citizens from an "I" orientation to a "We" orientation.[475]

In 1888, the book *Looking Backward* by Edward Bellamy became a best seller and had a huge influence on the thinking of that era. It gave readers a vision of a better society, told from the perspective of what life had evolved to in the year 2000. The book describes how by the envisioned 2000 future, we had evolved into a much more cooperative society. He describes an environment where people find it unbelievable that those in the 1880s lived as they did, with such corruption and contempt for the concerns of those without status or wealth. It doesn't predict our 2000 society very well. Still, it forged new transformative approaches in the 1880s by stirring the imaginations of the citizens, illustrating how the pen can be mightier than the sword in changing hearts.[476] The question is: how did such change come about? What inspired these new narratives, and what were they? Who brought about the change? What lessons can we take away from their struggles and successes?

## How Did the Changes Come About?

The movement began at a grassroots level, as women like Frances Perkins and Ida B. Wells began to take on moral crusades to change the circumstances of the poor. Perkins was a Mount Holyoke graduate who always imagined a life that consisted of marrying wealth, then becoming a philanthropist. Yet she was having tea with friends when she witnessed the devastating 1911 Triangle Shirtwaist fire in New York City. That was a pivotal moment in her life.[477] It was in the garment district at a facility that employed newly arrived immigrants as workers. Hundreds of helpless teenage girls were trapped inside a burning sweatshop where they worked on sewing machines 12 hours a day, 7 days a week.

Many died because there were limited routes out. With access to only one functional elevator that gave out during the fire, a narrow fire escape, and a locked front door to avoid employee theft, many leaped to their death by jumping out windows or down the elevator shaft in a vain attempt to save their lives. One hundred forty-six lives were lost. Two years earlier, they had called a strike to bring attention to the need for more safe and humane working conditions to no avail. There was too much corruption as the garment industry paid the politicians to ignore the unsafe conditions.[478]

After witnessing that, Perkins jumped into activism and politics, realizing that moralizing as an activist was not enough. She became the first woman in America to obtain a cabinet post as the Secretary of Labor under President Franklin Roosevelt in 1933. She was one of the thousands of women fighting these issues of neglect and focusing on changing the destitute conditions.

Ida B. Wells was another influential activist, an amazingly resilient and courageous woman, born into slavery in 1862. She managed to care for her siblings after the death of her parents by finding work at a young age and went on to teach high school while taking college courses. When asked to give up her first-class seat on a train, she refused and was thrown off the train; nevertheless, she sued the railroad company.

Her attempt was unsuccessful, but she didn't stop there. She wrote an impassioned article about her experience that launched her career as a journalist documenting racial inequality as the rise of Jim Crow took root. She fearlessly accounted the horrors of lynching, which was reduced by 90% by 1920, partly due to her increased attention to the issue. She wanted to join the women's suffrage movement, but her stance against lynching and racism put her at odds with the head of the Women's Christian Temperance Union.[479]

The activism started on a grassroots level and spread to both parties. Citizens were inspired by middle-class women taking up crusades to attack various issues. Some reformers were visionaries like Ida B. Wells, who was ahead of her time. Others were just tinkering around the edges. Yet the changes occurred on multiple levels as the grass-roots upswell continued to touch political leaders. Activists realized real reform had to include changes at the top. Many battles were framed as moral imperatives.

The approach used was more of what Putnam and Garret called "soul searching" rather than blaming one class or political party. Many of their efforts started by focusing on the atrocities due to wrong policies or neglect. This led to re-examining their shared values, summoning everyone to contribute to necessary activism. Their narratives also stressed how society was complicit and everyone should do their part to reshape problem areas.

Ministers worked to critique the sins of the time and amplify the moral imperative. [480] Walter Rausxhenbusch and others reframed Christianity into a framework for creating a just society through the Social Gospel movement from 1870 – 1920. The leaders were made up of liberal Protestant ministers who advocated for the abolition of child labor, a shorter work week, a living wage, and factory regulations.[481]

They were not ideologically driven; instead, they rallied around the call for doing the patriotic thing, which involved caring for each other and improving the country. They talked about restoring the moral health of the nation. The narratives also stressed using moral outrage to turn civic concern into activism, and people responded by becoming incredibly active on many levels.[482]

Progress sometimes rests on the slow accretion of greater truths that nag at a society until it finally endorses them. These narratives arose after a populist upsurge and in competition with calls for socialism. They didn't push for a revolution but managed slow and steady reform that built up, snowballing into more and more arenas over time. They balanced the tensions between the desire for personal liberty with the call for responsible business practices. Not all the narratives were endorsed at the time, but many laid the groundwork for the New Deal that came much later during Franklin Roosevelt's presidency. Others, the most profound voices like Ida B. Wells, laid the groundwork for the civil rights movement.

## WHO BROUGHT ABOUT THE CHANGES?

While middle-class, educated women were at the vanguard of the changes with their strong call for higher moral standards, it was also hugely popular with the young. High schools proliferated because Horace Mann's everyday school reform movement started in the 1830's so that by 1900, 78% of children ages 8-17 were going to school.[483] From 1890 – 1930, twenty million immigrants came to the United States.[484] Mann convinced people that more schooling would help the new immigrants assimilate more successfully into the culture. The young clamored for new perspectives to meet the new times as urbanization and industrialization shifted society into a wage-based system.

Yet the movement spanned throughout all levels, from the elite to the factory workers, as debates expanded about how to deal with the new parameters of society. Walter Lippman, a 25-year-old progressive journalist, wrote a book called *Drift and Mastery*, where he downplayed the value of utopian thinking and instead suggested that the changes had to be done collaboratively by the American people from all walks of life.

The changes were even brought on by some of the wealthiest men at the time. Tom Johnson, mayor of Cleveland (1901 – 1909), initiated innovative reforms that were far-reaching and emulated in other cities. Johnson was inspired by the writings of Henry George's book, *Progress, and Prosperity*. George advocated for ways to regulate the monopolistic practices that led to booms and busts in the economy and focused on society's moral obligation to reduce poverty. Over time, a handful of progressive mayors began spreading new approaches across the country as they bounced their ideas around as they were tried out in one city and passed to another.

Johnson was famous for selling his shares in the railroad companies that had brought him wealth and then advocated for the streetcars to become public property. His positive changes brought improved housing conditions, better sanitation, and policing; he built more parks on expensive waterfront property, community centers, and homes for the elderly and indigent.[485]

Over time, these changes percolated up to influence politicians in both parties as the clamor for change continued, even past the Progressive Era and into the New Deal. Theodore Roosevelt, at 42, was the youngest president to date ever elected to office, and he ran on a promise to implement progressive policies. President Wilson and Franklin Roosevelt also followed up on the foundation that progressive activists had generated. Their agenda was like something we might work on today, as Robert Putnam cites: universal, affordable healthcare, campaign finance reform, corruption and control by big business, progressive taxation, and environmental regulation.[486]

Muckrakers published magazine articles that objected to the corruption in city politics, inhumane tenement living conditions, the monopolistic practices of Standard Oil, and racism. In the end, they took on many different causes based on the revitalization of their shared values and created a shift away from the greed and self-centeredness of the first Gilded Age, and moved us towards a more collective caring sensibility, according to Putnam and Garret.

They conclude that the reformers in that era tackled many problems without an actual blueprint, but they were highly innovative. If we are to be as productive as they were, they also suggest we should avoid fashioning our reforms along the lines of polarization of today's debates. Instead, we should find ways to appeal to a broad base.

# CONCLUSION
## NEXT STEPS

Citizens must come together and use their collective intelligence to generate an effective discourse that can lead the country back in the right direction. Leaders can model a way forward that restores a virtuous cycle where integrity matters. In a way, powerful speakers are our superheroes now; they can rekindle patriotism in peoples' hearts and give them the courage to reject the toxic influences that are undermining our greatest traditions. Authentic speakers like Mario Savio from the Free Speech Movement would be helpful, so they can awaken the conscience of our nation, restoring respect for our highest values.

Our national discourse is like the lifeblood of our society, and it has been poisoned by divisive leaders. Yet fixing it is our work; together, we can generate new conversations that take us deeper into the heart of the matter, moving us away from the political grandstanding and towards reconnecting. We have forgotten that we are interlinked across a vast connection of webs from our beginnings in our family of origin to our partners, our children, our fellow citizens, to all the pockets of humanity across the globe, our Earth, and all the sacred elements of life on this planet.

Ultimately, it was through soul searching that the Gilded Age shifted and gave way to the better values of the Progressive Era. It was by asking everyone to examine their role in contributing to the failed norms of the time, not blaming and demonizing others. Innovative thinking was also a powerful force in creating the new era, coupled with a more profound moral awareness. These are changes that a bold movement could begin to initiate.

A strong pro-democracy movement could address multiple issues simultaneously. It should have a clear agenda that is designed collectively. It could appeal to the need to create a higher quality of life with a solid social safety net, reminding people that we would be better off if everyone is taken care of, the middle class is flourishing, and multigenerational poverty is eradicated. Central to a robust democracy is creating one where multiple needs are addressed simultaneously, and a sense of belonging encompasses everyone.

Our current levels of inequality are tearing our country apart. Following the lead of other strong democracies, we should recommit to policies that take us back toward a more balanced and sustainable country. We are, after all, a nation of immigrants, so it makes no sense to suddenly abandon our commitment to growing a healthy middle class from around the world.

Our goal should be to lean into our diversity and learn from each other. Our mantra should become that our diversity is not a liability, but our greatest asset. This is the next step in our evolution as a society. Catalyzing conversations with broad groups can be a springboard for igniting the necessary reforms that can be game-changing. The movement should lead us toward unlocking our collective wisdom and becoming the learning society called for in these times. Through understanding each other better, we can stretch and become wiser and more compassionate, moving toward creating the connections and understandings we need to become more emotionally intelligent in our interactions.

An excellent place to begin is by generating many types of conversations that can strengthen our national discourse. Healing conversations, where both sides feel heard, is a good beginning. We also need opportunities to reinvigorate our shared aspirations. While we may disagree on the solutions, the first step is to rekindle a shared consensus around our desires. Another step in this journey is creating better problem-solving conversations with people who want to serve as peace ambassadors. They can seed more authentic conversations into our national discourse that embrace compromise and honor the legitimacy of diverse opinions.

Reminding us of our connections is a critical issue in these times, because there is strength in numbers, and the more voices that spark that remembrance, the stronger the pull toward strengthening these bonds. Soul-searching questions also could bring us better conversations. What kind of society do we think we deserve?

All these tactics could encourage us to respectfully hold the tension between our differences. Instead of repeating the same old divisive dance steps, we could try new ones, flirt with nuance, sidestep the outrage, and offer something novel: another way forward that examines our everyday concerns. The solutions are there ... if we can shift our attitudes and be open to them.

Ultimately, we must create a politics that works for all of us, not just the elite. It is time to escape the strangling influences of special interests and return to being a government for the people and by the people. Our political system must also include more robust accountability measures so that people are vetted before they can run for office and held to specific ethical standards, so they can be forced to leave when they violate their oath.

Modernizing our democracy should be another high priority. New tools could bring the view of the people into play in a more dynamic way. Another important lesson for our time is that we must get better at sharing power and working in teams and partnerships. The complexity of these times calls for it, and people everywhere are yearning for it.

It is also essential to realize that the sooner we start to rise up to meet distant challenges, the better off we will be. Embracing the future entails using modern tools and adapting new ideas to enhance our democracy. Citizen Councils could be used to reflect the majority's desires more adequately than some other sources of authority these days. Citizens should also play a more vibrant role, getting involved at different levels of government. A modern government would also be more agile, adaptive, and able to implement changes more efficiently.

In the end, profound change is often driven by a fresh vision that emerges as new narratives inspire a spiritual shift where better values rise. We should use the powerful techniques of Appreciative Inquiry to help us build a new bold national vision for our democracy.

To generate a large coalition for a democracy movement, a broad umbrella helps. Many issues were included in the broad agenda during the progressive age, and the activists arose from different walks of life, philosophies, and parties. They also bridged different generations, with women and youth in the vanguard. It was less inclusive than our next movement must be. Still, it illustrated how a diverse, pragmatic move with a broad goal like improving the quality of life can galvanize various groups of activists to simultaneously push for innovative solutions on many fronts.

Younger generations, however, often have a significant role in bringing in the future. They deserve support and resources for their endeavors, so they will have the bandwidth they need to conquer our problems. They deserve to be free of extensive debt and schooled in universities that prepare them to be future leaders of an entirely different world.

Seeking connections across issues, generations, and political parties would also go a long way toward undoing the fractures in our culture. Before new conversations have any effect, we must restore a sense of empathy and compassion for our various struggles, especially the ones we don't share.

The creation of 21st Century Learning Hubs could inspire new conversations that reconnect us, and disperse valuable understandings simultaneously. They could also help develop stronger collaborative capacities and reduce some of the anxiety people feel about the rise of artificial intelligence and the massive loss of jobs it will entail. It will be smoother and more comfortable if we all work together and bring comfort to each other as we design and advocate for a future that matches our dreams.

Part of the challenge is that humans will need to learn how to share power and work collaboratively on a deeper level than ever before in order to design a society where the benefits of technology are enjoyed more equitably. Developing our emotional and collective intelligence will be critical to helping us navigate well through another high-tech revolution that could create a level of abundance we have never imagined. These encounters also offer opportunities to have conversations about how to strengthen our shared commitment to a more equitable society.

Learning hubs could also make people more aware of the dangers of fascism so we can reduce the appeal of a strongman. We also must find ways to regulate the news so we discourage creating propaganda that panders to people's fears, animosity, and irrationality, exacerbating the negative influence of those emotions on our society.

Establishing ways to put more political power in the hands of citizens, and keep it there, has to be an essential part of our learning as a society. Our destiny lies in our hands; there are no guarantees that we will follow the trajectory of the Progressive Era and shift from the current selfish orientation to a more collective one, where we create a healthier society for everyone. Yet throughout history, progress has often been stimulated by a small cohort of citizens taking leadership, motivating many to unite and create a new way forward.

If we are to collectively heal our differences and come together across our country, it will probably happen that way again, as it has many times in the past. We should not be afraid of the future either. We should, instead, come together and rise up to weave together the best traditions from our past with our future dreams, so we can begin to bring forth that more perfect world that is struggling to emerge.

# A Special Bonus from Ruth

Now that you have read *Igniting a Bold New Democracy*, you are aware of how you can help reform our country. You've hopefully been inspired by the stories of how change has happened in the past and are more informed about the transformations that are necessary and how to create them.

You can also receive a special bonus which is a comprehensive list of the various organizations that are working on these issues, so you can find ways to help change our country.

There are books out there that complain about our broken politics, but there are few that explain how to catalyze the transformations that are needed. With this additional information, you'll be armed with the skills required to become one of the sparks that helps ignite a new bolder approach to citizens improving our country.

Go to http://Ruthbackstrom/bonus to register for your gift. You'll also receive additional information about progress that organizations are making on creating deep reforms. You may, of course, unsubscribe at any time.

The sooner you start to become a powerful change agent, the better! Never underestimate the power of one person to help create profound transformations.

Let's come together and shift our country back towards being the democracy that reflects our best values and inspires us.

Let's create the game changing reforms that are needed together!

*Ruth Backstrom*

# ABOUT THE AUTHOR

Holding a BA in history and a PhD in education, Ruth Backstrom had always dreamed of writing a book since she was thirteen, but it took a pandemic to create a space and time without distractions for her to really do it.

The book evolved out of a series of talks that she gave at a local community center. Her talks came out of her experiences doing educational events with the center and in other arenas. She worked for ten years as an advocate for a more sustainable community and the creation of a food policy council. In the process of working with groups, the discussions after the talks were so rich that she realized people are yearning to have conversations about how to solve the problems in our country. Sharing her thoughts became a way of spreading these conversations to a broader audience, so more people could think together about how to handle these tumultuous times and enact the reforms we all want.

This book also sprang from a desire to spread new kinds of conversations across our country. She became interested in the profound power of certain facilitation techniques to bring out the collective intelligence in a room. She went on to learn various facilitation methods and was trained as a coach. Her experiences with collective intelligence inspired the birth of this book as she began to see the possibilities that could come alive if we could come together and have authentic problem-solving conversations again.

# GLOSSARY

**G.I. Bill** – The GI Bill was the short name given for the Servicemen's Readjustment Act of 1944. The bill offered a number of benefits to returning veterans from WWII. There were loans to small businesses, home mortgages, and free educational grants to veterans after WWII. G.I. stands for government issue.

**FDR's fireside chats** – President Franklin Delano Roosevelt (1933-45) used radio as a powerful medium to speak directly to the people, bypassing the press. He delivered a thousand talks directly to the homes of citizens through the radio. Reporters labeled these talks fireside chats. As a result of these personal entreaties, white house mail increased extensively, as people developed a more personal connection with the president through these broadcasts.

**ACLU** – The American Civil Liberty Union was started in 1920 to protect individual civil rights and stop the government, or other institutions, from violating the freedoms described in the Constitution, particularly freedom of expression. It continues to try to protect people from abusive behavior today and monitors problematic practices, as well.

**Antifa** – This movement's main goal is to fight fascism. It is made up of loosely connected individuals, and organizations.

They came to the United States in the 1970s. The Antifa movement believes that if citizens had resisted the Nazis in the streets, they would never have come to power. So, they have aggressively protested hate speech and white supremacists at rallies like Unite the Right in Charlottesville, Virginia, in August 2017.

**Jim Crow Laws** – These were a series of state and local laws and statutes that prohibited Black people from full participation in American society. Laws and policies were established to prohibit access to voting and other fundamental rights. They also established segregated eating, lodging, and restrooms. These codes and laws were in place after the 13th amendment abolished slavery in 1865. They lasted until 1968 when the civil rights movement forced congress to extend full citizenship rights to African Americans and created enforcement mechanisms to try to guarantee them.

**Nazi Trials at Nuremberg** – The Nuremberg trials consisted of 13 trials after the end of WWII, between 1945 – 49. At the trials. high-ranking Nazi officials were tried for crimes against humanity. The Nazi killings were responsible for an estimated 6 million European Jews being murdered, and it is estimated that another 4-6 million non-Jews were also killed.

**HUAC** – In the early 1950s, the House Un-American Activities Committee was created by the U.S. House of Representatives. Senator Joseph McCarthy used it to accuse celebrities and other prominent people of Communism. He particularly attacked the motion picture industry. If people refused to testify, they were blacklisted, often losing their jobs, and sometimes ending up in prison. By the late 1950s, its power was waning, and the anticommunist hysteria began to disappear.

**McCarthyism** – Senator Joseph McCarthy, from Wisconsin, lead HUAC. His aggressive pursuit of communists created a sense of fear among left-leaning liberals. His tactics often relied on intimidation, legitimizing hearsay evidence, and bullying tactics. His power over the committee lasted from 1950 – 54 and ended with him being censored by Congress for his behavior.

**Marshall Plan** – This was a four-year plan, enacted in 1948, to rebuild Europe after WWII; it included restoring cities, critical industries, and infrastructure. It was developed by Secretary of State George Marshall to modernize Europe and also prevent the spread of communism. They invested approximately $13 billion in the enterprise and it helped lead to the recovery of Europe.

**Cuban Missile Crisis** – This crisis lasted for 13 days in October 1962 after the Soviet Union installed nuclear missiles on Cuba, 90 miles from the U.S. shores. On October 22, 1962, Kennedy told the public that he was putting a military blockade around Cuba and also threatened to remove the missiles by force, if necessary. People were worried that we were on the brink of nuclear war. Through negotiations, they agreed to a compromise that led to the removal of the missiles in exchange for an agreement that President Kennedy would not invade Cuba and would remove U.S. missiles from Turkey as well. This compromise worked and averted a potential nuclear confrontation.

**Dynamic Facilitation** – A facilitation technique that Jim Rough developed and began teaching in the 1990s. He created it while working in the Simpson Timber Company in 1981. It is a technique that generates an environment that allows people to go into a choice-creating mode where people often produce deeper insights and solutions.

**Citizen Councils** – These are well-developed strategies that have been institutionalized in Vorarlberg, Austria. It is a method for getting citizen input on issues. The government sends out letters to a large group of citizens, and they chose a council from the individuals that express interest in participating (the size is between 12-24 people). The citizens are given all the data that is necessary for them to understand the issue fully when they come to the event. They meet for two and a half days with a facilitator who is trained in Dynamic Facilitation. At the end of that time, they come up with several key points that address the issue on a deep level. These resolutions are then shared with the wider public and refined with their input. A team then follows through on implementing the recommendations that come out of this process.

**Appreciative Inquiry** – The Appreciative Inquiry Model has its roots in David Cooperrider's 1986 dissertation. Later the model was expanded by others and became a powerful organizational development tool in the 1990s. This approach encourages groups to emphasize what is working, rather than just focus on the problems. Then it encourages people to use the strengths of an organization to address any areas that need to be improved. From there, it takes them through a process of collaboratively imagining and designing the future they want for their organization.

**Nonviolent Communication (NVC)** – Marshall Rosenberg developed Nonviolent Communication as a tool for helping diffuse violence and used it to help peacefully desegregate schools in the 1960s. Marshall stressed the fact that people are continually trying to honor their values and have their needs met simultaneously. Violence erupts when people cannot see any other way to get their needs met.

# Notes about Sources

## Endnotes

**Part I**

**Chapter 1**

1. Ashley Collman, "A Man Who Thought the Coronavirus was a "Scamdemic" Wrote a Powerful Essay Against Virus Deniers After He Hosted a Party and Got His Entire Family Sick," Business Insider, July 28, 2020

2. Lilliana Mason, *Uncivil Agreements, How Politics Became Our Identity*, University of Chicago Press, Chicago, Illinois, 2018, pgs. 21-22

3. Stephen Prothero, *Why Liberals Win (Even When they Lose Elections)*, Harper Collins, N.Y., N.Y., 2016, pg. 211

4. Ibid., pgs .9-10

5. Ibid., pg. 184

6. https://fpif.org/divide_and_conquer_as_imperial_rules/ 6

7. https://millercenter.org/president/fdroosevelt/life-in-brief

8. https://www.cnbc.com/id/100540655

9. https://www.defense.gov/News/Feature-Stories/story/Article/1727086/75-years-of-the-gi-bill-how-transformative-its-been/

10. http://recordsofrights.org/events/72/the-bonus-army-march-on-washington

11. Ibid.

12. https://www.legion.org/history

13. "Atherton Assails Rankin for Delay," New York Times Archive, April 24, 1944

14. https://www.neh.gov/humanities/2014/julyaugust/feature/how-the-gi-bill-became-law-in-spite-some-veterans-groups

15. https://tucson.com/news/arizonas-ernest-mcfarland-and-the-fight-for-the-gi-bill/article_a430950b-5612-5872-901f-e94f179e9b26.html

16. https://www.encyclopedia.com/social-sciences-and-law/law/law/gi-bill

17. https://www.neh.gov/humanities/2014/julyaugust/feature/how-the-gi-bill-became-law-in-spite-some-veterans-groups

18. https://www.cbsnews.com/news/how-the-gi-bill-changed-america/

19. https://www.neh.gov/humanities/2014/julyaugust/feature/how-the-gi-bill-became-law-in-spite-some-veterans-groups

20. Ibid.

21. Tom Brokaw, *The Greatest Generation*, Random House, N.Y., N.Y., 1998

22. https://www.apmreports.org/episode/2015/09/03/the-history-of-the-gi-bill

23. https://www.va.gov/opa/publications/celebrate/gi-bill.pdf

24. https://www.va.gov/opa/publications/celebrate/gi-bill.pdf

25. https://www.marketplace.org/2009/10/06/how-gi-bill-changed-economy/

26. https://veteranseducationsuccess.org/gi-bill-history

27. https://www.history.com/news/gi-bill-black-wwii-veterans-benefits

## CHAPTER 2

28. https://abcnews.go.com/Politics/Vote2008/full-transcript-sen-barack-obamas-victory-speech/story?id=6181477

29. Kevin Hechtkopf, "Obama Defends Rick Warren's Role at Inauguration," CBS News, December 19, 2008

30. https://www.cheatsheet.com/entertainment/15-ridiculous-moments-fox-news-attacked-barack-obama.html/

31. Norm Ornstein, "The Real Story of Obamacare's Birth," The Atlantic, July 7, 2015

32. https://www.britannica.com/story/barack-obamas-presidential-legacy

33. https://www.forbes.com/sites/gracemarieturner/2020/01/17/top-reasons-why-obamacare-is-wrong-for-america/

34. https://www.huffpost.com/entry/why-are-bankers-still-bei_b_194242

35. https://www.sentencingproject.org/about-us/

36. Neil Schoenherr, "The Costs of Incarceration in the U.S. is more than $1 trillion," Washington State University, St. Louis, September 7, 2016

37. https://www.latimes.com/archives/la-xpm-2001-feb-19-mn-27373-story.html

38. https://abcnews.go.com/US/federal-judge-regrets-55-year-marijuana-sentence/story?id=28869467

39. https://www.nytimes.com/2014/09/08/us/the-rise-of-the-swat-team-in-american-policing.html

40. https://www.nytimes.com/article/breonna-taylor-police.html

41. https://www.aclu.org/blog/smart-justice/mass-incarceration/another-day-another-124-violent-swat-raids

42. John Surico, "A Former Cop Describes Racist Police Quotas in New York," Vice, April 4, 2016

43. Peter Edelman, "How it became a crime to be poor in America," The Guardian, November 6, 2017

44. National Research Council, *The Growth of Incarceration in the United States: Exploring Causes and Consequences,* Washington, D.C., The National Academies Press, 2014

45. https://www.cnn.com/2020/09/15/us/breonna-taylor-louisville-settlement/index.html

46. https://abcnews.go.com/US/27-million-settlement-george-floyds-family-approved-minneapolis/story?id=76419755

47. Ta Neshi Coates, *Between the World and Me*, Penguin Random House, N.Y. N.Y., 2015, pgs. 77-82

48. https://www.usnews.com/news/cities/articles/2020-08-17/how-the-us-government-promoted-housing-segregation-in-us-cities

49. Lisa Cannell, insights from Gregory Fairchild, "Segregation in 2020: Why Aren't we moving Forward?", UVA Darden, Ideas to Actions, September 2020

50. https://www.brookings.edu/blog/how-we-rise/2021/06/11/time-will-not-heal-5-ways-to-address-the-inheritance-of-black-poverty-starting-now/

51. https://www.pewresearch.org/race-ethnicity/2022/08/30/black-americans-have-a-clear-vision-for-reducing-racism-but-little-hope-it-will-happen/

52. https://hcz.org/our-purpose/

53. https://abcnews.go.com/Politics/story?id=4608394&page=1

54. https://www.rev.com/blog/transcripts/a-more-perfect-union-speech-transcript-barack-obama

55. https://www.chicagotribune.com/nation-world/ct-full-text-of-obama-eulogy-in-charleston-20150626-story.html

56. https://www.nytimes.com/2015/06/21/us/dylann-storm-roof-photos-website-charleston-church-shooting.html

57. https://www.biography.com/activist/bree-newsome

58. https://www.esquire.com/news-politics/news/a35912/confederate-flag-banned/

## CHAPTER 3

59. https://www.jfklibrary.org/2022-profile-in-courage-ceremony

60. https://www.rev.com/blog/transcripts/liz-cheney-delivers-address-at-reagan-institute-6-29-22-transcript

61. https://news.yahoo.com/trump-tells-capitol-rioters-we-love-you-but-you-have-to-go-home-now-215650227.html

62. https://www.youtube.com/watch?v=ZZujB5tSqek&t=10s

63. https://www.nbcnews.com/politics/congress/read-full-remarks-rep-liz-cheney-delivers-closing-statement-prime-time-rcna39569

64. https://www.newsweek.com/donald-trump-poll-independents-2024-1741078

65. https://www.reuters.com/world/us/cracks-appear-trumps-standing-among-republicans-after-jan-6-hearings-2022-07-21/-

66. https://www.history.com/this-day-in-history/womens-march

67. https://www.forbes.com/sites/jackbrewster/2021/06/30/study-confirms-big-2020-takeaways-bidens-gains-with-suburban-voters-independents-won-him-election/?sh=b893610ba712

68. https://www.britannica.com/story/
why-did-joseph-mccarthys-influence-decline

69. https://www.biography.com/news/
artists-blacklisted-hollywood-red-scare

70. https://www.cbsnews.com/news/
edward-r-murrow-joseph-mccarthy-report-1954/

71. https://www.britannica.com/story/
why-did-joseph-mccarthys-influence-decline

72. https://www.nbcnews.com/politics/congress/read-full-
remarks-rep-liz-cheney-delivers-closing-statement-prime-time-
rcna39569

73. https://www.theguardian.com/environment/2019/sep/02/
greta-thunberg-responds-to-aspergers-critics-its-a-superpower

## PART II

74.      https://www.moreincommon.com/our-work/
what-we-do/

75.      Ibid.

## CHAPTER 4

76. Rachel Dickson, "Why We Should Commemorate
the 1963 Chicago Public School Boycott," October
22, 2013, 10:AM, WTTW News (https://news.wttw.
com/2013/10/22/1963-chicago-public-school-boycott)

77. Alexander Nazaryan, "School Segregation is as Bad Today as
it was in the 1960s," Newsweek, March 22, 2018

78. https://www.nytimes.com/1999/09/11/us/by-court-order-
busing-ends-where-it-began.html

79. Alexander Nazaryan, "School Segregation is as Bad Today as
it was in the 1960s," Newsweek, March 22, 2018

80. Ibid.

81. Ibid.

82. Elizabeth Hinton, *America on Fire, The untold History of Police Violence and Black Rebellion Since the 1960s,* W.W. Norton and Company, N.Y., N.Y., 2021, pg. 2

83. Christopher Wilson, "The Moment When Four Students Sat Down to Take a Stand," Smithsonian Magazine, January 31, 2020

84. https://www.abhmuseum.org/voting-Rights-for-blacks-and-poor-whites-in-the-jim-crow-south/

85. Aniko Bodroghkozy, "Media Historian on 'Bloody Sunday', the Late Representative John Lewis," The National Interest, July 20, 2020

86. Ibid.

87. Jeff Wallenfeldt, "Selma March," Britannica, July 28, 2020

88. Ibid.

89. Elizabeth Hinton, *America on Fire, The untold History of Police Violence and Black Rebellion Since the 1960s,* W.W. Norton and Company, N.Y., N.Y., 2021, pg. 2

90. Ibid., pg. 10

91. Ibid., pg. 3

92. Ibid., pgs. 41-2

93. Ibid., pgs. 74-6

94. Ibid., pgs. 146-7

95. Ibid., pg. 204

96. Ibid., pgs. 118-19

97. Ibid., pg. 4

98. Maurice Isserman & Michael Kazin, *America Divided, The Civil War of the 1960s,* Oxford University Press, N.Y., N.Y., pg. 242

99. https://www.christianpost.com/news/vonette-bright-dies-campus-crusade-for-christ-billy-graham-church-model.html

100. Ibid.

101. Stannsilov Grov, Erwin lLaszlo, & Peter, Russell, *The Conscious-ness Revolution*, Elf Rock Productions, Las Vegas, Nevada, 2003, pgs. 5-9

102. Ibid., pg. 168

103. Ibid., pgs. 260-62

104. Ibid., pg. 281

105. https://www.huffpost.com/entry/mass-incarceration-cost_n_57d82d99e4b09d7a687fde21

106. Andrew Hartman, *A War for the Soul of America: A History of the Culture War*, University of Chicago Press, Chicago, Ill, 2015, pg.4

**CHAPTER 5**

107. Waldo Martin, "Holding one Another, Mario Savio and the Freedom Struggle in Mississippi and Berkeley" in *The Free Speech Movement, Reflections on Berkeley in the 1960's*, edited by Robert Cohen and Reginald E. Zelnik, University of California Press, Berkeley, CA, 2002, pgs. 83-84

108. https://kinginstitute.stanford.edu/encyclopedia/freedom-summer

109. Waldo Martin, "Holding one Another, Mario Savio and the Freedom Struggle in Mississippi and Berkeley" in *The Free Speech Movement, Reflections on Berkeley in the 1960's*, edited by Robert Cohen and Reginald E. Zelnik, University of California Press, Berkeley, CA, 2002, pg. 83

110. https://kinginstitute.stanford.edu/encyclopedia/freedom-summer

111. Doug Rossinow, "Mario Savio and the Politics of Authenticity" in *The Free Speech Movement, Reflections on Berkeley in the 1960's*, edited by Robert Cohen and Reginald E. Zelnik, University of California Press, Berkeley, CA, 2002, pgs. 548-9

112. Waldo Martin, "Holding one Another, Mario Savio and the Freedom Struggle in Mississippi and Berkeley" in *The Free Speech Movement, Reflections on Berkeley in the 1960's*, edited by Robert Cohen and Reginald E. Zelnik, University of California Press, Berkeley, CA, 2002, pgs. 86-87

113. Mario Savio, "Thirty Years Later," Reflections on the FSM," in *The Free Speech Movement, Reflections on Berkeley in the 1960's*, edited by Robert Cohen and Reginald E. Zelnik, University of California Press, Berkeley, CA, 2002, pgs. 59-61

114. Michael Rossman, "The "Rossman" Report, A Memoir of Making History," in *The Free Speech Movement, Reflections on Berkeley in the 1960's*, edited by Robert Cohen and Reginald E. Zelnik, University of California Press, Berkeley, CA, 2002, pg. 192

115. https://fsm.berkeley.edu/free-speech-movement-timeline/

116. http://www.slatearchives.org/chronology.htm

117. Ibid., pg. 10

118. Michael Rossman, "The "Rossman" Report, A Memoir of Making History," in *The Free Speech Movement, Reflections on Berkeley in the 1960's*, edited by Robert Cohen and Reginald E. Zelnik, University of California Press, Berkeley, CA, 2002, ibid., pgs.194-195

119. Robert Cohen, "The Many Meanings of the FSM," in *The Free Speech Movement, Reflections on Berkeley in the 1960's*, (eds Robert Cohen and Reginald E. Zelnik), University of California Press, Berkeley, CA, pgs. 5-6

120. https://fsm.berkeley.edu/free-speech-movement-timeline/

121. Doug Rossinow, "Mario Savio and the Politics of Authenticity" in *The Free Speech Movement, Reflections on Berkeley in the 1960's*, edited by Robert Cohen and Reginald E. Zelnik, University of California Press, Berkeley, CA, pg. 533

122. Robert Cohen, "The Many Meanings of the FSM," in *The Free Speech Movement, Reflections on Berkeley in the 1960's*, (eds Robert Cohen and Reginald E. Zelnik), University of California Press, Berkeley, CA, pgs. 40-41

123. Ibid., pg. 119

124. https://www.metrotimes.com/news/mario-savios-bodies-upon-the-gears-speech-50-years-later-2271095

125. https://www.vhlf.org/havel-in-the-media/vaclav-havels-lessons-on-how-to-create-a-parallel-polis/

126. Doug Rossinow, "Mario Savio and the Politics of Authenticity" in *The Free Speech Movement, Reflections on Berkeley in the 1960's*, edited by Robert Cohen and Reginald E. Zelnik, University of California Press, Berkeley, CA, pg. 548

127. Malcolm Burnstein, "A Movement lawyer's Perspective," in Robert Cohen and Reginald E. Zelnik (eds), *The Free Speech Movement, Reflections on Berkeley in the 1960's*, University of California Press, Berkeley, CA, 2002, pg. 437

128. https://www.democracynow.org/2003/11/21/the_free_speech_movement_reflections_on

129. Robert Cole, "December 1964," in Robert Cohen and Reginald E. Zelnik (eds), *The Free Speech Movement, Reflections on Berkeley in the 1960's*, University of California Press, Berkeley, CA, 2002, pgs. 422-9

130. Reginald E. Zelnik in "On the Side of the Angels," in Robert Cohen and Reginald E. Zelnik (eds), *The Free Speech Movement, Reflections on Berkeley in the 1960's*, University of California Press, Berkeley, CA, 2002, pg. 313

131. Robert Cohen, "The Many Meanings of the FSM," in Robert Cohen and Reginald E. Zelnik (eds), *The Free Speech Movement, Reflections on Berkeley in the 1960's*, University of California Press, Berkeley, CA, 2002, pg. 12

132. Robert Cohen, "The Many Meanings of the FSM," in Robert Cohen and Reginald E. Zelnik (eds), *The Free Speech Movement, Reflections on Berkeley in the 1960's*, University of California Press, Berkeley, CA, 2002, pg. 25

133. https://www.berkeley.edu/news/media/releases/2004/06/08_reagan.shtml

134. Robert Cohen, "The Many Meanings of the FSM," in Robert Cohen and Reginald E. Zelnik (eds), *The Free Speech Movement, Reflections on Berkeley in the 1960's*, University of California Press, Berkeley, CA, 2002, pg. 26

135. https://www.berkeley.edu/news/media/releases/2004/06/08_reagan.shtml

136. Ibid.

137. Sean Burns, *Free Speech Movement Legacies and the Promise of Community Engaged Scholarship*, Blum Center for Developing Economies, October 1, 2014

138. Ibid.

139. Robert Cohen, "The Many Meanings of the FSM," in Robert Cohen and Reginald E. Zelnik (eds), *The Free Speech Movement, Reflections on Berkeley in the 1960's*, University of California Press, Berkeley, CA, 2002, pg. 3

140. Samuel Farber, "The Free Speech Movement 56 Years Later," Jacobin Magazine, September 3, 2020

141. https://www.history.com/this-day-in-history/eisenhower-warns-of-military-industrial-complex

142. Bill Zimmerman, "The Four Stages of the Antiwar Movement," The New York Times, Opinion, October 24, 2017

143. https://www.newyorker.com/magazine/2018/02/26/what-went-wrong-in-vietnam

144. https://timesmachine.nytimes.com/timesmachine/1965/04/18/issue.html

145. https://www.healthline.com/health-news/ lingering-health-effects-of-agent-orange

146. https://www.history.com/topics/vietnam-war/ vietnam-war-history

147. Ibid.

148. Christopher J. Levesque, "The Truth Behind the My Lai Massacre," The New York Times, Opinion, March 16, 2018

149. https://www.newyorker.com/magazine/2018/02/26/ what-went-wrong-in-vietnam

150. Bill Zimmerman, "The Four Stages of the Antiwar Movement," The New York Times, Opinion, October 24, 2017

151. https://www.theguardian.com/film/2003/jul/04/ artsfeatures2

152. Ibid.

153. Ellen Kershner, "How many Americans Were Killed in the Vietnam War?" History. World Atlas.com, June 10, 2020, https://www.worldatlas.com/articles/how-many-americans-were-killed-in-the-vietnam-war.html

154. https://www.nixonfoundation.org/2020/04/fifty-years-ago-president-nixon-announces-cambodia-incursion/

155. Bill Zimmerman, "The Four Stages of the Antiwar Movement," The New York Times, Opinion, October 24, 2017

156. https://timesmachine.nytimes.com/timesmachine/1970/05/02/issue.html

157. https://www.nbcnews.com/news/us-news/kent-state-massacre-shootings-college-campus-50-years-ago-changed-n1197676

158. https://www.huffpost.com/entry/ may-4-1970-national-guard_b_1476017

159. https://www.jacobinmag.com/2015/04/ khmer-rouge-cambodian-genocide-united-states/

160. https://www.bbc.com/news/world-asia-pacific-10684399

161. Zeigler, Daniel et al, (Directors), 2005, Sir! *No Sir* (title) Displaced Films, and Page Productions (Production Companies)

## CHAPTER 6

162. Al Gore, *The Assault on Reason*, Penguin Press, N.Y., N.Y., 2007, pg. 9

163. https://www.cnbc.com/2020/10/28/2020-election-spending-to-hit-nearly-14-billion-a-record.html

164. https://www.dw.com/en/german-election-party-and-campaign-financing/a-58807353

165. https://sunlightfoundation.com/2014/11/10/u-s-political-finance-americans-spend-more-on-elections-but-they-lead-from-behind/

166. https://thewordenreport-governmentandmarkets.blogspot.com/2015/09/blue-collar-lawmakers-access-to-maines.html

167. https://www.brennancenter.org/our-work/court-cases/arizona-free-enterprise-club-v-bennett

168. https://www.npr.org/2012/11/15/165220138/doris-kearns-goodwin-on-lincoln-and-his-team-of-rivals

169. Jonathan Haidt, "Why the Past Ten Years of American Life Have Been Uniquely Stupid," Atlantic Magazine, April 11, 2022

170. DiAngelo, Robin J., *White Fragility*: *Why It's so Hard for White People to Talk about Racism*. Boston: Beacon Press, 2018, pgs. 90-91

171. Haidt Jonathan Haidt, "Why the Past Ten Years of American Life Have Been Uniquely Stupid," Atlantic Magazine, April 11, 2022

172. Ibid.

173. https://knpr.org/npr/2021-02/tech-ethicist-tristan-harris-says-digital-democracy-needed-correct-system-harms

174. Jonathan Rauch, *The Constitution of Knowledge, A Defense of Truth*, Brookings Institution Press, Washington, D.C., 2021, pgs. 76-77

175. Al Gore, *The Assault on Reason*, Penguin Press, N.Y., N.Y., 2007, pg. 26

176. Robert McChesney, *Rich Media, Poor Democracy*, University of Illinois Press, Urbana, Chicago, 1999, pg. 240

177. Ibid., pgs. 17-18

178. Ibid., pg. 9

179. https://www.monticello.org/site/jefferson/educated-citizenry-vital-requisite-our-survival-free-people-quotation

180. https://www.jagranjosh.com/general-knowledge/democracy-index-2021-1644567197-1

181. Celine Castronuovo, "U.S. Score falls in Economist's annual Democracy Index," The Hill, February 2, 2021

182. https://www.msnbc.com/rachel-maddow-show/maddowblog/supreme-court-reactionary-rampage-rcna36362

183. https://www.msnbc.com/msnbc/take-andrew-jackson-the-20-bill-msna622951

184. https://thehill.com/opinion/op-ed/60439-why-the-citizens-united-decision-undermines-democracy/

185. https://thebndstory.nd.gov/the-early-years/the-nonpartisan-league/

186. Monica Davey, "A Placid North Dakota Asks, Recession? What Recession?" New York Times, December 5, 2008

187. Ibid.

188. Ibid.

## PART III
## CHAPTER 7

189. https://www.washingtonpost.com/archive/opin-ions/1998/03/15/for-arguments-sake/04636e38-6298-4c2c-90d3-db0726e60b28/?utm_term=.607ec20dfc7e

190. Ibid.

191. John and Julia Gottman, Doug Abrams, Rachel Abrams, *Eight dates, essential conversations for a lifetime of love,* Workman Publishing Company, N.Y., N.Y., 2018, pg. 75

192. Atlee, Tom, with Rosa Zubizarreta, *Tao of Democracy, Using Co-Intelligence to Create a World That Works for All,* The Writer's Collective, Cranston, Rhode Island, 2003, pgs. xiii-v

193. Virginia Hughes, "How to Change Minds? A Study Makes the Case for Talking it Out," New York Times, September 16, 2022

194. Atlee, Tom, with Rosa Zubizarreta, *Tao of Democracy, Using Co-Intelligence to Create a World That Works for All,* The Writer's Collective, Cranston, RI, 2003, pgs. 4-9

195. Tom Atlee, *Empowering Public Wisdom, A Practical Vision of Citizen-Led Politics,* Evolver Editions, Berkeley, CA, 2012, pg. 12

196. Ibid., pg. 34

197. Ibid., pgs. 58-59

198. https://www.co-intelligence.org/Macleans1991Experiment.html

199. Judith Glaser, *Conversational Intelligence,* Bibliomotion, Brookline, MA, 2014, pg. 71

200. Ibid., pgs. 190-191

201. Ibid., pgs. 70-71

202. https://www.conversationalintelligence.com/benchmark/clients

203.   Rosa Zubizarreta, *From Conflict to Collaboration, A User's Guide to Dynamic Facilitation*, Two Harbors Press, Minneapolis, MN, 2015, pg. xiv

204.  Ibid., pg. xiii

## CHAPTER 8

205.  Jim Rough, personal conversation

206.  Jim Rough, *Society's Breakthrough! Releasing Essential Wisdom and Virtue in All the People*, Bloomington, IN, 2002, pgs. 73-94

207.  https://www.zmescience.com/research/chimps-enjoy-solving-puzzles-just-for-the-thrill-of-it/

208.  Rosa Zubizarreta, *From Conflict to Collaboration, A User's Guide to Dynamic Facilitation*, Two Harbors Press, Minneapolis, MN, 2015, pg. 12

209.  Rough, Jim, *Society's Breakthrough! Releasing Essential Wisdom and Virtue in All the People*, Bloomington, IN, 2002, pgs. 39-60

210.  Ibid., pgs. 36-38

211.  https://www.wisedemocracy.org/wisdom-councils-in-austria.html

212.  Ibid.

213.  Juanita Brown and David Isaacs and the World Café Community, *The World Café: Shaping Our Future Through Conversations That Matter*, Berret-Koehler, San Francisco, CA, 2005

214.  Manfred Hellrigi video at https://www.wisedemocracy.org/wisdom-councils-in-austria.html

215.  Rosa Zubizarreta, Andy Paice and Martha Cuffy, "Citizens' councils: What are they and why are they so popular in Austria?", Research and Development Note, New Democracy, August 27, 2020, (http://www.democracy.com.au)

216.  Ibid.

217. Ibid.

218. https://www.wisedemocracy.org/wisdom-councils-in-austria. html

219. Jim Rough, personal conversation

220. https://www.wisedemocracy.org/wisdom-councils-in-austria. html

221. Jim Rough, personal conversation

222. Jim Rough, personal conversation

223. https://www.wisedemocracy.org/wisdom-councils-in-austria. html

224. Jim Rough, personal conversation

225. https://www.wisedemocracy.org/mauthausen-example.html

226. Manfred Helrigl, personal conversation

227. Jim Rough, *Society's Breakthrough! Releasing Essential Wisdom and Virtue in All the People,* Bloomington, IN, 2002, pgs. 10-11

228. https://www.buergerrat.net/english-version/

## CHAPTER 9

229. Jackie Stavros and Cheri Torres, *Conversations Worth Having,* 2nd addition, Berett-Koehler, Oakland, CA, 2022, pg. 31

230. Ibid., pgs. 74-6

231. https://www.researchgate.net/publication/235344292_ Appreciative_inquiry_The_power_of_the_uncondi- tional_positive_question/link/54de683c0cf2510fcee3b52a/ download

232. Catherine Moore, Psychologist, "What is Appreciative Inquiry? A Brief History and Real-Life Examples," in Positive-Psychology.com, June 2, 2022

233. https://weatherhead.case.edu/faculty/Ronald-Fry

234. Catherine Moore, Psychologist, "What is Appreciative Inquiry? A Brief History and Real-Life Examples," in Positive-Psychology.com, June 2, 2022

235. https://appreciativeinquiry.champlain.edu/learn/appreciative-inquiry-brief-history/

236. Ibid.

237. Jackie Stavros and Cherri Torres, *Conversations Worth Having*, 2nd addition, Berett-Koehler, Oakland, CA, 2022, pg. 92

238. Ibid., pgs. 92-93

239. Linda Bark, personal conversation

240. https://www.researchgate.net/publication/235344292_Appreciative_inquiry_The_power_of_the_uncondi-tional_positive_question/link/54de683c0cf2510fcee3b52a/download

241. Jackie Stavros and Cheri Torres designed the pilot interview

## CHAPTER 10

242. https://www.cnvc.org/training/resource/needs-inventory

243. https://www.cnvc.org/about/marshall

244. https://www.cnvc.org/training/resource/book-chapter-1

245. Marshall Rosenberg, *Living Nonviolent Communication*, Sounds True, Boulder, CO, 80306, pgs. 12-14

246. https://www.cnvc.org/training/resource/book-chapter-1

247. Ibid., pg. 91

248. https://www.theguardian.com/technology/2016/jul/20/milo-yiannopoulos-nero-permanently-banned-twitter

249. Greg Lukianoff, and Jonathan Haidt, *The Coddling of the American Mind, How Good Intentions and Bad Ideas are Setting Up a Generation for Failure*, Penguin Press, N.Y., N.Y., 2018, pgs. 81-3

250. Jon Rouson, "How One Stupid Tweet Blew Up Justine Sacco's Life," New York Times Magazine, February 12, 2015, N.Y., NY.

251. https://podcast.app/brene-on-shame-and-accountability-e102939801/

252. Robin Young, "Stanford Researchers Bring Together People with Different Political Views," WBUR, October 7, 2019 https://www.wbur.org/hereandnow/2019/10/17/people-with-different-political-views

253. Vignesh Ramachandran, "Stanford Students Help Bridge Political Divide," Stanford/News, October 16, 2019

254. Robin Young, "Stanford Researchers Bring Together People with Different Political Views," WBUR, October 7, 2019 https://www.wbur.org/hereandnow/2019/10/17/people-with-different-political-views

**PART IV**

**CHAPTER 11**

255. https://www.history.com/topics/1960s/1968-democratic-convention

256. Ibid

257. Joel Achenbach, "'A Party that had lost its mind': In 1968; Democrats held one of history's most disastrous conventions," Washington Post, August 24, 2018

258. https://www.thehistoryreader.com/military-history/nixon_vietnam_war/

259. Rick Perlstein, *Nixonland, the Rise of a President and the fracturing of America*, Scribner, N.Y., NY, 2008, pg. xiii

260. William E. Leuchtenburg, *The American President, from Teddy Roosevelt to Bill Clinton*, Oxford University Press, NY, NY, 2015, pg. 471

261. Jerald Podair, Zach Messitte, Charles Holden, "The man who pioneered Trumpism," Washington Post, November 15, 2018

262. Ibid

263. McKay Coppins, "The man who broke politics," The Atlantic, November 2018

264. https://www.huffpost.com/entry/the-gingrich-revolution-a_b_8272054

265. McKay Coppins, "The man who broke politics," The Atlantic, November 2018

266. Ibid

267. Parker Palmer, *Healing the Heart of Democracy: The Courage to Create a Politics Worthy of the Human Spirit*, Jossey Bass, San Francisco, CA, 2011, pgs. 13-14

268. https://reclaimdemocracy.org/powell_memo_lewis/

269. http://billmoyers.com/content/the-powell-memo-a-call-to-arms-for-corporations/

270. Ibid.

271. https://www.statista.com/statistics/257340/number-of-lobbyists-in-the-us/

272. http://billmoyers.com/content/the-powell-memo-a-call-to-arms-for-corporations/

273. https://www.politico.com/story/2011/02/the-end-of-the-dlc-era-049041

274. http://www.huffingtonpost.com/entry/the-roots-of-the-democratic- debacle_us_584ec983e4b04c8e2bb0a779?section=us politics

275. Lawrence Lessig, "How to Get Our Democracy Back," The Nation, 2/22/2010

276. Ibid

277. https://www.commondreams.org/newswire/2016/03/24/report-reveals-dangerous-influence-american-legislative-exchange-council-alec

278. Naomi Oreskes and Erik M. Conway, *Merchants of Doubt*, Bloomsbury Press, NY, NY, 2010, pg. 35

279. Ibid, pg.7

280. Ibid, pg.125

281. Ibid, pgs. 246-7

282. Stephen Prothero, *Why Liberals Win, Even When they Lose Elections*, Harper Collins, N.Y., NY, 2016, pgs. 189-190

283. Ibid, pgs. 193-194

284. Ibid, pgs. 199-200

285. Richard L. Berke, "Religious Right Candidates Gain as GOP Turnout Rises," New York Times, November 12, 1994

286. Michael Lofgren, *The party is Over: How the Republicans went crazy, the Democrats became useless, and the Middle Class got shafted.*, Penguin Books, NY, NY, 2012

287. https://www.salon.com/2014/04/19/reaganomics_killed_americas_middle_class_partner/

288. https://truthout.org/articles/top-1-percent-in-us-now-have-more-wealth-than-entire-middle-class-combined/

289. https://www.sfweekly.com/news/the-great-eliminator-how-ronald-reagan-made-homelessness-permanent/

290. Ibid

291. https://sfgov.org/scorecards/safety-net/homeless-population

292. Alan S. Blinder, and Janet Yellin, *The Fabulous Decade, Macroeconomic Lessons from the 1990s*, A Century Foundation Report, July 1, 2001, NY Century Foundation Press, NY, NY.

293. Ibid

294. https://www.themoscowtimes.com/2019/04/12/richest-3-russians-hold-90-of-countrys-financial-assets-study-a65213

## Chapter 12

295. https://www.pewresearch.org/politics/2021/05/17/public-trust-in-government-1958-2021/

296. Bandy X. Lee, *Profile of a Nation: Trump's Mind, America's Soul*, World Mental Health Coalition, N.Y., N.Y., pg. 123

297. Jonathan Haidt, *A Righteous Mind*, Random House, N.Y., N.Y., 2012, pgs. 245-246

298. Mike Robinson, "Sense of Belonging: Characteristics, Importance and Examples", Its Psychology, October 10, 2022

299. Its Psychology, "Sense of Belonging: Characteristics, Importance and Examples," February 24, 2019

300. Bandy X. Lee, *Profile of a Nation: Trump's Mind, America's Soul*, World Mental Health Coalition, N.Y., N.Y., pg. 76

301. Ibid., pgs. 29-30

302. Ibid., pg. 32

303. https://www.splcenter.org/news/2020/03/18/year-hate-and-extremism-2019

304. Ibid., pg. 31

305. Michael Greenwald, "How Everything Became the Culture War," Politico Magazine, November/December 2018

306. Ibid., pg. 70

307. Will Stone, "What's coming this winter? Here's How Many More Could Die in the Pandemic," NPR, October 16, 2020

308. https://thehill.com/homenews/administration/469058-poll-62-of-trump-supporters-say-nothing-the-president-could-do-would

309. https://thehill.com/homenews/533531-after-capitol-siege-majority-of-americans-say-trump-should-be-removed-from-office

310. Jason Stanley, *How Fascism Works, The Politics of Us and Them*, Random House, N.Y., N.Y. 2018

311. Ibid., pgs. 3-5

312. Bandy X. Lee, *Profile of a Nation: Trump's Mind, America's Soul*, World Mental Health Coalition, Inc., N.Y., N.Y., 2020, pg. 30

313. Jason Stanley, *How Fascism Works, The Politics of Us and Them*, Random House, N.Y., N.Y. 2018, pg. 51

314. Ibid., pgs. 78-80

315. https://www.msnbc.com/msnbc/totally-accurate-trump-defends-calling-mexican-immigrants-rapists-msna629836

316. https://www.washingtonpost.com/media/2021/01/07/some-fox-newss-trump-supporters-now-declare-his-political-career-is-done/

317. Jason Stanley, *How Fascism Works, The Politics of Us* and *Them*, Random House, N.Y., N.Y. 2018, pg., xxix

318. Ibid., pg. 35

319. Ibid., pg. 94

320. https://www.nytimes.com/interactive/2017/09/18/upshot/black-white-wealth-gap-perceptions.html

321. Jason Stanley, *How Fascism Works, The Politics of Us and Them*, Random House, N.Y., N.Y., pg. 94

322. Ibid., pg. 44

323. Ibid., pgs. 52-53

324. Bruce Y. Lee, "Steve Bannon suggests Beheading Fauci, What to do about Threats to Health Experts," Forbes, November 6, 2020

325. https://people.com/health/dr-fauci-received-death-threats-letter-filled-with-power-while-working-for-trump/

326. Jason Stanley, *How Fascism Works, The Politics of Us and Them*, Random House, N.Y., N.Y., pg. 57

327. Ibid., pgs. 57-66

328. https://www.jewishvirtuallibrary.org/joseph-goebbels-on-the-quot-big-lie-quot

329. Arie W. Kruglanski, "What drives the pro-Trump Mob?" Boston Globe, January 11, 2021

330. https://www.rasmussenreports.com/public_content/politics/elections/election_2020/most_say_mail_in_voting_worked_but_47_say_fraud_likely

331. Jason Stanley, *How Fascism Works, The Politics of Us and Them*, Random House, N.Y., N.Y., ibid., pg. 71

332. https://www.theguardian.com/commentisfree/2019/jul/19/donald-trump-archetypal-far-right-charismatic-leader

333. Bandy X. Lee, *Profile of a Nation: Trump's Mind, America's Soul*, World Mental Health Coalition, Inc., N.Y., N.Y., 2020, pg. 121

334. Ibid., pg. 27

335. Ibid., pg. 54

336. Ibid., pg. 76

337. Ibid., pg. 71

338. Ibid., pg. 76

339. Ibid., pg. 121

340. Joost A. M. Meerloo, MD, *The Rape of the Mind, The Psychology of Thought Control, Menticide and Brainwashing*, Martino Publishing, Mansfield Center, CT, 2015, (original copyright 1959), pgs. 73-88

341. Bandy X. Lee, *Profile of a Nation: Trump's Mind, America's Soul*, World Mental Health Coalition, Inc., N.Y., N.Y., pg. 90

342. https://news.stanford.edu/2010/09/23/naimark-stalin-genocide-092310/

343. Bandy X. Lee, *Profile of a Nation: Trump's Mind, America's Soul*, World Mental Health Coalition, Inc., N.Y., N.Y., pgs. 93-103

344. https://www.nytimes.com/2017/01/31/opinion/the-republican-fausts.html

**CHAPTER 13**

345. Parker Palmer, *Healing the Heart of Democracy: The Courage to Create a Politics Worthy of the Human Spirit*, Jossey Bass, San Francisco, CA, 2011, pg. 7

346. https://www.inverse.com/article/38457-inequality-study-nature-revolution

347. https://www.brookings.edu/blog/up-front/2019/06/25/six-facts-about-wealth-in-the-united-states/

348. Bandy X. Lee, *Profile of a Nation: Trump's Mind, America's Soul*, World Mental Health Coalition, Inc., N.Y., N.Y.,2020 pgs. 92-93

349. https://www.worldometers.info/world-population/canada-population/

350. Eric Liu and Nick Hanauer, *The Gardens of Democracy, A New American Story of Citizenship, the Economy and the Role of Government*, Sasquatch Books, Seattle, Washington, 2011, pg. 125

351. https://drugabusestatistics.org/opioid-epidemic/

352. https://www.theguardian.com/us-news/2018/feb/13/meet-the-sacklers-the-family-feuding-over-blame-for-the-opioid-crisis,

353. https://www.nytimes.com/2019/11/27/nyregion/brooklyn-opioid-investigation.html

354. https://www.upmc.com/media/
news/092018-burke-od-dynamics

355. https://www.washingtontimes.com/news/2020/nov/6/
andrew-yang-something-deeply-wrong-with-democratic/

356. https://twitter.com/ZachandMattShow/
status/1324518032719433728

357. Benjamin Fearnow, "Millennials Control just 4.2% of U.S.
Wealth," Newsweek, 10/8/2020

358. https://www.statista.com/statistics/296974/us-popula-
tion-share-by-generation/#:~:text=The%20statistic%20
depicts%20the%20distribution,population%20in%20the%20
United%20States.

359. https://www.addictioncenter.com/community/
millennials-alcohol-drugs-suicide/

360. Olga Khazan, "The Millennial Mental-Health Crisis,"
The Atlantic, June 11, 2020

361. Ibid.

362. https://worldpopulationreview.com/country-rankings/
gun-deaths-by-country

363. https://www.cnbc.com/2022/02/28/why-health-care-costs-
are-rising-in-the-us-more-than-anywhere-else-.html

364. Bandy X. Lee, *Profile of a Nation: Trump's Mind, America's Soul*,
World Mental Health Coalition, Inc., N.Y., N.Y., 2020, pg.126

365. https://www.youtube.com/watch?v=hNDgcjVGHIw

366. Ibid.

367. https://www.nytimes.com/2021/11/23/books/review/san-
fransicko-michael-shellenberger.html

368. https://www.davisvanguard.org/2019/12/presentation-dis-
cusses-ways-to-prevent-and-reduce-homelessness/

369. Ibid.

370. https://caufsociety.com/cities-solving-homelessness/

371. https://www.huffpost.com/entry/red-blue-states-covid-cases-deaths-wapo_n_613d675fe4b0640100a5a973

372. Edited by Jerry Schwartz, "Divided America, An A.P. Guide to the Fracturing of a Nation," Associated Press, 2016, pgs. 2-10

373. Sahil Chinoy, "What happened to America's Political Center of Gravity," New York Times, June 26, 2019

374. Thomas B. Edsall, "We Aren't Seeing White Support for Trump for what it is. Exodus of White College Educated votes from Republican party," New York Times, August 28, 2019

375. Parker Palmer, *Healing the Heart of Democracy: The Courage to Create a Politics Worthy of the Human Spirit*, Jossey Bass, San Francisco, CA, 2011, pgs. 75-76

## Part V
## Chapter 14

376. Peter H. Diamandis & Steve Kotler, *Abundance, The Future is Better Than You Think*, Free Press, Simon & Shuster, N.Y., N.Y., 2012, pg. 11

377. Ibid., pg. 13

378. Sally Goerner, Robert G. Dyck and Dorothy Lagerroos, *The New Science of Sustainability, Building a foundation for Great Change*, Triangle Center for Complex Systems, Chapel Hill, NC, 2008, pgs.10-11

379. https://www.bbc.com/news/science-environment-58494391

380. Sally Goerner, Robert G. Dyck and Dorothy Lagerroos, *The New Science of Sustainability, Building a foundation for Great Change*, Triangle Center for Complex Systems, Chapel Hill, NC, 2008, pgs.10-11

381. Ibid., pgs. 117-129

382. Ibid., pgs. 329-330

383. Ibid., pgs. 13-14

384. Ibid., pgs. 15-16

385. https://www.opednews.com/articles/3/Jean-Gebser-and-the-Recove-by-Blair-Gelbond-Awareness_Consciousness_Freedom_God-180810-900.html

386. https://www.cdc.gov/nchs/pressroom/nchs_press_releases/2018/201811_Yoga_Meditation.html

387. https://wiki.p2pfoundation.net/Evolution_of_Consciousness_According_to_Jean_Gebser

388. Arie Kruglanski, "What drives the pro-Trump Mob?" Boston Globe, January 11, 2021

389. https://wiki.p2pfoundation.net/Evolution_of_Consciousness_According_to_Jean_Gebser

390. Sally Goerner, Robert G. Dyck and Dorothy Lagerroos, *The New Science of Sustainability, Building a foundation for Great Change,* Triangle Center for Complex Systems, Chapel Hill, NC 2008, pg.10

391. https://homecare.com/resources/blog/fast-food-and-obesity-the-cause-and-effect-relationship/

392. https://shsnews.org/23233/opinion/high-school-students-discover-they-are-not-prepared-for-college/

393. Ibid.

394. https://wiki.p2pfoundation.net/Evolution_of_Consciousness_According_to_Jean_Gebser

395. Sally Goerner et al., Robert G. Dyck, and Dorothy Lagerroos, *The New Science of Sustainability, Building a foundation for Great Change,* Triangle Center for Complex Systems, Chapel Hill, NC, 2008, pgs. 65-99

396. http://www.fountainmagazine.com/Issue/detail/Understanding-Todays-Schools-with-Chaos-Theory

397.  Ibid.

398.  http://www.cosmopolisproject.org/gaia-theory-in-a-nutshell/

399.  Sally Goerner et al., Robert G. Dyck, and Dorothy Lagerroos, *The New Science of Sustainability, Building a foundation for Great Change,* Triangle Center for Complex Systems, Chapel Hill, NC, 2008, pg. 53

400.  Ibid, pgs.65-78

401.  Ibid., pg. 17

402.  https://www.gaiamind.org/Gebser.html

403.  https://features.slashdot.org/story/05/04/18/164213/the-early-history-of-nupedia-and-wikipedia-a-memoir

404.  https://thenextweb.com/news/the-nuts-bolts-wikipedia-how-it-works

405.  https://www.goodreads.com/quotes/133403-we-should-do-away-with-the-absolutely-specious-notion-that

406.  https://www.openculture.com/2015/10/bertrand-russell-buckminster-fuller-on-why-we-should-spend-less-time-working.html

## CHAPTER 15

407.  Teachers College, Columbia University. (n.d.). Maxine Greene Collection. Retrieved August 4, 2019, from PocketKnowledge website.

408.  https://plato.stanford.edu/entries/dewey/

409.  https://www.tc.columbia.edu/articles/2014/may/maxine-greene-tcs-great-philosopher-dies-at-96/

410.  Teachers College, Columbia University. (n.d.). Maxine Greene Collection. Retrieved August 4, 2019, from PocketKnowledge website.

411.  https://creativeleaps.org/resources/articles/releasing-the-imagination-by-maxine-greene-book-review

412. Marshall Sahlins, "Teach-Ins Helped galvanize Student Activism. They Can So Again Today." The Nation, April 6, 2017

413. Ibid.

414. https://nces.ed.gov/programs/coe/indicator/cta

415. Marshall Sahlins, "Teach-Ins Helped galvanize Student Activism. They Can So Again Today." The Nation, April 6, 2017

416. https://www.forbes.com/sites/zackfriedman/2020/02/03/student-loan-debt-statistics/?sh=6db993db281f

417. https://oneclass.com/blog/featured/181364-how-do-us-college-costs-compare-to-other-countries3F.en.html

418. Jonathan Haidt, *A Righteous Mind, Why Good people are Divided by Politics and Religion,* Vintage Books, N.Y., N.Y., 2013

419. https://academiamag.com/finland-most-resilient-to-misinformation-in-classroom-milieu/

420. https://www.thoughtco.com/what-is-political-correctness-4178215

421. Emanuella Grinberg, Elliot C. McLaughlin, CNN, "Against its wishes, Auburn hosts white nationalist Richard Spencer," CNN, April 19, 2017

422. Erwin Chemerinsky, "Hate Speech is Protected Free Speech Even on College Campuses," Vox, December 26, 2017

423. https://www.insidehighered.com/news/2019/09/16/states-passing-laws-protect-college-students-free-speech

424. Jeremy Peters, "In the Name of Free Speech, States Crack Down on Campus Protests," N.Y. Times, 6/14/2018

425. Ibid.

426. Ibid.

427. Aaron R. Hanlon, "Why Colleges Have a Right to Reject Hateful Speakers like Ann Coulter," The New Republic, April 24, 2017

428. Erwin Chemerinsky, "Hate Speech is Protected Free Speech Even on College Campuses," Vox, December 26, 2017

**CHAPTER 16**

429. Frances Moore Lappe, *Democracies Edge, Choosing to Save Our country by bringing democracy to life*, Jossey Bass, San Francisco, CA, pg.7

430. https://www.21global.ucsb.edu/global-e/march-2017/what-has-happened-public-imagination-and-why

431. Ibid.

432. Eric Liu, *You're More powerful than You Think, A Citizen's Guide to Making Change Happen*, Public Affairs, N.Y., N.Y., 2017, pgs. 32-33

433. Eric Liu and Nick Hanauer, *The Gardens of Democracy, A New American Story of Citizenship, the Economy and the Role of Government*, Sasquatch Books, Seattle, Washington, 2011, pg. 9

434. https://www.americanbar.org/groups/crsj/publications/human_rights_magazine_home/the-state-of-healthcare-in-the-united- states/health-care-as-a-human-right/

435. https://www.commondreams.org/news/2022/02/10/progressives-call-democrats-endorse-21st-century-economic-bill-rights

436. Eric Liu, *You're More powerful than You Think, A Citizen's Guide to Making Change Happen*, Public Affairs, N.Y., N.Y., 2017, pg. 61

437. https://citizenuniversity.us/eric-liu/

438. https://www.ted.com/talks/eric_liu_how_to_revive_your_belief_in_democracy

439. Eric Lui, *You're More Powerful than you Think, A Citizen's Guide to Making Change Happen*, Hatchett Book Group, N.Y., N.Y., 2017, pgs. 75-119

440. Ibid.

441. Ibid., pgs. 77-78

442. Linda Stout, *Collective Visioning, How Groups Can Work Together for a Just and Sustainable Future*, Berrett-Koehler, San Francisco, CA, pgs. 96-169

443. https://todayinclh.com/?event=a-philip-randolph-meets-with-fdr-in-white-house-protests-segregation-in-military

444. https://coloradosun.com/2019/06/04/peak-health-summit-county-lower-health-care-costs/

445. https://www.coloradohealthinstitute.org/research/peak-health-alliance-summit-sight

446. https://stateofreform.com/featured/2022/06/colorado-continues-innovative-approach-to-reducing-health-care-costs/

447. https://blogs.lse.ac.uk/usappblog/2017/12/13/evidence-from-oregon-shows-that-citizens-initiative-reviews-can-improve-voters-decision-making-about-ballot-measures/

## CHAPTER 17

448. https://www.21global.ucsb.edu/global-e/march-2017/what-has-happened-public-imagination-and-why

449. https://founders.archives.gov/documents/Adams/99-02-02-3102

450. Don Lansky, *Peeling an Artichoke, Opening to the heart of Spiritual Awakening*, Land and Sky Publishing, Charlottesville, VA, 2021, pg.11

451. https://www.quotes.net/quote/4412

452. Jovi, Bon, "You Give Love a Bad Name," Slippery When Wet (album), Mercury Records, 1986, CD

453. George Marshall, *DON'T EVEN TALK ABOUT IT, Why our Brains are wired to ignore Climate Change*, Bloomsbury Publishing, N.Y., N.Y., 2014, pg. 236

454. Ibid., pg. 234

455. Ibid., pgs. 36-38

456. Ibid., pg. 93

457. Thomas Berry, *The Great Work, Our way Into the Future,* Three Rivers Press, N.Y., N.Y., 1999, pg. 49

458. https://www.theepochtimes.com/right-life-mayan-people_1518929.html?welcomeuser=1

459. Michael Reynolds, *Journey,* Earthship Biotecture, P.O. Box 1041, Taos, NM, pg. 7

460. Nick Aspinwall, "These homes are off-grid and climate-resilient. They're also built of trash," The Washington Post, January 4, 2022

461. Michael Reynolds, *Journey,* Earthship Biotecture, P.O. Box 1041, Taos, NM, pg. 7

462. Nick Aspinwall, "These homes are off-grid and climate-resilient. They're also built of trash," The Washington Post, January 4, 2022

463. https://safarisafricana.com/which-country-has-the-most-national-parks/

464. John Gottman and Nan Silver, *The Seven Principles for Making Marriage Work,* Three Rivers Press, N.Y., N.Y., 1999, pgs. 23-4.

465. Michael Lerner, *The Left Hand of God, Healing America's Political and Spiritual Crisis,* Harper, San Francisco, 2007

466. Ibid., pg. 41

467. Ibid., pg. 75

468. https://www.youtube.com/watch?v=18Zh7X-u0jI, How to Talk About Race During Black Lives Matter with David Campt, June 9, 2020

469. Ibid.

470. https://www.youtube.com/watch?v=hFhDidan9Vc, Dr. David Campt, "From Slacktivism to Activism! How Allies can Step up to the Moment" June 3, 2020

471. Ian Haney Lopez, *Merge Left, Fusing Race and Class, Winning Elections, and Saving America*, The New Press, N.Y., N.Y., 2019, pg. 9

472. https://tmforveterans.org/research-on-tm-and-substance-abuse/

473. Robert Putnam and Shaylyn Garret, *The Upswing, How America Came Together a Century Ago, and How We Can Do It Again*, Simon and Shuster, N.Y., N.Y., 2020, pg. 328

**CHAPTER 18**

474. http://nationalhumanitiescenter.org/tserve/twenty/tkeyinfo/socgospel.htm

475. Ibid., pg. 335

476. Ibid., pgs. 315-6

477. Ibid., pgs. 319-320

478. https://www.history.com/topics/early-20th-century-us/triangle-shirtwaist-fire

479. Robert Putnam & Shaylyn Garret, *The Upswing, How America Came Together a Century Ago, and How We Can Do It Again*, Simon & Schuster, N.Y., N.Y., 2020, pgs. 321-4

480. Ibid., pg. 328

481. https://www.britannica.com/event/Social-Gospel

482. Robert Putnam & Shaylyn Garret, *The Upswing, How America Came Together a Century Ago, and How We Can Do It Again*, Simon & Schuster, N.Y., N.Y., 2020, pg. 329

483. https://www.encyclopedia.com/social-sciences/culture-magazines/1900s-education-overview

484. https://www.encyclopedia.com/social-sci-
ences/news-wires-white-papers-and-books/
education-reform-movement

485. Robert Putnam and Shaylyn Garret, *The Upswing, How America Came Together a Century Ago, and How We Can Do It Again*, Simon & Schuster, N.Y., N.Y., 2020, pgs. 226 -7

486. Ibid., pg. 335

www.ingramcontent.com/pod-product-compliance
Lightning Source LLC
Chambersburg PA
CBHW062116020426
42335CB00013B/993